RECOGNIZING ISLAM

Hugh Roseby

November 1983.

D1501022

MICHAEL GILSENAN

Recognizing Islam

AN ANTHROPOLOGIST'S INTRODUCTION

CROOM HELM
London & Canberra

British Library Cataloguing in Publication Data

Gilsenan, Michael
   Recognizing Islam.
   1. Islam
   I. Title
   297   BP161.2

   ISBN 0-7099-1119-X
       0-7099-1139-4 Pbk

Printed and bound in Great Britain by
Biddles Ltd, Guildford and King's Lynn

CONTENTS

ACKNOWLEDGMENTS

The texture of any book derives from many sources and experiences. Teachers leave their imprint as much in their attitude to the world as in intellectual approaches. A.F.L. Beeston and Albert Hourani and the late Sir E.E. Evans-Pritchard all in their different ways channeled my energies and ideas about Middle Eastern societies and the moral as well as academic complexities that being a student entails. Friends and colleagues who have read the manuscript in whole or in part, in draft or final form, have been invaluable guides even and especially when I took a different path — Peter Brown, Clifford Geertz, Ernest Gellner, Abdullah Hammoudi, Geoffrey Hawthorn, John Stewart, Peter von Sivers, and Aram Yengoyan.

I owe to the Social Science Research Council of Great Britain (SSRC) support for six months at CRESM (Centre of Mediterranean Studies) at Aix-en-Provence in 1976, and members of that center were enormously kind and helpful to me. The SSRC also funded a Research Lectureship (1970-1973) at the University of Manchester in the anthropology department under Emrys Peters for work in and on Lebanese society. From that program comes much of the material within these pages. Earlier, from 1964-1966, the Social

Research Centre of the American University in Cairo supported my work on the Sufi brotherhoods of Egypt, and to them I am very grateful. A most valuable year at the Institute for Advanced Study in Princeton gave me the opportunity to edit and rewrite the manuscript. Peggy Clarke, Portia Edwards, and Catherine Rhubart could not have given better secretarial help nor have been more accommodating to an endless and unreasonable series of requests for additions and subtractions to what they had impeccably typed and copied. The social sciences division of the institute proved an oasis of calm and sociability and was enormously beneficial to me. My thanks to everyone there for all their encouragement.

The members of the Hamidiya Shaziliya brotherhood of Egypt placed me forever in their debt by their welcoming and generous acceptance of a young and confused graduate student. The people of the village of Berqayl in north Lebanon and other Lebanese friends showed me a different universe. My deep gratitude to them is dyed in sadness at the destruction and brutality that have shattered their world.

Patrick Seale and Mary Bruton have been patient and encouraging above and beyond the call of duty, and I am amazed at their kind perseverance.

Ken Brown, Robin Ostle, and Raoul Weexsteen have kept a watchful eye on my wilder flights, and their support has been vital to me. Alain and Bernice Ricard have been of more help than they can ever know, and to them this book is particularly offered.

Michael Gilsenan

CHAPTER 1

An Anthropologist's Introduction

My own experience of Islam began with a surprised and uncomfortable recognition that things are not what they seem.

As a nineteen-year-old preuniversity member of a British organization called Voluntary Service Overseas, I was doing a year of teaching in what was then (1959) the colony of Aden and the Protectorates and is now the People's Democratic Republic of Yemen. A friend and I were in Seyyun, one of the ancient towns of the great eastern wadi of the Hadhramaut, ruled by a British-appointed family of sultans and dominated by a highly influential clan of sherifs, descendants of the Prophet Muhammed.

Two young men of that family met us in the street, walking in the heat of the morning. The green band around their turbans, their flowing cream-coloured outer garments, and their trim beards all signified the holiness and precedence of their position.* Their wealth, from large local landholdings and overseas business in Indonesia, showed in the quality of the fine material of their clothes and in the size and equal

---

* No other groups could use these insignia of rank and status. That they never carried weapons was a further sign of the nature of their authority, though by this time that fact was of less practical importance than it had been.

elegance of the luxurious house to which we were being guided.

It was all an enchantment, a desert, an oasis, a holy town, an age-old tradition. The fullness of sanctity and a ritualized sense of gracious order and harmony were added to when a student of mine encountered in the street stooped respectfully to kiss the young sherifs' hands as we passed, thus marking his respect and acknowledgment of their position. The world was a perfectly formed magic garden. And I was entranced. All my images of Islam and Arab society were brought unquestioningly together.

The front door slammed behind us. The spell was broken. Our companions swiftly closed the window shutters so that no one could see us, lights were switched on, a Grundig tape recorder played Western pop music, and the strictly forbidden whiskey came out of the cupboard. Turbans were quickly doffed, and there was no talk of religion but only of stifling boredom, the ignorance of local people, the cost of alcohol, and how wonderful life had been in Indonesia.

To a naive adolescent, pious not to say sanctimonious in the face of the culture of this strange and marvelous society newly opened to him, the shock was enormous.

Was the street scene nothing but a scene? A show of holiness, a mere facade maintained by the elite, who had to hide from the very marks and duties of their authoritative position? Such signs of religion and hierarchy were used to dominate others, but, for some of the young sherifs at least, in the isolation of their houses were clearly an almost insupportable burden.

A day later I met the student, a boy in his late teens like myself. He delivered the second blow. "We kiss their hands now," he said, "but just wait till tomorrow." He was a Nasserist, a word that to the British and sherifian authorities meant subversion, communism, and an enemy to be bitterly resisted. A member of the first generation of peasants to be educated, he belonged to a cultural club in which most of the young men were sympathizers with the cause of the Egyptian president, then at the height of his power. That cause was identified as that of all Arabs against imperialism and the control of conservative and reactionary forces. He would talk to me, but I, too, was part of the apparatus of colonial administration, a fact that he realized much more clearly than I did.

The hand-kissing was a show, but a show with diametrically opposed meanings for the actors. It secreted hidden interpretations, reversals, and denials.

Both sides had strong definitions of true religion. The sherifs' whole position rested on their descent, ritual competence, and the belief in their power to bring blessing, education, and knowledge of Islamic law, all symbolized by their dress. For them the student was perilously close to unbelief and certainly tainted by socialism. The whiskey drinkers might acknowledge their own imperfect conduct but not see any link between this and a challenge to their authority. For the student, the men whose hands he kissed were not only obstacles to independence but had nothing to do with a true Islam, which had no need of sherifs, no need of reverence for wealthy merchants and landowners in green turbans or of deference to a religious hierarchy. The real Islam was free of such mediations with God and was embodied in the Quran and the traditions. It was an egalitarian force for the unity of all members of the community and part of a global struggle, an Islam that went hand in hand with a fight against local sources of corruption and alien power.

That moment in south Arabia contained many of the conflicts and traces of religion that, twenty years later, I have come to write about here: class opposition, groups and individuals using the same signs and codes but seeing events in quite different ways, concealed significances in social life, complex relations to wider historical changes in power relations and the economy. Finally, and not least, it draws attention to the danger of stereotypical images of another society and another religion. This is only one of the problems involved in learning about Islam in practice, where it is inextricably bound up with many dimensions of social life in ways that are frequently not at all what they initially appear to be.

These themes have run through my studies as an anthropologist, bringing new shocks and recognitions. My fieldwork has been carried out in circumstances where economic and political power, and sometimes overt violence and coercion, were crucial elements in social relations in which I myself was a participant.

In Egypt in the period 1964 to 1966 my work on the Sufi mystical brotherhoods was pursued among the urban poor, the low-paid unskilled and skilled workers, and new immigrants to the city from the countryside.* Other members were drawn from elements of the petty bourgeoisie, who were struggling to maintain a precarious status and were living on the margins of poverty, since their small businesses, trades, clerkships, or minor civil service positions were insecure and ill rewarded. They lived in a world of major political changes as Nasserism replaced British rule and an irreversible break with the past seemed to have been made. For them Islam was all the more important as society shifted in ways difficult to grasp. Yet the sheikhs of the great Islamic University of al-Azhar in Cairo assured me that these brotherhoods had nothing to do with Islam at all and that I was not only wasting my time but giving a false impression of what the true religion is. The brotherhood members in turn regarded many of the sheikhs as quite irrelevant to an experience of the inner truths of the ways to God and to the practice of Islam in general.

I was later (in 1971/72) to carry out field study in a semifeudal sector of Lebanese society in the impoverished northern region of Akkar. Here is a culture giving great weight to individualism, violence, and status honor. This code flourishes in a population composed mainly of extremely poor agricultural laborers, tractor drivers, construction workers, sharecroppers, and servants. The lords who dominated and exploited the village and owned much of the land did so through laws that were used almost as a personal instrument, through coercion, patron-client ties, and a twisted skein of shifting alliances and oppositions.

The perspectives on the world into which I was educated by villagers with very different views and practices of their own seemed full of contradictions and unease. There appeared to be an underlying radical refusal to believe that anyone acted for anything other than personal interest, whatever the vocabulary of religion, honor, or kinship that was used, or

* See my *Saint and Sufi in Modern Egypt: An Essay in the Sociology of Religion*, Oxford: The Clarendon Press, 1973 for a discussion of Sufi brotherhoods in Egypt.

that what was said or done was more than a cover for quite different secret intentions and purposes. Really to live in such a world involved practical mastery of both inner and outer realities as people conceived them. At the heart of reality might lie the core truth of religion, but who knew where that heart of reality lay or how to discover it? All this made for a multiplicity of interpretations, questionings, and almost theatrical social encounters. The rules and conditions of such forms might be shaped by overall social and economic conditions, but the everyday manifestations were kaleidoscopically variable. The relationship between these two dimensions is an unending problem that is present in everything that follows.

These kinds of experiences, so different and so similar, have been the main formative influences on my own construction of the meanings of Islam in society. The social classes among whom I anomalously moved are usually little considered in work on religion and belief. Historical documents give only inadequate and scattered accounts of what ordinary people are supposed to believe, and then only as seen through the eyes of literate specialists whose own position often includes the tacit or overt proposition that this cannot be true Islam. Both sheikhs and non-Muslim scholars can be found slipping into such attitudes and exclusions. That they do so is interesting and perhaps not very surprising. But such views are far too limited and partial.

The social strata of which I have spoken and among whom I have worked make up the broad mass of the population of many Islamic societies. They are usually not politically or socially dominant in a direct way, but they are of critical importance. States and regimes depend on their active or passive support, or on controlling them. They are "the people" as that phrase is generally used. It is this fact that gives a more general scope to the material presented here, beyond the range of the immediate context, be it Egypt, Lebanon, Turkey, Morocco, or any society to which I refer.

The significance of these classes and groupings has increased enormously in the modern period. They are its creation, born out of change. Their societies have all experienced the world transformations of the past century and a half, through colonial or imperial control, the development of the world capitalist market and consequent major shifts in production, technology, land tenure, and property relations. The forms and functions of the state have expanded and altered in a whole range of forms: monarchical, military, secular socialist, attempts at realizations of different conceptions of Muslim political institutions, state socialist, state capitalist, and others.

The whole nature of the relationship between town and country, too, has been transformed. The cities now dominate the rural areas to a far greater degree and in far more direct ways than before. Urban patterns of social life and organization have emerged that are quite different from those of the precapitalist period. The migration of peasants and agricultural laborers from villages to the cities and later to the factories and service industries of Europe is on a vast scale. New class structures have developed and are developing in societies that are still, for the most part, in various kinds of dependent status vis-à-vis the capitalist world. The mechanics, chauffeurs, and sharecroppers of north Lebanon and the unemployed workers, shopkeepers, clerks, and petty traders of Cairo have their counterparts in the whole region. They represent an enormous and ever-increasing proportion of the population of these societies.

For everyone the nature and meaning of society have become a central problem. The domination exercised in the Middle East, particularly by Britain, France, and the United States, has deep repercussions. Political orders have been overturned and with them often the authority of Muslim rulers and Muslim law. The very bases of political legitimacy and claims to authority are questions of constant relevance and sharply contesting points of view. Social and cultural institutions once part of the taken-for-granted everyday world are equally open to fiercely divergent interpretation. Many of the suppositions and predispositions that make up culture have come into conscious and often very critical and self-conscious reflection. What Islam means for Muslims in the modern world is now an issue for debate and action in the context of the politics of nation states, the struggle for energy supplies, superpower rivalry, and dependency. What is the *umma*, the Islamic community, and how and where is *ijma'*, or consensus, to be formed? What is Islamic government and in what forms and institutions must it be embodied?

As the forces of nationalism and anti-imperialism have generated their own contradictions and taken sometimes acutely opposed directions that have divided, as much as unified, the idea of a pure tradition takes on a renewed vitality. Tradition: that which we have always done and believed and from which we have derived our social forms. But what is the authentic tradition with which we are to face the forces of unbelief, corruption, and oppression?

It is a confrontation. The insistence on a self-conscious examination is born out of contest. As a leading Arab intellectual has said, "Tradition is born in confrontation with military or commercial aggression . . . . Slavism, *brahmo saraj*, the reinterpretation of Confucius by *Kang Yu-Wei*, salafiyya – these responses are doubtless different but nonetheless display the same structure."*

Tradition, therefore, is put together in all manner of different ways in contemporary conditions of crisis; it is a term that is in fact highly variable and shifting in content. It changes, though all who use it do so to mark out truths and principles they regard as essentially unchanging. In the name of tradition many traditions are born and come into opposition with others. It becomes a language, a weapon against internal and external enemies, a refuge, an evasion, or part of the entitlement to domination and authority over others. One of the single most important elements in what is often called Islamic fundamentalism is precisely this struggle over the definition of what is the tradition. This means not only a religious interpretation but a whole form of life. Such pro-. cesses, as Laroui's remarks make clear, have been worldwide in the past two centuries, as capitalism has spread, and are by no means confined to Islamic communities.

The basic building blocks of these ideologies of Islamic tradition are largely shared. It is the relations between them and the stress on a particular interpretation of a given element that are significant for the distinctions between movements and groups.

The fundamentals can be set out quite simply. Islam which

* Abdullah Laroui, *The Crisis of the Arab Intellectual*, trans. Diarmid Cammell, Berkeley/Los Angeles. University of California Press, 1976, p. 87. The *Salafiyya* is a very important reformist movement in modern Islam (see chapter 7).

means submission to God, is constructed upon what Muslims believe is a direct Revelation in Arabic from God: the Quran. This recitation or reading, for that is what the word *Quran* means, is the miraculous source of the umma, the Islamic community. It is the Word. And the conception and communal experience of the Word in prayer, in study, in talismans, in chanting of the sacred verses, in *zikr* (Sufi rituals of remembrance), in the telling of beads, in curing, in social etiquette, and in a hundred other ways are at the root of being a Muslim. The directness of the relationship with Allah through the Word and its intensely abstract, intensely concrete force is extremely difficult to evoke, let alone analyze, for members of societies dominated by print and the notion of words standing for things.

It is yet more difficult when we realize that the shape and form of the letters making up the Quranic verses that adorn mosques and homes, for example, are not decorative in any Western sense but are part of this essential directness of the Revelation and are felt as intrinsically full of divine energy and grace.

This recitation that gave birth to the community was given to the Prophet Muhammed, whose duty it was to transmit it to the society of early-seventh-century-A.D. western Arabia in his role as a "warner," as the Quran calls him, and as the last, or "seal," of the prophets. The Revelation had come down before, to the Jews and the Christians through their prophets, acknowledged as such in the Quran, but it had been distorted by the rabbis and the priests. This is the last chance. There will be no other after it. Muhammed is not a wonder-worker, the miracles are made by God, and one of the greatest miracles is the divine language of the Quran itself.

Nonetheless, the figure of Muhammed obviously occupied an extraordinary position, and the family of the Prophet came to be especially revered. Often the ruler had to claim to be of that family of the Qureish, and groups of holy men, such as the sherifs I have already mentioned, based their authoritative positions on such a sacred genealogy. No other principle had been established by Muhammed before his death in A.D. 632, or the year 11 of the Muslim calendar, so that his succession was left problematic to his followers and to generations after.

The practice of the Prophet, the *sunna*, became a model for all Muslims, and it was recorded and elaborated in what became a large number of texts, on which, together with the Quran, the Islamic law was based. The traditions of Muhammed and his Companions, known as the *hadith*, developed into a framework for defining what the community is, and this framework became the basis of education and learning as much as of practical life.

Practical is a key word in my view. For God and His umma are active in history. They have a covenant that is lived out not only in the five pillars — the profession of faith that "there is no God but Allah, and Muhammed is his Prophet," the observance of fasting during the daylight hours of the holy month of Ramadan, the giving of alms, the making of the five daily prayers, and going on the great pilgrimage to the holy cities of Mecca and Medina. It entails also a general sense of practical readiness for whatever the power of God disposes in small matters or in great. Believers have their guide and model in the sunna and the hadith, which deal with the most mundane aspects of everyday life and behavior as well as the general principles directing the community.

This practical readiness is far closer to a simple characterization of the Islam of my experience than is any image of either passive resignation or fanatical impulse.

The Book, the Family, the Tradition. All three are interpreted and acted on, their meanings in life fired and turned into a personal and collective enterprise. These are the fundamental elements in contemporary movements that call for a return to a true Islam. But they are by no means the only ones, and the ways in which they are understood vary widely.

Muslims have always been aware of differences and variations in the way traditions were viewed and actions demanded. In the Middle Ages local and regional pilgrimages, as well as the great pilgrimage to Mecca and Medina, were points at which people from quite separate social and economic orders gathered. The collective quest for blessing or knowledge was one that gave form and substance to the idea of the umma. These pilgrimages served as channels of information. Ideas and beliefs flowed through them at startling speed. Such gatherings at a shrine were frequently markets as well, centers of distribution and exchange in an economy that might have direct or indirect links over thousands of miles of caravan route. The disappearance of the caravans has not diminished the importance of modern pilgrimages. The social, political, and symbolic weight of such gatherings has, if anything, increased. The sense in which Islam forms a world ideological system has deepened and become more actual as the means of communication have developed.

Religious men in Indonesia would, by the late nineteenth century, know very well of the reformist or Sufi mystical currents in Morocco, Egypt, Syria, Iran, or India. They would know of the revolts, rebellions, constitutional movements, and peasant insurrections in the name of Islam against internal and external foes. Books were published and read by the learned men. Popular hymns, exhortations, and lives of saints could be purchased, memorized, and repeated by an ever-expanding audience. The meanings of Islam were both quickened and challenged at the same moment. The tape recordings of the Ayatollah Khomeini's speeches smuggled into Iran spread the revolutionary message in ways security apparatuses were unable to prevent. This is but the most recent example of the speed at which ideas and calls to action are diffused.

The notion and fact of diversity in the Islamic world is therefore no more a new one for Muslims than is the call for a return to the first principles, or rather, first practices, of the community. The so-called revival of Islam in the 1970s and after is not a revival at all but a continuation. Religious movements of all kinds — austere and ecstatic, legalistic and mystic, activist and quietist — have been socially and politically highly significant since the late eighteenth century, as European and capitalist influence became predominant. There have been two hundred years of what Westerners treat as a ten-year wonder. The reference is to a long history; the forms, contexts, and relations are constantly renewed.

All of this means that Islam is very much at the center of the cultural and political stage, or appears to be.

Appears to be. Memories of a hand kiss in a street in south Arabia make me hesitate. Contemporary events are dangerous guides to thought. Islam has become so much of a preoccupation of Western politics and media that we are tempted to think of it as a single, unitary, and all-determining object, a "thing" out there with a will of its own. There is a strong notion of a powerful, irrational force that, from Morocco to Indonesia, moves whole societies into cultural assertiveness, political intransigence, and economic influence.

Another version of this idea is the notion that religion is the key to the "Arab mind" or, at a wider level, that something called the "Muslim mind" or "Islamic civilization," explains a whole series of events and structures that are otherwise totally baffling and alarming. Islam is seen as the key to the secret and as part of the nature and essence of these people. The Iranian revolution is one of the most startling phenomena that have catalyzed and continue to stimulate this sense of Islam as a total and threatening mysterious presence.

In this book I want to dissolve such conceptions and give you a more cautious awareness of what the term *Islam* comes to mean in quite different economic, political, and social structures and relations.

Anthropologists see the meaning of a particular social role or myth or ritual or event as being the product of its relations and contrasts with other roles, myths, rituals, and events. The implications of this approach are that Islam will be discussed not as a single, rigidly bounded set of structures determining or interacting with other total structures but rather as a word that identifies varying relations of practice, representation, symbol, concept, and worldview within the same society and between different societies. There are patterns in these relations, and they have changed in very important ways over time. My aim is not to persuade the reader to substitute a relativized and fragmented vision for one of global unity. Rather it is to situate some of these religious, cultural, and ideological forms and practices that people regard as Islamic in the life and development of their societies.

There are therefore whole sections of the book in which topics and themes are dealt with that do not appear at first glance to have much to do with Islam or religion: the furnishing of the *salon* of the Lebanese bourgeoisie; sexuality, honor, and violation linked to God's grace; the street plan of modern Cairo; tribal markets; family feuds; genealogies; and so forth. To take any element on its own or only in relation to other elements defined as "religious" would not yield its social meaning. And we have to be prepared to find that religion is often only a very minor influence.

What these topics also show is how much there is in common between the experience of the Lebanese and Egyptian working classes and petite bourgeoisie and those same classes in other societies of the Third World in which Islam does not figure at all. An Indian village is not a Lebanese village, and Rio de Janeiro is not Cairo, of course. But I think you will see that as well as the specific differences there are many things in common generated by the complex strains of a system of dependency that is worldwide. The way in which the economy, patterns in the use of public and domestic space, and conceptions of power and identity operate are at least as alike as they are distinct. Third World societies have been exposed to the same forces in various shapes and guises, and the chapters that follow illustrate this point and show that those forces themselves may not be quite what we think: "It has been observed that Hegel studied English political economy before thinking about Napoleonic expansionism, and it is true that it was not the Decembrists or the savants accompanying Bonaparte's expeditions who overturned societies, whether Russian or Egyptian, but English furniture."*

English furniture? Well, yes. Furniture, ways of sitting, modes of dress, politeness, photography, table manners, and gestures overturn societies, too. Such conventions, techniques, and ways of acting in and on the world are as important as any religion, and changes in them may be as dislocating as changes in belief. So we should be especially wary of assuming that it is Islam that is the most important area on which to focus. We do not have to accept or impose the primacy of religion over social, economic, or political factors. This book is an attempt to demystify our standard approaches to Islam, just as my own views were so radically shaken in south Arabia.

There are many writers who, from different perspectives and disciplines, are attempting this kind of rethinking.

---

* Laroui, *Crisis of the Arab Intellectual*, p. 87. Napoleon landed in Egypt in 1798 accompanied by a group of French intellectuals and scholars, as well as by an army. They were the savants referred to.

Edward Said has launched a full-scale attack on traditional modes of Orientalist scholarship.* Abdallah Laroui has dissected the role of Arab intellectuals from within. Groups of French and English students have subjected the texts they were brought up on to highly critical appraisal. The sense that it is time for a basic shift in the ways in which we think about Islam in society has become more and more urgent in the last two decades.

This is a reaction to previously dominant modes of thought in anthropology, political science, history, and Oriental studies. The first emphasized functional interrelations, with units usually defined as villages or tribes, and put the rest of the world "in brackets" or in a brief section on something called social change. The second, political science, stressed elites, a division between essential forms of society called traditional and modern and a view of politics very close to current Western political interests in the area. History in most cases seemed not to have caught up with the innovations in theory and method that occurred in other branches of the subject since World War II, notably in social history and the history of those classes often disregarded in the narrative of events. Orientalism operated within a tradition that had become ossified, seeing texts to be commented on often with the reverence of a medieval divine, adoring Islam but suspicious of Muslims, and frequently downright hostile to and uncomprehending of political movements in the contemporary Middle East.

Intellectual space has opened up, space that had previously seemed totally filled by such perspectives. Writers such as Maxime Rodinson, whose work had not had the general impact it deserved, came to the notice of a much wider public. We have begun — and in many ways intellectuals are slower than tortoises — to catch up with the changes that have long since taken place in the societies we study, and in the disciplines to which we belong. In journalism, too, amid a pile of instant books there are now versions of the travel book that make the fact that the author starts off knowing nothing into a virtue. But it is not patronizing of excellent

* Edward W. Said, *Orientalism* (New York: Pantheon Books; London: Routledge and Kegan Paul, 1978). See Select Bibliography for other works of a critical nature.

writers such as Jonathan Raban to say that this kind of trained innocence is not an instrument that can, or is designed to, dig too deep analytically.*

My own basic procedure has been to use a lot of material drawn from personal experience of Islam and to try to re-create the surprise of the moment when my work really began, that moment when realization collided with illusion in south Arabia. The writings of others are of course here, explicitly or implicitly, in all that follows. I certainly had no wish to limit this book so dramatically as to exclude a whole range of studies of different societies. But I have used my own work as the main source and concentrated on communities in the Middle East and have not tried to give a summary of other studies or a state-of-the-field type of discussion. That has its place no doubt, but it is not my project here. This book is my point of view on what "studying Islam" means, and it does not pretend to be a survey of all Muslim societies or religious behaviors.

This means ignoring such countries as Indonesia and Pakistan, which would be very important for a wider picture of Islam in social terms. It entails concentrating mainly, as too many do, on Arab societies, which is misleading to the degree that the numerical majority of Muslims in the world from Africa to Asia are not Arab and, equally, not all Arabs are Muslims. Yet the main themes of our inquiry can be discussed in more limited terms, and should be if the reader is not to be overwhelmed with material. So the best principle of selection has seemed to me to be that of looking at what I know best, partial and uncertain though that very often is.

The book begins with the basic theme of the formation and transformation of power and authority within Muslim societies and elaborates a set of variations on this theme. It moves from a discussion of the highly institutionalized positions and functions of the religious scholars to the more shifting patterns of the establishment of a given holy man's relations to specific local groupings and what people take to be the legitimating signs of grace.

The second chapter concentrates on the scholars: those who have been a key mediating element between the Holy Book and the Traditions and the Community, and who have

* Jonathan Raban, *Arabia through the Looking Glass* (London: Collins, 1979).

necessarily, therefore, been tangled in the webs of power woven by dominant classes and the political and cultural apparatuses of states and communities. What I want most to show about these 'ulema, as they are called in Arabic, is how their structural positions have varied across different kinds of economic and political systems, or within the same system as it has changed over time. Though the 'ulema do not form a class, the class origins of members of this stratum, and the relations they had and have to the ruling economic and political groups, is one of the first questions the anthropologist must raise.

This is not to say that class origin is some kind of master key, particularly when we are dealing with precapitalist societies, where the nature and relations of class are often far too schematically presented. But where the 'ulema played an important role in the appropriation of the agricultural surplus of the direct producers working the land — as tax farmers, for example — or were intimately linked to the merchant class of the bazaars, there are obviously primary interests that carry considerable weight.* For such factors, allied to their legal and educative functions as guardians of the Revelation, constitute a complex of authority and potential power of great significance. So I discuss such complexes in two different and changing social settings — at the center of the Ottoman Empire in the late eighteenth and early nineteenth centuries and at the fringes in Morocco over the same period — to show the institutional and cultural mechanisms at work in these contrasted sets of social relations.

One consequence of this emphasis is to avoid a purely internal analysis of the law of which they were the formulators and reproducers by means of theological and legal discourse, schools, courts, and exegeses. I do this because I share the point of view expressed by the French sociologist Pierre Bourdieu, among others, which bears not so much on the explicit ideology and legitimations that a group produces or inculcates as on "those ideological effects . . . which have no need of words, and ask no more than a

---

* These connections and their importance in contemporary Iran have been discussed in Michael Fischer *Iran: From Religious Dispute to Revolution* (Cambridge, Mass.: Harvard University Press, 1980), particularly at page 93.

complicitous silence."* The nature of the silences and the complicity is what has to be explained.

In the third chapter I turn to the Shi'ite tradition of Islam, and examine the place of suffering in the religious culture of Iran (at the state level) and Lebanon (at the village level). In both cases it emerges as only one strand in a pattern of relations that is itself changing under the impact of capitalism. The two settings are again very different, and the authority and social position of the religious specialists is constructed on correspondingly different grounds. "The same" cultural themes take on a variety of significances and express reversals of the world order that are quite other than their apparent message.

This variation is extended through the following three chapters (4, 5, and 6). These trace out the paths of cultural signs of religious authority that are not those of the 'ulema. Now we are in a realm of grace and miracles, of holy descent and mystical Sufi brotherhoods, of the outer forms and inner realities that people take to be the fundamental building blocks of the world. But we are also in the realm of the working class and *lumpenproletariat* of contemporary Egypt and Morocco, of the feudal lords and holy men of north Lebanon, and of the contradictions and tensions of cultural practice in social life. Miracles that seem to deny the class politics of society in a hidden way confirm them; a religious sheikh who gives all the right signs of grace is discredited without his realizing it; ascetic Sufi leaders sweep around Senegal in Cadillacs. As always, the blessings of the poor and the blessings of the rich turn out to be part of quite distinct forms and institutions with quite distinct and often opposed meanings, even though the terms in which they are understood initially appear to be identical.

This leads us into what I might call another key, a key whose dominant is colonialism and the struggle over the body and soul of whole societies (chapter 7). This battle, epitomized here in phases of the French domination of Algeria and the rule of the Italians in Libya, goes through succeeding stages in which religion itself comes to be redefined as new classes and kinds of opposition to the colonial order become

* Pierre Bourdieu, *Outline of a Theory of Practice* (Cambridge: Cambridge University Press, 1977), p. 188.

paramount. In Algeria the leadership of the Sufi brother-hoods gives way to that of fractions of the bourgeoisie and the "reformers," intent on producing an austere and militant Islam that will be purified of what they see as accretions and used as a weapon against the power of the outsider. The ultimate success of the Algerian revolution, associated with reformist ideology, leads in time to a different emphasis in which Islam and socialism are proclaimed with increasing insistence to be closely allied. But that stress is not only an article of faith on the part of the state; it may also turn into a critique of the state by those who feel that the self-styled purity of the reformers' Islam is in fact a perversion and an instrument of class interest.

In the more "tribal" society of Libya, militant Islam emerges, in the context of an equally total and brutal colonial form, under the guise of a Sufi order. The Sanusiya eventually become the germ of an independent state. But they in turn are displaced by a revolution whose discourse is marked by a Nasserism and Arab socialism and also by a radical attempt at a kind of permanent revolution whose ideological base is claimed to be that of a true and renewed Islam.

Both the following chapters (8 and 9) develop further the question of how power is imposed and struggled for in dimensions of space. Spatial forms are not of course a given part of the natural order of things, though crucially they may come to be apprehended in that way. They are constructed, imposed, used, and defined in different ways at different times by different classes. They entail profound and often unconscious relations of ideology and hierarchy. When major changes occur in traditional models, the effect may be to recast the cultural and practical vocabulary in terms that cannot simply be incorporated into the old. Rather, they put the old in a new perspective, moral and political as well as spatial, and contradict key elements of what dominant groups take to be, in the most pejorative sense of the word, traditional. This category itself becomes a symbolic force that diminishes and discredits, rather than justifies and legitimates, a way of existence. A new kind of opposition and incoherence is introduced into the world at a fundamental level. Whole city forms and functions are transformed in ways that are determined by a different economic and cultural logic, one of whose basic properties is to deny and dislocate the already existing logic. House design and the furnishing of the *salon* are thus indicators of far wider processes as a part of which the whole perception and ideology of the city changes.

The sense of a world turned inside out lies at the heart of chapter 10, which focuses in some detail on modern Egypt. Large numbers of movements, groupings, and associations have arisen there to challenge the present on the basis of a vision of what a true Islam dictates and imposes absolutely on the community. Such movements are full of tensions, political and cultural. Yet they help to form one kind of response to the upheavals of history molded above all by imperial control, by capitalism, and by nationalism. New classes anchored in the cities oscillate in their ideological commitments. State apparatuses and government policies toward religion have alternately repressed and encouraged what are often called fundamentalist currents in answer to changes in the constellations of power in Egypt. The Sufi orders, too, in their own way show the disruptive effects of a conjunction of different social classes within the same mode of religious organization.

These, in brief, are the concerns of this book. It is my own introduction to Islam as well as an introduction for others, which returns me to the previously indicated dimension of autobiography. Perhaps these chapters retroactively help me to realize what it is that I have been doing in studying the Middle East for the last twenty years. Certainly they have often surprised me in the writing with the sense that this is what I have been really doing. If they give the reader some sense of discovery as well, then they will have more than served their purpose.

CHAPTER 2

The Men of Learning and Authority

The Prophet departed, the Revelation remained. A religious and political community was being formed, but there was no line of succession to the leadership of that as yet newly born umma. Nor could the shapes it was to take in conquest and expansion be revealed other than in their unfolding over time. Change, radical change, was of the essence. But for this to be so without the destruction of Islam as a vision and a model of a world order, the religiocultural system had to be made into a system, elaborated and institutionalized around the Quran and the sunna. The Holy Book had to take its definitive and final organized structure. The path or tradition had to be brought into existence and authoritatively sanctioned.

As the community became in effect many diverse communities with different historical, political, and linguistic roots, the unity of a normative, legal, and legitimating Islam was of crucial significance. The divisions of the polity that occurred from the death of the Prophet onward, and the great Umayyad and Abbasid empires of the succeeding three centuries, made all the more vital the preservation of unquestionable Truth and its diffusion in society. If dynasties frequently seemed to rule in ways contrary to the Word of

God, so much the more important was it for Islam to be seen as the real underlying and continuous foundation of society, whatever the acts of the rulers.

This preservation was a creative process. It had to be. Islam was, in theory, to regulate not only the correct position for the making of the prayers but also taxation, not simply the pious life but land tenure. If in fact local customs were often incorporated into the evolving administrative practices of empire as well as what became Islamic culture, they had to be reunderstood as Islamic. If innovations and personal judgments by legists had to be made as part of the heroic religious virtuosity of the early period, it was to ensure that religion should and could be experienced as unified and constant in a transforming universe.

Belief and practice that are regarded as eternal, unchangeable in essence if not in every detail, and as given by a higher and nonhuman power still have to be carried on. They have constantly to be re-created in social life. Even if the pious fiction is that things are just as they were and that the sacred tradition is unaltered, the myths unchanging, the genealogies fixed forever, we know that in fact things do change. What is regarded as totally orthodox in one age is not so regarded in another; myths appear and disappear or are interpreted in different ways by different groups; genealogies contain strange gaps and often leave out as many people as they include. They must do so in one way or another to stay alive and significant as a society changes or as, say, a religious system becomes part of new economic and political orders.

Certain vital questions lie always just below the surface of everyday life, breaking through in times of crisis. Since the Prophet Muhammed gave no rules for the succession, who would lead the community and what duties would such a person have? What would "the Islamic community" mean in practice? Who was to say? In other words, which persons would possess the authority to certify as legitimately Islamic a given office, institution, or action, and on what basis would they do so? What characteristics would a society have to possess that would make it manifestly a Muslim society?

These are fundamental interrogations of contemporary life as well as of the first centuries of Islam, and they have all kinds of social, economic, and political implications. The responses, often very different, appeal to various sources of authority. First, of course, is the Quran itself and the law that is held to be derived from it. Beyond that is the whole body of canonical tradition, the hadith, which relates to what the Prophet or his Companions said or did in certain circumstances. This body of knowledge in theory goes back to the Prophet himself or to members of the original community. But we know that, in historical terms, many of the hadith do not go back that far, but rather emerged in the three hundred or so years after the Prophet's death, as society encountered new kinds of problems and demands.*

These traditions and the notion of the sunna, or path of the rightly guided community, embody a model of social practice. Indeed the whole idea of a model (the Prophet's life and acts are a prime example) became and remains enormously important. But hadith and sunna do not grow on trees. They have to be continually re-created and reproduced in social life, just as the Revelation itself has to be preserved and imparted to the faithful of all classes and groups. What kinds of persons could accomplish these functions?

Descendants of the Prophet (the sherifs) became privileged, or at least able to claim some kind of privileged status and respect. Men of learning, who in some cases were also sherifs, studied, organized, and interpreted the Book and became another category of figures of authority. Others, associated with the rich and many-sided Sufi mystical tradition, claimed descent by blessing, a chain of grace that linked particular holy men to the family of the Prophet or to that of a saint, or through mystical powers to perform miraculous acts that testified to their special religious favor in the eyes of the Divinity.

Part of the vitality and dynamism of Islam in society springs from the tensions, competition, and contradictions inherent in the ranks of the different specialists and holy men, who may at one moment be completely and publicly at odds, asserting their sole control of a given power or path to blessing, and at another moment be happily cooperative or even unified. Such tension is part of the way in which religion

* Much critical sifting was carried out by Muslim scholars and jurists to establish as far as they could which traditions did go back to the Prophet and which did not, which were genuine, which doubtful, and which to be rejected.

is constantly transformed in relation to, and as part of, other social institutions and structures.

Relations within the same institution or body of specialists are equally important given the varying possibilities of schism and dispute over structure and doctrine. But for all such groups and categories similar questions arise. How is their authority defined and in what fields are they regarded as competent or having jurisdiction? How does one become, remain, and cease to be such a person? What is their "cultural capital," their justification and signs of legitimacy, and how is it translated into wider patterns within social life?

The Ideal Type of 'Alim

The 'ulema (singular 'alim) have been pre-eminently guardians and interpreters of the sacred texts. They performed the great historical function of organizing a body of law and practice derived from the Quran and the traditions of the Prophet and the Companions. Often associated with the ruling groups within society, they have occupied and still hold a major place in defining an official version of Islamic belief and practice. The explanation of, and commentary on, the Quran, the sifting of different traditions to judge their validity, and the administration and elaboration of law that came to be enshrined in four great "schools" — the Hanbali, Hanafi, Shafe'i, and Maliki — were and are the core of their position as the learned doctors of scripture. Their control of law and education up to the modern period also meant a powerful influence on the ways in which the Arabic language itself and styles of thought and argument were developed. In the historical evolution of Islam the guardians of scripture played a vital part as formulators, preservers, and interpreters of the Book and the Law.

Note that they are not what Westerners would call by the term *clergy*. The 'ulema do not possess or monopolize a unique mediating role between the believer and God; they cannot promise or refuse salvation or grace, and the keys to hell or paradise are not in their hands. There is no mechanism of confession or penitences that they operate, and they are not God's substitutes on earth. They are different, therefore, from a Church hierarchy through which the believer must go to approach the Divinity.

The 'ulema saw themselves as the proper guardians of "the Word," the Revelation. More specifically, we could say that they guarded the Word as *text*. Now, this notion of the text seems to me of particular sociological importance when trying to characterize their social role and the bases of their authority. Inasmuch as the Quran is the major symbolic source and resource of a society that regards itself as Muslim, the 'ulema in effect reproduced it as a text of which they were the keepers. As such it is written down, commented upon, and held to be sacred, unchanging, and unchanged. As commentary piles on commentary (each commentary, of course, being itself a text and part of a growing body of knowledge), so it becomes less and less likely that anyone will understand, or be permitted to think that he possibly could understand, "the meaning," unless he has specialized training. This process necessitates further commentaries! So commentaries and interpretations, while apparently elucidating meaning, in effect restrict it to the body of specialists and to some extent serve to withdraw the "original" from daily life and to mediate its relation with the rest of the community. The text is made esoteric and becomes the special preserve of scholars, who are self-defined as the only ones who can really understand it.

The text becomes an instrument of authority and a way of excluding others or regulating their access to it. It can be used to show that others are wrong and we are right; what is more, we have the right to be right and they do not! We *know*. So Revelation is controlled and becomes a potential mode of control. If we remember that the Quran appeared during a particular period and in a particular style that became the basis of an evolving "high" language and culture largely inaccessible to the masses, and that anyhow the masses were generally illiterate and possessed the spoken but not the written word, the importance of establishing it as a text becomes even clearer.

A second notion, perhaps equally significant, is what we may call the impersonal nature of the 'ulema's authority. Learning is acquired through training, and not, for example, through personal sanctity. An 'alim goes through a process of study and examination, that depersonalizes and objectifies both the learning itself and the position of the learned in general. At the same time, such a process is ideally universal and neutral. It is the same for everyone. It depends in theory on the objectively judged competence of the student, who performs according to criteria that are applied to all students. It is not tied to a particular person or setting but has, or claims, authority everywhere, regardless of the individual character of anyone who has been through the training and has acquired skills. So 'ulema are always being produced through the system of religious schools and universities, and the text is continually reproduced as a text.

Clearly this institution contributes to the particular social order within which it is located at any given time and place. Because as long as the 'ulema system continues, it helps to guarantee the political and ideological structures of which it is a part as being Islamic, as having legitimacy, even if absolutely no direct reference to the characteristics of the particular political and social order in question is ever made.

The 'ulema therefore had (and have) a rather different kind of knowledge, formulated in a different kind of way from that of other people. Text and training are crucial. On that basis the 'alim has the authority and legitimacy of a man of knowledge who guards and ensures the purity of the central core of Revelation and Law, which are so vital in Muslim societies. This means that they help to create what the official meaning of Islam should be for members of any given society, and in that sense they establish the yardstick for locally defining what is Islam and what is not.

This function of providing the official version clearly has and had both advantages and dangers. In conditions of dynastic instability, of the incorporation of new groups and societies (many of whom might not have Arabic as their native tongue and for whom, therefore, the Quran and the Law would be in a foreign language), or of the splitting of empires and the emergence of local powers, the maintenance of a textual tradition and the building up of an enormous apparatus of interpretations, legal judgments, and exegeses preserved the Islamic tradition as something present and continuous. In times of flux it could be taken as a fixed point. Its very repetitiveness, its endless replications of previous established ideas, might be a highly positive quality. In the often changing and uncertain conditions of the world the tradition carries on because it is so rigid, formalized, apparently sealed, opposed to innovation. Only in the face of the massive qualitative change of the coming of colonial and capitalist power might the tradition itself seem threatened and the 'ulema suddenly appear a desperately inadequate guarantee of its survival.

On the other hand, the dangers were of equal significance. The 'ulema might be well and truly buried under their commentaries and legalisms. There existed the constant possibility of becoming ever more introverted and esoteric until the whole system would become totally ossified and cut off from the social world. The specialists might do their job too well, depriving the system of any flexibility or those creative powers it must have in order to survive. Ultimately the rigidity of such a system might in fact help to produce what it aimed to avoid: a situation in which the mass of the people, excluded from the elitist learning, created their own men of authority who might be highly suspect and even heretical in 'ulema terms. Heterodoxies might flourish. If the 'ulema were closely associated with the ruling political powers, the implications of such heterodoxies would also necessarily be political. There could arise miracles and miracle workers, healers, mystical groups, new ritual forms, and a host of beliefs and symbols put together in a patch-work quilt to make sense of everyday life. Much of this might be thought by the masses to be genuinely Islamic and perfectly orthodox, even if in 'ulema eyes there would be scandalous theological and legal perversions of the 'ulema version of "the Truth." The Quran might be given interpretations many miles from those endlessly reproduced in the great religious schools, in part because the great schools were shut off from the people.

Many factors have historically moderated these dangers, and the ideal typical picture of the 'alim that I have drawn. Believers do not depend on the 'ulema for performing the basic religious duties (the so-called five pillars), and the Quran is there to be heard, chanted, memorized, or, by the literate, read. The sacred tradition, therefore, could never simply be taken over by the state through the control of a compliant or dependent body of scholar-lawyers.

Other roles and specialists emerged with other powers that were asserted to be Islamic, the Sufi sheikhs being the classic example. Moreover, the general category of holy or learned man could in many cases embrace being 'alim and Sufi and curer and teacher and mediator all at once without any sense of contradiction. For many people a given individual came to be regarded as a religious authority competent to give legal guidance and judgment as much on the basis of his locally acquired reputation for learning and insight, position of influence in the community, descent, even wealth and kinship connections, as on any background of formal training in one of the great schools or universities. The dynamics of such a process are very close to those that go to make up the authority of holy men who are not in institutional terms 'ulema at all, as we shall see in a later discussion of the position of sheikhs in north Lebanon.

In addition to this, let us remember that many people, particularly nomads and villagers and poor townspeople, had only extremely limited dealings with the 'ulema. Beliefs and practices that the latter might consider un-Islamic were regarded as perfectly Islamic by their practitioners and constantly blended into the popular cultural tradition.

Now, it is quite true that in the modern period particularly, the 'ulema have often been criticized for inflexibility and a blind following of precedent. But we should remember that in the process of law, cases had to take account of the enormously wide range of social problems and situations, and there was often a pragmatic flexibility under the apparently rigid framework.

Finally, it should be noted that the membership of the body of 'ulema was and is in many cases drawn from all levels of society, since becoming an 'alim was traditionally one of the relatively few means of social mobility. They are generally not recruited from a single class. A wide spread of backgrounds and social experience has continually fed into religious teaching because of this degree of social openness.

In spite of these qualifications, one fundamental point remains. In a very general sense the entire apparatus of judicial administration, the different realms of law, from the commercial to the personal, the definition and judging of crime, gives legitimacy to a whole social system and codifies crucial relationships — for example, those of property.

The law further establishes shared and enforceable models of right conduct. When closely integrated with what it defines as proper religious belief and organization filtered through the apparatus of courts and educational institutions, it is a means for the creation of authority and ideas about the whole nature of social life that is of immense influence.

It is not only what the law prohibits or regulates in one way or another that is crucial, however, but also the fact that it takes for granted or passes over in silence certain kinds of social structures, acts, and relationships.

So if the rulers enforce religious law in the "appropriate" areas, then a society can be claimed to be properly Islamic and to be based on religion. Since the religious law is defined as being in force, cooperation with an unjust ruler can be tolerated. Very different political and economic structures are thereby justified, placed beyond argument, or rendered "invisible" or irrelevant. Although the religious law may therefore appear largely indifferent to the wider political economy, in practice it provides that political and economic system with a moral and ideological underpinning.

The fact, too, that "the law," which is "eternal" and part of "the Truth" with a capital T, is dependent on certain social groups and in a real sense is produced by them and not merely administered, is dissimulated. So also is the fact that those social groups have their own specific economic and political relations and interests, including the relationship with the dominant strata to which many of them, in this case the 'ulema, may belong.

This is a topic of the widest cultural as well as political interest. For hadith and the sunna and the Holy Book were not theological texts in a narrow sense. Versions of traditions and of legal judgments in different local understandings, interpretations of what the proper path is according to various authorities, and invocations of the Prophet's actions and Quranic injunctions were woven into the everyday language of the ordinary people — workers, artisans, trades-men, cultivators, even pastoralists. In argument, discussion, punctuating conversation, and talk in what were until recently largely nonliterate societies, the sacred word was circulated and became part of the fabric of life, as it still continues to be.

The power of oral culture, the integration of sacred formulas into everyday speech, constantly created and reinforced more general structures of authority in society: the power of the father, the seniority of age, the restrictions on the position of women, the weight of model, right behavior. This discourse of authority was shot through with religious reference, and for practical purposes it made Islamic any number of locally derived forms of acts and relations. The 'ulema were thus directly and indirectly linked to what people took to be the sense of things, order in life, through these widely permeating forms of cultural practice as well as through the law and education.

The 'Ulema and the Emerging Nation State

One of the clichés of the eighteenth-century Enlightenment and its nineteenth-century successors was that the mystifying and irrational forces of religion had to be swept from the minds of human beings if they were to enter the age of reason, science and, increasingly, technology. Religion, it was held, might have dominated an early stage of history or characterized a phase in the development of society. But it had to give way to new forms of association and social relations. For some it might still have its place in the scheme of things. In England at the zenith of her industrial and commercial power there was a vital place for duty, rectitude, and the sense of hierarchy that the Established Church could buttress; for stern Victorian family piety; for the "muscular Christianity" of the English public school; and for the missionary zeal that saved the "heathen" to be part of the imperial heaven.

For others, it epitomized the political reaction and false consciousness that had to be exposed for what it was if the workers were to lose their chains. Peoples had to take back for themselves their own powers that were mirrored in the distorting glass of religion.

The place of organized religion in society was thus a very uneasy one. If progress was the supreme value of the new dominant bourgeoisie, the institutions of the sacred might be a help or a hindrance. Certain churches might ally themselves with the ruling ideology (as in England) or might be strongly identified with royal courts, the landed aristocracy, and conservative elements in the peasantry to create powerful reactionary coalitions.

The nation state developed in its different forms through this period by an ever-increasing expansion of bureaucratization and centralized control through the public administrations, the legal apparatus, forms of education, and such agencies of coercion as the army and the police. Religion took on a more specifically defined and limited place. The ideological cosmos of the nation state and of the capitalist commercial and industrial division of labor subordinated and absorbed the old powers of the sacred. "Secularization," a word used in a rather general and fuzzy way to indicate a loss of religious influence over public institutions and private habits and motivations, came to seem to many to be a necessary condition for the transformation of society. Such countries in Europe as Spain, Italy, or Ireland, in which religion maintained a central place, tended to be, and to be regarded by others as, marginal or peripheral to the great world centers of the new economic order in England, Germany, and later the United States. Whether democratic, autocratic, or socialistic, centralizing states have kept a watchful eye on the religious specialists, whose sacred mandate, not to mention their material resources, might well under certain circumstances exceed the state's own and present an alternative pole of authority and legitimacy.

Such trends also marked the Middle East from the nineteenth century onward, as relations with a Europe now economically and militarily much stronger threatened the very existence of that former world order, the Ottoman Empire. I can best illustrate these processes by looking at two contrasting settings: a Turkish state attempting both to recapture its hold over its own provinces throughout the empire and to resist Europe by adopting many of Europe's own economic and political forms; and a Moroccan society, on the edge of empire both geographically and in terms of its independence of Istanbul, in which the state was limited in scale and control and the 'ulema were enmeshed in far more fluid sets of relations.

1. *Young Turks, Old Institutions: The Triumph of a Secularizing State?*

At the imperial center of the Ottoman Empire in the early nineteenth century the position of the 'ulema was highly institutionalized. They were appointed as mosque functionaries, judges, teachers, and jurisconsults, which gave them control of law and education. The top 'ulema were ensconced in the palace and were on the Imperial Council. They were given ranks and titles in the course of their careers. As members of the ruling *askeri*, or military estate, they were incorporated into the political elite. Moreover, certain 'ulema not only were integral to the state bureaucracy but were part of the important social stratum of merchants and tax farmers, which gave them a significant articulating role in the political economy of the empire. They were exempt from taxation, unlike their fellow askeris, and their estates were not subject to confiscation on death but could be passed on to their heirs.

The administration of *awqaf* (lands and buildings made over as religious endowments) gave them a financial base largely independent of the central government. There was an increase in the number of sons of pashas from the Ottoman aristocracy entering the corps of 'ulema to qualify for passing on property, which means that there was some penetration by the political and military class.

Religious endowments and taxes, learning and bureaucracy, law and state legitimacy — these were powerful elements in the position of a religious establishment. Religion appeared as the cultural-legal framework of the social order, enforced by the political and military powers of the state. The 'ulema played a fundamental part in many dimensions of the running of the empire and were essential to its maintenance in its traditional, that is to say precapitalist and pre-European-domination, forms.*

---

* The reader will find interesting material in the article on which I have particularly drawn for this section: Richard L. Chambers, "The Ottoman Ulema and the Tanzimat" in *Scholars, Saints, and Sufis: Muslim Religious Institutions since 1500*, ed. Nikki Keddie (Berkeley/Los Angeles: University of California Press, 1978), pp. 33-46. Tax farming was the practice whereby the tax revenues of a given area were granted to an official who surrendered the assessed amount to the state and could keep whatever he could collect surplus to that amount. This had become a major way of raising revenue by this period.

Yet this very centrality and dependence on the ruling dynasty for office and privilege might make them very vulnerable in the event of any major shift in the nature of the political and economic system. And such a shift was occurring. By the late eighteenth and early nineteenth centuries European political influence and commercial penetration were intensifying throughout the Mediterranean and other parts of the empire. The Ottoman state as a whole was being integrated into a new world system based essentially on northern Europe. It was becoming a peripheral zone ever more subordinated to the strategic and commercial interests of European powers at the center. Such pressures represented structurally different forces, which the Ottomans were ill equipped to counter but attempted to resist.

One dimension of resistance was the incorporation and adaptation of key institutional forms identified as being crucial to the creation of a modern and progressive order in Europe. Here the relation of the state to organized religion became a contentious issue. The expanding European presence might see Islam as a threat and source of potential opposition. Yet, for very different reasons, so did locally developing groups and classes in Turkey itself. By the mid nineteenth century these latter, made up of a new professional military corps, civil servants, engineers, members of the professions, and a small commercial and industrial bourgeoisie, also wanted to remove the "irrational" barrier to progress that Islamic institutions were taken to be. Society had to be opened for the technological, administrative, economic, and political changes that these groups saw as necessary for the establishment of a reformed social order in which they would play a central role. One instrument in these transformations would be the secularization of the state in ideology, law, education, and bureaucracy.

This raised questions that in various ways continue to haunt many Islamic societies, hovering over the heads of ruling elites and apparatuses. Can religion in its diverse manifestations be controlled and appropriated by the state and the ruling classes? What are the practical social implications of attempts to assert that control? Can a universalist and egalitarian Islamic ideology be regulated by national and class particularities?

Not a few students of this topic have felt that, beginning precisely with the Ottoman state in the mid nineteenth century, Islamic society was secularized and religion effectively removed as a basic element in political, economic, and even social life. Since contemporary events show that in fact the degree to which Islam in its different shapes has been effectively relegated to the private domain is, to put it mildly, extremely variable, let us go back to that crucial period when the process of freeing society from religion is thought to have begun.

There is no doubt that the major reforms were of great significance in the Ottoman Empire. The sultan diminished the autonomy of the 'ulema by starting to bureaucratize the religious administration and at the same time to establish affairs of state as separate from those of religion. A Directorate of Waqf was founded, and some of the privileges of the scholar-lawyers were permitted to civil officers (who now acquired the very important right to pass on material goods to heirs, for example). In the field of education there was emphasis on creating a new technical-military elite with a broader base of literacy among the population through reform of the schools from which such an elite might be recruited. Translation schools for feeding in Western science and knowledge came into existence. In law, Western-style codification of a part of Muslim religious law was a vital part of legal reforms. New commercial and penal codes were similarly introduced, more or less based on French models. The new Imperial Penal Code of 1858 was also derived in the main from French law. Finally, as Richard Chambers puts it, "the Land Code was produced by applying Western methods of classification and codification to traditional law on a selective basis and adapted to the contemporary situation."*

Much of what occurred can be summed up as a rationalization and strengthening of state power from the sultan's position and the elimination or neutralization of any group opposed to it. There was an emphasis on military efficiency and new forms of training, a new form of knowledge, a technocratic and bureaucratic elite at the disposal of the state and legitimated by the fact of being its servants and by the new ideology of "reform" and "reason." This very nineteenth-

* Ibid., p. 44.

century European program would be used to defend the empire against the Europeans and to ensure its survival.

The foundation of the policy and the impact of modernization are not to be found in the reforms themselves, which are as much the expression as the substance of change. The foundations lie in the disruption of the economic and political structures of Turkish society by European capitalism. We have had indications of this in the changes in the legal system, specifically as it affected economic and commercial affairs. The new commercial code of 1841, the codification of holy law (the *shari'a*), the Imperial Penal Code, and the Land Code were all formed by and modeled on European practice, dictated by European needs and interests in the exploitation of the Ottoman Empire at that period. The phrase already quoted, that "the Land Code was produced by applying Western methods of classification and codification to traditional law on a selective basis and adapted to the contemporary situation" in a way conceals far more than it reveals. It passes in silence over the key issue, which is the transformation of forms of property, rights of individuals and social groups to land — the primary element of production in such a society — and the enormous shift in the pattern of relations of town with countryside. In other words, it ignores the significance of law as an instrument and ideology of foreign, in this case European, capitalist control.

Some clues are given to the importance of these changes for whole strata of the population. Chambers points out, for instance, that "the economic impact of the West upon the rural Ottoman economy was being acutely felt by the 1840s and 1850s." Most relevant to the question of the 'ulema, we discover that "despite the fact that the medreses [religious schools] were also feeling the pinch of rising prices and diversion of some evkaf [religious endowments] revenues, their endowments still provided at least a subsistence living for many of the impoverished peasant youths who were entering the cities in large numbers."* This means that the Land Code, among many other factors, had the effect of beginning the fragmentation and pauperization of the rural strata and driving them into the expanding cities as a large pool of unskilled labor. This process of breaking up the rural

* Ibid., p. 37.

society's traditional units and forms of property and production has occurred in different forms in many modern societies, often through colonial rule and the application of regulations of the type of the Ottoman Land Code. It is such factors — the demands of the European powers and the nature of the overall developing economic system — that determine the broad outlines and purposes of such processes.

Yet were the 'ulema really quite as unseeing as is sometimes suggested? Were their links with the population as diminished and secularization as rampant as we might initially think? Under frontal attack by the state power, which was ultimately in a position to control at least their economic resources and like privileges, they behaved with a necessary circumspection. Their role of ideological production of the social system was undercut by the new techno-military-bureaucratic elites and the realities of European influence. Integration into and dependence upon the state, once the key to influence and privilege, became a disadvantage as the state changed its character. They were pushed out to the periphery of political office and power.

Given this context, they appear to have been fairly clear as to where they could and where they could not operate. For example, it was only when the Grand Vezir Reçid Pasha declared that "the Holy Law has nothing to do with the matter" that they reacted violently, and successfully, against the new commercial code. On their own ground of the Holy Law, on which the Pasha was unwise enough to place himself and the matters at hand, they were triumphant. Much of the creation of the "modern, secular" education system went without opposition. But the attempt to make them change their traditional attire, again a contest that was on their ground of symbols of traditional office and authority and of the identity of the 'alim, failed.

The 'ulema seem to have had a clear sense of where their competence and authority lay. Many reforms went through without problems being raised. I would suggest that this was partly because they would not have dreamed or even have been able to consider infringing on the competence of the political power that possessed its own particular realm.

Note finally that there is far more than meets the eye to the nature and degree of secularization. Given that the medreses provided subsistence living for many of the impoverished peasant youths who were part of a growing class of urban working people and *lumpenproletariat*, it may well be that the links of the 'ulema with the mass of the population were being radically strengthened. The Tanzimat reforms may, in this sense, have crystallized and integrated religious elements even more firmly than before among a people subject to violent dislocation of their whole social order. No longer a privileged elite, the 'ulema were allowed to become popular. The formally defined "Islamic character" of the Ottoman state may have been diminished. The "Islamic character" of Ottoman society and the new urban and rural lower classes may have been considerably intensified.

Since, if this view is correct, the strengthened association to which I refer occurred predominantly among the rural and urban laboring classes, we might expect the 'ulema (and religion in general) to be identified *by the new ruling strata* as "reactionary" and "a block to progress." The rational-technical ideology of the ruling group and that group's composition made "religion" an irrelevant irritant at the state level, a sign of backwardness to be superseded by reason and science, and largely the concern of the lower orders, who were now viewed as "traditional."*

The fact that for many the "traditional" social organization had been smashed and their lives radically disrupted by the state and market forces was masked by the instrumental notion so dear to technocrats that such social strata were "conservative" (when there was very little left to conserve) and possessed "attitudes" that had to be changed in order for them to be made useful for the general planned progress of the state. The structural characteristics of the lower strata and comprehension of their situation were walled off behind the ideology of modernization. The only religion appropriate to the new elites was one that was "properly" organized, responsible to the state, limited in its functions to carefully defined spheres, and concerned with a sober, "rationalist" reading of scripture.

In this context religious forces became a framework for

* The spread of a technocratic ideology of progress as being determined purely in the realm of economic and social engineering "problems" and "solutions" continues in our own time in societies as different as Algeria and Morocco.

the expression of the otherwise more or less disorganized and unorganized interests of the disprivileged and exploited, the heart of a heartless world, in Marx's phrase. Its symbols and idioms were interpreted by the poor as enshrining their identity (in a very idealized way), and what was perceived as another order of existence established on divine prescript and prophecy rather than that order (or disorder) in which in fact they were compelled to spend their daily lives. Since the Holy Law and the Quran and the 'ulema and other religious figures existed and may have served to canalize and structure such resentment and nascent class sentiment, religion was transformed from a pillar of the state served by a privileged elite who were part of the politically dominant stratum into a form of latent rebellion on the part of the uprooted. The determining forces of this very slow transformation were ultimately Western capitalism, and proximately state-directed "reforms."

Every attack upon those ideas and institutions that had once been part of the basic symbolic capital and legitimacy of state and society but that were now being discarded in the name of modernity further crystallized and defined Islam for the poor and for those classes who were marginal to this new order as "their" religion. In this sense state policy worked very directly against itself. Every attack, therefore, did not necessarily diminish religion but helped to increase that polarization and antagonism of social groups that was being produced by economic change, the growth of the modern state, and European power. The latter used its law as instrument and ideology and displaced the previous, local framework and its guardians (the 'ulema). The displacement did *not* mean the secularization of society. It meant, rather, the shift in the social signification of religion and the nature of the strata who would begin to regard themselves as "the true believers."

The state, despite itself, enshrined religion. It made religion a potential source and language of opposition to what may be seen as political and economic structures that fell altogether outside "Islamic society." Diminishing the role of the 'ulema, inevitable in these circumstances, also diminished the ways in which they helped to guarantee the legitimacy of power. Previously they could argue for collaboration, even with an unjust ruler, as long as religious law was preserved. But what if it was not? What if it was quite explicitly restricted and excluded from domains over which it had once been sovereign? The emerging dominant classes would free themselves of the traditional ideology. What of those who, like the peasants and landless coming into the towns or the displaced artisans, were dragged willy-nilly into the new order? Their lives were transformed by it, but they were and may have seen themselves as merely its instruments, they were far from grasping how it arose historically from outside.

At the same time, however, this intensification in the expression for the poor of a religious system of symbols and forms imposed its own limitations. The forces acting on them were identified in a demonology of foreigners, "nonbelievers," and so forth, rather than as the overall capitalist and market system of relations within which, without comprehending in what or how, they found themselves enmeshed and their lives determined.

So religion gave vivid expression and form to an objective process within the society. It also concealed and transcendentalized the determinants of that process.

As Islam, for different reasons and with different connotations, became identified with the old order by both sides, so the political and social meaning of religion as a vehicle for group and class interest was increased.* For the state, which created the notion of traditionalism, religion was something to be separated off and relegated to a controlled and subordinate role. It was regarded as an abstraction and a mode of thought that was part of the distressingly traditional attitudes of the rural and urban disprivileged (whose traditional life had been shattered). One of the paradoxes of the Turkish pattern of modernization is that the state thereby lost control over and understanding of religion at the precise historical moment that it unwittingly helped to endow it with greater and more profound social significance. The reforming sultan and the Young Turks were as ideologically

* For the state the old order was something to be rejected and displaced. For those who are displaced it was liable to be viewed rather as the authentic way, the true path, the real basis of social life, "ours," or, rather, "us." It furnished, too, a demonology of the new order. This kind of contradiction has the most profound implications for the contemporary condition of Muslim societies. The Iranian revolution demonstrates the significance of those processes very well.

incapable of comprehending this as the lower strata were of escaping their demonology at this stage of the process. Both positions are heavy with implications for the later history and evolution of the society.

Once this is understood, it is difficult to assert that it was only the 'ulema who failed to grasp the consequences of the reforms. Yet the state had its triumph, even if it was not understood at the time! While it was true that for the dis-privileged the forms and symbols of religion were now made more all-embracing in their social reference, an important change did take place. Religion started to become identified as such and as distinct from other forms of ideology and views of the world, rather than being taken for granted as an integrated and axiomatic part of everyday life. It was in this sense made more conscious and thereby perhaps in the long run more vulnerable to the challenges of social and cultural transformation.

2. Morocco in the Nineteenth Century: A Diffused Authority

The first point to note is the difference between Morocco and our previous example. This was a far less centralized and bureaucratized society. The degree of control that a sultan could at any time exert fluctuated enormously, and the zone that came under his military and fiscal power at a given moment was constantly varying. The ranges of the Atlas Mountains and a dispersed peasant and transhumant popula-tion for whom warfare was as much a form of social organiza-tion as herding made life very difficult for the would-be authority at the would-be "center." Great tribal leaders, representing the pastoral and transhumant groups that played a major role in the economy, were powerful rivals. The prominent families of the cities were equally able to resist a ruler by their astute use of multiple sources of authority and influence. They might be sherifs (descendants of the Prophet), heads of Sufi mystical brotherhoods, judges, traders, and a great deal more besides. We have already seen two examples earlier of the degree to which they could combine many roles and functions with effortless ease. Being an 'alim was but one string to the bow.

There was therefore a lesser degree of dominance of the "official" model of Islam, more or less opposed to what was regarded as the vulgar and popular forms, than was the case in Ottoman Turkey. The fluctuations in the authority of the established central government made this aspect of religious legitimacy and production not only less appropriate to the many-sided nature of the situation but positively limiting to the elite itself, for whom the greater the range of cultural and social alternatives that could be employed, the better. It was in their interest to maintain office, the bureaucracy, and areas of power in relatively uncrystallized, ambiguous, and multistranded forms. The model of Islam was similarly more fluid in its boundaries.

Land and building grants, office, taxation privileges (sherifs were immune from taxation, but then so, de facto, were a lot of people), and the income from religious offerings at shrines attached to certain town families were all part of their economic base. Local ties were very important in determining who got what and at whose expense in the way of judicial positions.

The status and class positions of 'ulema varied enormously. In tribal and transhumant areas they were very often absent altogether unless a merchant, a man of political influence, or a government official, who was also an 'alim, happened to have economic or political relations with a particular group or area. Trade, commerce, and market networks linked very different social units: tribes, peasants, and the towns, which were the centers of merchants, officials, artisans, laborers.

This fluidity also involved a relative indifference to the presence of many different kinds of religious statuses, practices, and symbolic forms that in Ottoman Turkey were sometimes regarded as opposed to 'ulema-defined orthodoxy. Saints and holy men, all kinds of Sufi groupings, *baraka* (blessings) and miracles, talismans and curing, shrines and sacred sites, and a whole complex of local beliefs and rites could exist and indeed be quite central to what Islam and "Islamic society" were taken to be by ordinary people without raising serious problems of correctness or appropriateness.

'Ulema who were also members of the upper bourgeoisie of the urban centers such as Fez might despise or regard as signs of ignorance the practices of the peasants and tribesmen, but this is as much a mark of their class position as of religious scrupulousness. The dissident hinterlands were

47

typically imaged as places of darkness, and naturally as practicing forms of religion that would not in purist terms be well regarded; religion in these benighted areas centered more on the powers of persons and acts of grace or miracles than on the sober, proper, learned religion of the urban elite, with its strong self-image as the repository of civilization.

Moroccan society was characterized by constantly balancing and unbalancing political alliances and conflicts. All ideas of a single, unitary status group of 'ulema and a clearly defined orthodox model of Islam here dissolved into the cultivation of a necessary ambiguity and a multiplicity of sources for social and cultural legitimacy. Military force was there for the tribal leaders as well as the sultan's use. Since being an 'alim was but one strand of social identity, and the possibility of combination with other factors was so great, there was less mutually exclusive competition among religious specialists claiming different bases over the same or overlapping territory.

At the same time the development of urban life and a tradition of learning and "high" culture permitted the production and elaboration of a legal-literary domain by the great families of the towns. These regarded themselves as the embodiment of civilization surrounded by the turbulent hordes of the countryside and the mountains. But for that production and that notion of a civilized few surrounded by a savage many to exist, rights in land, taxation exemptions, and inheritance were fundamental. Association with the merchant strata, the most important group of notables outside the rulers themselves in both our examples, made a relationship of law and commerce that was vital to both.

Take these two cases cited by the American historian Edmund Burke, a student of Moroccan society. The Mufti al-Wazzani in the late nineteenth century held legal office (*mufti* is the title for a canon lawyer entitled to issue *fatwas* or legal opinions), was a professor at the religious university, a leading member of a holy lineage, an Idrisi sherif, the leader of a religious brotherhood, and a landowner, not to mention all the personal ties and alliances made possible by this embarrassment of spiritual and worldly riches. The chief qadi (judge) of Fez at the same period was a teacher as well, and he had been a financial agent, a provincial judge, and a customs agent. Such examples could be repeated, certainly for that time and for the 'ulema elite, for most Muslim societies. A plethora of influences, positions, powers, alliances, relations, and interests all crystallized in particular individuals who would appeal to different sources of authority and power.*

Note, however, that we are dealing here very much with the elite. For them it was a whole configuration of elements that went to make up their social statuses and rank and not only their position as 'ulema, important though that was. Lower down the social scale the less fortunate brethren, who did not already possess the advantage of highly placed families, major offices in the administration, access to the rulers, political backing, inherited wealth, or whatever other resources, would not have found that the identity of men of learning in itself opened many doors, or even gave them enough to live on!

At this level, too, there were multiple ties all centered on the religious order in its more everyday and less socially exalted level. Speaking of a small market town, the well-known American anthropologist Clifford Geertz shows how the income from religious endowments funds not only the mosques, religious schools, and saints' shrines but also provides for those who service the buildings, lead the prayers, give sermons, read the Quran for public and family occasions, and teach or study the religious texts. In an important observation he emphasizes the link this makes with the different strata of bazaar and town society:

> As virtually all these people — known collectively, the janitors and such aside, as *tulba* (sq. *ṭāleb*), "religious scholars" (literally, "devoted, eternal students") — are also market traders, often prominent and influential ones, habus money not only mostly gets back into the bazaar economy from which, mostly, it originally comes, but acts to fuse the religious and economic elites of the town.†

* Edmund Burke III, "The Moroccan Ulema, 1860-1912: An Introduction" in *Scholars, Saints, and Sufis: Muslim Religious Institutions since 1500*, ed. Nikki R. Keddie (Berkeley/Los Angeles: University of California Press, 1972), pp. 93-125.

† Clifford Geertz, "Suq: The Bazaar Economy in Sefrou" in *Meaning and Order in Moroccan Society*, ed. C. Geertz, H. Geertz, and L. Rosen (Cambridge: Cambridge University Press, 1979), p. 152. *Habus* is a term glossed by Geertz as "properties deeded by their original owners . . . . to God's community of believing Muslims, the *umma*." (p. 131). It is the equivalent of waqf property.

Though taken from an account of a contemporary setting, this seems to me to pick out elements that were central to the religious institution a hundred years ago. One with the identity of learned man or mosque functionary or specialist in religious law or shrine attendant was and is part of a multi-dimensional world in which Islam moves through the capillaries of the social system, through property relations, rents, market relations, pilgrimages, offerings at saints' tombs, and law. But *moves through* does not mean dominate. I must not sweep the reader away in a cloudy vision of a timeless arabesque of fascinatingly complex relations. Religion does not structure the local and regional forms of the market, however important its institutions may be. Nor, equally to be remembered, does the small Moroccan town of Sefrou represent some unchanging essence of Islam in society.

Geertz makes this clear enough in his description of the bazaar as a local arena for "an increasing number of increasingly marginal traders and artisans [who] tried to crowd themselves into a slowly expanding economic niche, a niche whose size and nature were in good part reflexes of developments elsewhere."* This "development of underdevelopment" inexorably forms local relations, framing them in the context of a peripheral part of a peripheral economy.

Such peripheralization could not produce the official secularization that the Turkish state attempted in its efforts at self-transformation through European forms. The position of the sultan in Morocco depended far more on his ideological legitimation as a sherif and as Commander of the Faithful, all the more so in the absence of highly developed state apparatuses. Political and social networks and strongly localized identities characterized a society that preserved intensely personal and regional modes of political action. In Morocco, in considerable contrast with Turkey, the 'ulema became *more* influential as central government grew slowly stronger and the semiautonomy of some tribal groupings diminished.

Part of the expanding political and cultural influence of the 'ulema in the late nineteenth and early twentieth centuries was thus translated by them into the language of the purification of the religious tradition. A new traditionalism came out of their reforms of religious teaching and practice, the negative

* Ibid., pp. 233-34.

and critical aspects of which grew out of hostility to "unorthoxody" and "superstitions." There would be only the most controlled space for mysticism in the emerging official religious culture, especially those popular forms of mysticism enshrined in the Sufi brotherhoods and holy men with personal followings and all the host of local practices that were precisely local rather than universal.

In actuality this meant an increasing cultural separation between the major towns, centers of the 'ulema reformers, and the countryside, the small towns, villages, and tribal groupings, precisely in the historical period when economic and political integration was forcing them together.

Conclusion: Renewal and Fossilization

Running through all this material are some very general themes out of which particular histories have woven complex variations. Let me pick them out again before returning to more specific questions.

One basic theme is cultural and religious. The 'ulema are men of knowledge ('ilm) defined as springing from religious sources of the Book and tradition of law. It is through the 'ulema, though not exclusively, that the sacred texts are reproduced and authoritative tradition is constituted. Both pass into popular culture and practice through formal processes of religious education and legal judgment, as well as through myriad channels that go from mosque to market to linguistic etiquette.

This religious framework of holy texts proclaiming a universal umma, the Islamic community, articulates with a second major theme, which is political and ideological. The cultural role of the 'ulema generated authority for the holders of power. It guaranteed the order of society as being Muslim. Here the Holy Law is crucial, in theory and in practice. The fact that the 'ulema are its keepers and that through it they helped to regulate not only questions arising out of property relations but also issues in personal and family life is most important. This double aspect entails the presence of the 'ulema in the apparatus of the courts and in legal discourse, and also at the most significant stages of the life of the individual. As the servants of a higher power expressed in Revelation and Law, they have an authority that has great practical relevance for the everyday world.

Their legitimation is not ideologically constituted by a state institution, however powerful. The fact that they are servants of that other power manifested in the Divine Message means that they have a symbolic and ideological base that is, and can be seen to be, distinct from that of the rulers, even though they might in certain circumstances be subservient to and dependent upon the politically dominant groups. Moreover, the Quran and the umma go far beyond the range of particular local dynasties or beliefs. They are universalistic terms. There is always an inherent tension between them and such particularistic forces as a given regime's attempts to appropriate religion to itself as an instrument of power or, in our modern day, state-dominated nationalism.

At the same time we have to remember that the Islam of the Book leaves little room for mediators between God and His human creation. The scholar-legists have no monopoly on the sacred texts. Compliant 'ulema who are unwilling or unable to confront the rulers may easily find themselves denounced and ignored in the name of a true Islam that has no place for politically obedient graybeards.

The third theme that needs elaboration is that of the 'ulema as a social category. It is true that in the examples I have cited the control of religious endowments and the participation of some 'ulema in tax farming gave to certain individuals a position in the structure of economic relations at different levels from the local community to the state. Those who were tax farmers were integral to the administration that extracted the agricultural surplus from the rural population. Such 'ulema were part, therefore, of relations of debt and usury in the countryside. It is also true that the administration of *waqf* (religiously endowed) lands and property provided an economic base that was largely exempt from the otherwise arbitrary and destabilizing effects of economic policy by the state (changes in tax rates, additional financial imposition, sequestration of assets), which hampered the development of a strong merchant class up to the later nineteenth century. With all this, however, the 'ulema are not and have never been either a social class or even a corporate group. They are drawn from and found at quite distinct structural and social positions.

Our two examples of Morocco and Ottoman Turkey show quite contrary developments in the period of increasing European and capitalist penetration. In Morocco the upper levels of the 'ulema were most important in formulating a cultural response to colonialism. Confrontation with the powerful external forces represented by France was above all conducted at the level of values, symbols, and culture. The 'ulema reformist tendency could be allied with a liberal nationalism in which "tradition" was constructed as a vital bulwark against a Western absorption of the Moroccan identity. There existed the social, economic, and political space for the 'ulema elite to be seen as champions and agents of a renaissance of society, not through European modes of "progress" (as in Turkey) but through making new by restoring the original purity of the Islamic message — as they interpreted it. Elements that the 'ulema saw as corrupted versions of Islamic practice — the cults of saints and shrines, for example — were attacked in the name of true religion. The localism that such cults expressed was to be subordinated and controlled.

For many commentators the Moroccan 'ulema served as guardians of the cultural heart of the nation. For others, such as Abdullah Laroui, they perpetuated a form of alienation and mystification all the more dangerous because it appealed to apparently authentic and indigenous forms. In Laroui's view this identification of pure religion with the nation was and is a kind of sanctification of society in an archaic mode. It is an "exaggerated medievalisation" that blocks a true apprehension of history through a "quasi-magical" evocation of classical Arabic culture. Language and culture are fossilized, not renewed. The reformers are lost in an illusion of renaissance.*

In this reading the 'ulema have acted to freeze the language of being, religion, and authority even while permitting the development of capitalist types of organization in business, industry, and bureaucracy.

The emergent Turkish ruling class, on the other hand,

* Abdullah Laroui, *The Crisis of the Arab Intellectual*, trans. Diarmid Cammell (Berkeley/Los Angeles: University of California Press, 1976), p. 156.

introduced a radical "European"-influenced program of secularization. For them tradition meant backwardness. The whole point here was to break with major aspects of Ottoman organization up to that time. The downgrading and control of the 'ulema religious establishment was central to their policy. So, too, was the desire for a revolution in mentality and intellectual training, at least at the level of the administrative and military elites. National identity was to be separated from religion. The legitimization of the imperial state would no longer depend on archaic notions of the guardianship of the faithful or the carrying out of the pre-scriptions of the Holy Law.

Religion was to cease to be crucial to the ideological reproduction of the state and to its bureaucratic and economic system. Quite separate languages of tradition and modernity developed. Religious symbolism was left to the masses who were outside and merely objects of the reforms of the central power. Secularization by decree would enable Turkey to make the quantum leap into a new kind of autocratic system built on different foundations from the old.

Far from playing an important social and cultural part in the articulation of increasingly dependent societies with the capitalist world system, as in North Africa, the 'ulema in Turkey were excluded from any effective role.

CHAPTER 3

The Community of Suffering and the World Reversed

One of the important factors we have to consider in the study of the practical forms of Islam is the existence or nonexistence of a tradition and cultural theme of resistance to the political power by the representatives of the religious tradition. Such a tradition does exist in the communities that are called *Shi'ite*. It provides a rich repertoire of symbols and interpretations within which the idea of a suffering community of believers can be formulated and dramatically expressed. There are provided, too, as in all religions, modes of giving meaning and form to suffering and explanations for the fact that the evil flourish as the green bay tree while the good are oppressed. Such an explanation is usually called by sociologists (following Max Weber) a *theodicy*. In the previous pages we have in fact sketched out the conditions for the emergence of such a theodicy among the disprivileged in Turkish society. I want to try to show here how the form and social significance of a theodicy of suffering are largely determined by social factors; and how "the same" core of symbols may bear very contrasting meanings in different contexts.

The dominant set of symbols within the Shi'ite tradition concerns the martyrdom of the Prophet Muhammed's grandson Hussein at the Battle of Kerbela (A.D. 680), the triumph of the evil, worldly forces responsible for his death (the Umayyad dynasty), and the leadership of the community of believers by an elite of the spiritually elect. That elite is constituted at two levels: the first is the line of Imams, to whom alone authority and legitimate rule belong. The founder of this line was the father of the Imam Hussein, 'Ali ibn abi Talib, the fourth of the four "rightly-guided" caliphs who followed the death of the Prophet, who is regarded by many as of a quasi-divine nature. He, too, was murdered.

The historical charter is therefore from its inception marked by the theme of the legitimate ruler of the Muslim community, and he who can be said to define the meaning of being a Shi'ite, being cheated of his rightful succession and suffering death at the hands of the oppressors who displace him. His son is likewise a victim to tyranny, being defeated and murdered by the oppressors.

The Imams are infallible, again in some versions treated almost as divine in nature. For the "Twelver" Shi'ites at a certain point in time the Twelfth Imam of the line went into concealment and the community awaits, suffering under the political rule of the unjust, the return of this concealed Imam as savior. The notion of the concealment of the Imam and of the reversal of the true and legitimate order of the world is central.

The second level is that of the guidance of the community until the day of the return by religious specialists who can serve as teachers of religious precept and practice. In Iran such a specialist is called a *mujtahid*, and the one who is selected by the believer as his guide is "the source of imitation" (*marja'-i taqlid*). The notion of the model figure and practice, important enough as we have seen in the Sunni version, here receives a transforming and intensifying force, not least because it is by definition in some degree of permanent tension with the temporal power.

The following set of themes of Twelver Shi'ism is quite different from those shown in our discussion of the role of the Sunni 'ulema:

1. A community of suffering "consecrated" by that suffering
2. The martyrdom of the quasi-divine figure, historically

and symbolically seen as the cause of the suffering
3. The successors (Imams) as a spiritually perfect elite
4. The Imams ultimately forced into concealment
5. The expected revelation of the hidden Imam and his return
6. His triumph over an unjust political order with whom the believers have always been in overt or covert tension and opposition
7. The guidance of the community meanwhile by the mujtahids and the "sources of imitation"

The vital importance of the spiritual guide for each believer produces a notion of personally established authority and a model of action and thought of a very radical nature. The idea of suffering, divine leadership, and personal model come together in the re-enactment in passion plays of the drama of the Imam Hussein.

Such, in simple terms, is the core of the cultural tradition. Let us see how it is socially produced in very different societies, focusing on the role of the men of religious learning.

Iran in the Nineteenth Century: Dramas and Constitutionalism

The major issue that is usually raised concerns the alliance between the 'ulema and the constitutionalist reformers. As a noted scholar of Iran, Hamid Algar, remarks, this alliance is generally seen as anomalous. He himself in one study has explained it in terms (by now familiar to us) of the failure of the 'ulema to see the real implications of constitutionalism for state and society. He goes on to suggest in a later article that the importance of the doctrine and ideology of the opposition to tyranny may in fact have much greater bearing on the case than has previously been allowed and may help us to understand the apparent alliance with the reformers.*

* Hamid Algar, "The Oppositional Role of the Ulama in Twentieth-Century Iran" in *Scholars, Saints, and Sufis: Muslim Religious Institutions since 1500*, ed. Nikki Keddie (Berkeley/Los Angles: University of California Press, 1972), pp. 231-55.

The rulers in Iran in the nineteenth century were the Qajar dynasty, and it was against them that the 'ulema invoked the language and imagery furnished by the Shi'ite tradition. The passion plays commemorating the martyrdom of the Imam Hussein, the recital of religious verses on the same themes, the use of the highly charged rhetoric of opposition (the Qajars were "the Umayyads" of the age, the Imam Hussein was claimed as the founder of the secret societies that existed at the period, and so forth) all reached a peak at this time. The Battle of Kerbela became a kind of dominant symbol for and of the community. That is to say, it was presented as an organizing image and metaphor within which could be found a correlation to the present experience of the people under an oppressive dynasty. It identified or asserted a correspondence between the founding myth of the community and the community's actual contemporary situation. The myth became part of a vivid present for the individual and the group consciousness, as a model and ground of their social and spiritual condition.

It must be stressed that from a sociological point of view, the power of the image of the Imam is in part a function of the power of the evil of the forces opposed to him. As usual, it is the theologians (the 'ulema) who paint the most vivid and terrifying pictures of the devil. They need him more than anyone else, after all. It is therefore most important, if the myth is to be turned into an influential political ideology under the auspices of the 'ulema, that the Qajars be damned as the tyrants of the age. This "tyranny" seems to have a liberal admixture of mythology, as might be expected. Scholars have noted, in fact, that the Qajar dynasty was relatively feeble, with an uncertain economic base, limited armed power (whereas the 'ulema sometimes had their own private militias), and restricted authority outside the capital. The state was not really as strong as the myth proclaimed.

The position of the 'ulema was very different from that of the rest of the population. They were a spiritual elect who had acquired a far more authoritative role and function than their Sunni counterparts in Turkey or Egypt. Unlike those in other societies, they had powers largely independent of the state. Furthermore, since religious law governed commerce in the sense that many commercial matters had to go through the religious courts, we find the same alliance and inter-relationships of merchant and 'ulema groups as elsewhere. Algar notes that donations and religious taxes the merchants paid to the 'ulema were the second most important form of income after awqaf revenues. Tithes that were supposed to go to the poor passed through their hands as well, giving them a significant "popular" function in addition to all their other religious competences.

This alliance of merchants and 'ulema was given further substance by the direct threat to its interests by the Qajars' relative powerlessness in the face of European economic and political activity. Not only did Westernization, or the threat of it, impinge on 'ulema legal privileges, it endangered the very basis of the merchant-artisan-'ulema strata, who feared that they might find themselves in direct and very unequal competition with European commerce.

This danger of the destruction or profound modification of local forms of production and exchange seems to be the fundamental factor in considering the opposition of the 'ulema to the state and the intensification of the available powerful symbols of the struggle of the community against oppression.

This does *not* mean that the cultural tradition was insignificant or merely a kind of emotive window dressing. Not at all. It was of enormous power in summoning up the founding myth of the community, focusing on a primordial identity now put at risk in a very real sense by new modes of domination, and concentrating opposition to the rulers. For all strata could find in their own experience different critical areas of correspondence with those martyred by the unjust and unbelieving. It does mean, however, that it would be dangerous to take the doctrine and ideology as the determining factor in the conduct of the 'ulema, at least at this stage. It was a determining factor in the conduct of their followers.

The opposition of the 'ulema therefore seems to have had a double aspect. One side was the support of constitutionalism by a merchant-'ulema stratum, whose position and status were threatened by Qajar and European policy. The other, more specifically associated in public terms with the religious specialists, was the invocation of certain basic cultural symbols for interpreting the situation of European penetration backed by the Qajars. These two different kinds of political and social discourse were operated by the same group at the same time — liberal-bourgeois constitutionalism and the martyrdom of the Imam Hussein by the evil power of the worldly usurpers (Umayyads equals Qajars).

We should note that the drama of suffering and salvation was in part a defence of social, economic, and cultural privilege against European expansion and the state. The great advantage of the passion play was that it reached all levels of society and that into it each individual and group could pour their own particular shades of meaning and find their own subjective experience of the evil of the times expressed in a transcendental and intensely political form. It thus generalized what might otherwise have been a particular and limited struggle between different sectors of the dominant strata (the Qajars and the 'ulema) and located the sources of injustice in a dynasty, not in a social system.

Yet the dream had a certain ambivalence after all. Liberating while attempting to control all the resentment and sense of oppression of the lower strata was notoriously liable to backfire on those confident enough to undertake the task, even if such resentment was couched in cultural terms from which such leaders also derived their legitimacy. The control of the meaning of symbols is an uncertain operation. Who knows what understandings may not be found in the drama and the variations in the significance to be found in it? The drama also held out a promise, as well as an image, of martyrdom. The concealed Imam would return one day. Perhaps, in anticipating or prophesying his coming and in seeing all around the conditions for his triumph, social forces would be let loose that might threaten even the religious specialists and their monopoly of sanctity.

It is interesting, therefore, that many of the 'ulema supported constitutionalism rather than calling for a Messianic upsurge and foreshadowing the emergence of the savior from concealment. It was, if I may put it this way, rather important that the Imam remain hidden. And he was hidden, and the bases of the social crises were also hidden, behind a rhetoric and deeply felt discourse of martyrdom. At the same time the more decorous and worldly plant of constitutionalism was nourished. One could support it in good conscience because one did not in any case expect the Holy Law to be the law of the state while the Imam was hidden . . . .

So the concealed Imam had many meanings and served many functions, including that of displacing expectancies of change until the last day, sanctifying the role of the 'ulema, and postponing a confrontation with the fundamental nature of the situation. He was being used to defend covertly the established order of economic and political relations in which the 'ulema actually had so large a stake.

The Passion Play and Social Stratifications: A Lebanese Village

The Iranian 'ulema in opposition to the state encouraged the passion play, which took its immediate social meaning from that opposition to partly mythologized political power as wielded by the Qajars, and to European political and economic penetration. The martyrdom of Hussein offered an image of the world as it is (the oppressors are triumphant), showing that the "true" order of things is reversed by the actual historical order; the world is seen as morally and politically upside down, and the source of religious and social authority is contained in the hidden Imam figure.

This reversal of the world can be taken in diametrically opposed ways. In the passive sense it offers an image of suffering to be endured and an experience of oppression that is mythologically and historically the fate of the community. True believers can only await the return of the savior at some unspecified and uncertain point in the future. The play sanctifies suffering, makes of it a sign of the true community, and becomes a kind of dream, a nostalgic myth, a cry of lament by a helpless yet righteous people.

Alternatively, in the active mode, this reversal of the world contains a potential for mass mobilization and an extremely dynamic view of the community's role and duty. It radically exposes the illegitimate power of the rulers and asserts the legitimate authority of the believers who await — with what dangerous impatience! — the emergence of the concealed Imam. The dominant interpretation was formed in the

Iranian case within a given historical and social context under the leadership of the 'ulema (who with the merchant stratum made up one wing of the ruling order), who were the champions of righteousness in double form — as constitutionalist reformers and as sources of imitation, teaching, and guardianship of the founding tradition.

Faithful to our general theme of variation and transformation, let us now look at a more limited village setting, in which the drama of Hussein becomes an overt attempt to confirm rather than to deny the order of the world. It delivers a message that preaches the dangers of the established form of things being turned on its head, rather than exposing the illegitimacy of existing power and authority and calling for their overthrow. This allows us to examine a situation in which it is the learned men themselves who have represented power and authority but who are now inexorably losing their place in the community, even at the moment when they appear symbolically in the play to be its leaders and the key to its identity.

In a Shi'ite village in south Lebanon in the first half of the 1950s we find religious specialists with a rather different structural position from that of the Iranian 'ulema, though also challenged by the impact of the European-dominated capitalism.* There are two main groups that go to make up "the Learned Families" in the village: the sheikhs and the sayyeds. The position of the largest group, the sheikhs, is theoretically based on learning. As the local "keeper of the culture" (a learned guardian of the genealogies and lore of the group) put it: "We are like one family, because we are of one weave, *and that is knowledge*" (my emphasis). Very few have actually been to the Shi'a University of Najaf in Iraq, but the cultivation of literacy and literary abilities on religious subjects is a major mark of group identity. They also claim descent from a follower of the founding sacred figure, one al-Hurr, who is said to have fought alongside the Imam Hussein at his last battle.

---

* I have drawn extensively on two articles by Emrys L. Peters for the material on south Lebanon: "Aspects of Rank and Status among Muslims in a Lebanese Village" in *Mediterranean Countrymen*, ed. Julian Pitt-Rivers (Paris/La Haye: Mouton, 1963), pp. 159-200; and "Shifts in Power in a Lebanese Village" in *Rural Politics and Social Change in the Middle East*, ed. Richard Antoun and Ilya Harik (Bloomington/London: University of Indiana Press, 1972), pp. 165-97.

A more specifically sacred ancestry is claimed by the sayyeds, who form the other wing of the Learned Families and make up about one fifth of the whole group. They wear the green turban as a sign of kinship with the Holy Family itself through the son of the Imam Hussein ('Ali as-Saghir), who survived Kerbela and became the fourth in the line of twelve Imams. It is this direct link, rather than learning per se, that identifies the sayyeds as having a separate status and the power of blessing (baraka).

Within the overall group of the Learned Families, therefore, we find the two major principles of authority: learning, and blessing through genealogical and spiritual descent from the founding ancestor, in this case the Imam 'Ali as-Saghir. The group thus encapsulates both elements in the Shi'ite tradition — a relation with the semidivine Imams and knowledge of the sacred tradition. The two principles are here completely complementary.

The sheikhs conduct prayers and the major rituals of the life cycle (marriages and funerals), witness wills and property transfers, and pronounce divorce. The sayyeds say prayers for the dead, attend religious rituals, and embody the notion of the pious life (a recurrence of the theme of the model for imitation). These particular competences — authority and literacy — also gave them a monopoly on administrative and teaching posts in the village up to the 1950s, as well as theoretically putting large areas of personal, family, and moral life within their sphere of influence as dispensers of advice.

Now the question of descent is crucial for two main reasons. In the first place, it limits access to the religious elite to what is defined as a single group into which (with a few exceptions) one is born. This is important for the acquisition or representation of knowledge, too, since in fact one "goes to Najaf" or "is learned" because one is a sheikh, rather than being a sheikh because one has been to Najaf. In contrast to the Sunni 'ulema, therefore, at this local level the boundaries round the elite are drawn by birth, not by training (though the theory is that learning is the reason for the title of sheikh).

Group frontiers are further reinforced in social practice by restricting the marriage of women of the group (women, it should be noted, can inherit property, a fact that gives them a pivotal position in calculations of marriage relations). They should marry either within the village and from other Learned Families or to those outside but of the same status. There is nothing specifically *religious* about these prescriptions as social rules of inclusion and exclusion, and there is no doctrine of caste pollution in operation here.

In the second place, descent is vital because the Learned Families as a whole are a major landholding group, if not the only one. Though the historical details are not clear, this control over the key factor of production at a time when the local economy was still relatively undisturbed by wider changes in the Lebanese economy must have given a solid base to their village prestige, influence, and dominance vis-à-vis a largely peasant and sharecropper population living off small plots of land.

Descent therefore took on a double ideological role: as a principle of religious and moral authority and a link with the figures by reference to whom the community is defined (the Imam and the heroes of Kerbela); and as a mode of definition and drawing of boundaries around an elite that predominated in production and the village economy and that had a monopoly over vital cultural resources.

Both these factors mean that the genealogy is not primarily a question of historical authenticity at all, but rather of specific religious, political, and economic significance. That is to say, it is a way of reflecting and conceptualizing a series of changes that take place on the ground in the social order. Groups are incorporated or drop out for different reasons. A particular family line dies out or loses its land, which means that it is no longer worth recording. It happens, too, that men are added to the genealogy who have earned or claimed the title of sheikh perhaps in the name of a learned relative but more concretely because of wealth. Yet others owe their place in this form of social mapping to the education of sons in Beirut or local influence achieved by whatever means.

As a corollary of this, the genealogy structures and makes possible a set of choices all of which can be regarded as legitimate. Its complexity is the key element in this flexibility, all the more so because different groups are perpetually competing over marriage and land arrangements and making often opposing claims in the name of the "sacred genealogy." They can do so in all righteousness because the descent charter in fact permits, even creates, ambiguities, areas of uncertainty, zones where very opposed interpretations can be given to particular links between individuals and which link has the priority and so forth. In a sense everyone can have his own version of the genealogy within limits, because no one has *the* version. The "received truth" in the guardianship of the keeper of the culture actually exists on a basis of multiple possible truths; the "sacred text," as always, can be taken in any number of ways. And note that it is said to be so complex that only one man (the keeper of the culture) dares to claim to know the exact relations.

The genealogy thus plays a very important ideological role in the reproduction of the social order. The sheikhs and sayyeds have a group interest in maintaining and producing it continually over time as a mode of inclusion for themselves and exclusion of others; as a text, a legitimating charter, and a social record of relations of power, marriage, and property.

One additional point: It is also a weapon of factional struggles and division within the Learned Family stratum. Contained within the same flexibility that is so crucial for its operation is the possibility of furious disputes arising that are encoded in the language of genealogy but which the genealogy cannot of itself resolve, *because* it contains too many possibilities. People speak as though descent determines social relations, but the truth is rather the reverse. Conflicts may be stated and claims made in the formulas of descent, but their outcome is determined by the relative power and influence of the opposing groups (who may have equal resources and become trapped in an enduring situation of stalemate and rancor). Genealogy becomes a source of discord as well as of authority. The ideology, classically, contains the seeds of its own negation.

This aspect becomes of particular significance when we locate the Learned Families more firmly within the context of changes in the Lebanese economy.

Clearly in the past and up to the period of the 1950s, they were "freed for religion" by the labor of a sharecropping and small-plot-owning peasantry. It was the latter who in fact made possible one of the main status boundary markers of the learned: They did not work. Labor was and is undignified, incompatible with authority. They were concerned with producing knowledge, not crops. Sheikhs received produce and the means for them to live out their roles and being as sheikhs through the mediation of peasant labor and a monopoly of knowledge. Since teaching and administrative posts were also in their hands, they initially controlled and profited from the formal links with the new if limited structures of the Lebanese administration as these emerged in the period after World War I. These services were part of a system of exchange, which was the basis for sanctity: learning for labor, blessing for tithe (the sayyeds supposedly receiving a religious tax of 10 per cent of agricultural produce), literacy for money, payment in kind, or other services.

It is equally clear that by the 1950s structural changes in the Lebanese economy had quite altered the nature and context of social relations and exchanges at the level within which this local landowning group had their prominence. The country was rapidly increasing the scale and range of its basically service-dominated economy (banks, tourism, restaurants, construction, and every kind of middleman and entrepreneurial activity). Thanks to its place in the Middle Eastern financial markets and the relations of Lebanon to the West, Beirut had virtually swallowed up the political and economic resources of the other regions, which were reduced to an underdeveloped status within Lebanon itself. The capital was the main center of employment, education, and consumption, and it offered the means or the illusion of social mobility and grew enormously through an accelerated internal migration.

Where did this migration come from? From the countryside, where agriculture became less and less productive and of less and less overall economic significance in the percentage of gross national product that it generated and the limited investment that it received. On the land labor grew scarcer and more expensive as migration increased and the cost of living rose. In the rural areas the infrastructure (of roads, wells, electricity, and so on) remained only sporadically developed.

This lopsided development was perfectly represented in the social picture of Beirut itself. The glossy shopping streets and luxury apartment blocks jostled bidonvilles* and the impoverished dwellings of a migrant rural peasantry, often Shi'ite ex-cultivators from villages in south Lebanon.

Moving in the opposite direction, the cash economy reached into the rural areas and absorbed them, just as the small coastal towns and Beirut had absorbed so much of their population. More and more small shops opened in the villages, more and more small commercial enterprises sprang up. The whole range of occupations changed, and there were new educational and economic paths emerging.

Some were able to take full advantage of this process. For many, however, the fact that by and large the Shi'ite community of the south was one of the last to be incorporated into the modern social and economic structures meant that they entered a system that was already well developed. It had its own groups and elites and boundaries and no longer permitted easy social mobility. On the contrary. There were new exclusions and new limits that operated behind the facade of apparent free access. With a bit of luck a tractor driver might become a taxi driver, let us say. But it might be very difficult for him to become a taxi owner. Sectors of the rural population were released from the constraints of one system into the structures of another in which, in very different ways, they were also the disprivileged and marginal.

The effects of these processes on the particular local village situation with which we are concerned are profound. By the 1960s some four to five hundred people spent all or part of the year out of the village altogether (in a population of approximately eleven hundred), and the numbers fluctuated considerably from season to season. There was a local shortage of labor, and the Learned Families now had to compete for the labor of the agricultural workers. Moreover, the major relations and exchanges of the peasant stratum were more and more with the small shopkeepers and traders (produced by the capitalist cash economy), to whom they were bound by short- and long-term credit arrangements. Sheikh-peasant relations, on the other hand, tended not to be long-lasting and to be marked by tension, even by competition. Though the religious specialists still apparently had

* The French word deriving from *bidon*, meaning large tin can. It refers to shanty-towns constructed in metal from this kind of source.

about 50 per cent of the land, much of the produce went to the sharecroppers. The religious men had no alliance with a trader-merchant stratum (one of the strengths of the Iranian 'ulema) and no control over distribution and exchange. More important, land was no longer the chief factor of production and means of livelihood, either nationally or locally.

The system of exchanges that made sanctity possible and within which the privileged status of the Learned Familes was located was therefore heavily disrupted. Literacy ceased to be a monopoly of the few, and specifically religious expertise was not the qualification sought for in dealing with the problems of bureaucracy, political patrons, and the market. The range of services they could offer, particularly given their parochial setting whereas others were being incorporated into wider socioeconomic relations, became increasingly limited. Religious status no longer guaranteed, or was a powerful ideological weapon in, economic and political dominance. For the material underpinnings of that status were transformed by the impact of capitalism and the services-dominated national economy. Even blessing became a service to be paid for. In this setting the Learned Families were not in alliance with but were opposed to and by trader-peasant strata bound by credit and other exchange relations.

We can now see the significance of the disputes and factionalism among this sheikhly group that had become basically a declining village landowning stratum and the reasons for their almost equally busy concern with the genealogy relations. Given that the nature and social meaning of land and learning so changed, one is almost tempted to say that the sheikhs were condemned to an ever-increasing internal factionalism and genealogy mongering. The form and speed of social change alone must have made the latter a full-time occupation and a rich source of disagreement! As the material bases of privilege grew ever more insecure, and as factors outside their control diminished their class position and influence, so they were left to squabble ferociously over exactly who had the right to what, and which woman (with her rights of inheritance) should be married to which member of which family.

Since their social position was ideologically legitimated by the statuses of sheikh and sayyed, learning and descent, they were forced into a kind of cul-de-sac — cultivating an ideology that was less and less anchored in patterns of social relations that might make it viable. It was they, rather than any of the other groups, who were trapped within their own ideology and least able to transcend it. It was the once-dominant stratum that was least equipped to adapt to social change.

This is the situation in which the village performance of the drama of the death of the Imam Hussein takes on a particular irony.

In the play the sheikhs and the sayyeds took the part of the Imam and his forces, the shopkeepers and the peasants played the Umayyad generals and army. The "traitor" figure was suitably taken by a discreditable character who had served time in jail. The battle was duly and inevitably won by the forces of oppression, but the latter, as they made a final march to the village square lamented and beat themselves with chains and swords for their evil and for what they had accomplished.

In other words, the play might be taken as a statement of the authority of the sheikhs and sayyeds, which can only be flouted by the unrighteous; as a picture of the Shi'ite community at large headed by the Learned Men; and as a "glimpse of the world they [the audience] could anticipate when evil triumphs."* The play is a confirmation of the social order incarnated by the Learned Families, not an image of the world as out of joint.

Unfortunately, by the 1950s the world was out of joint from the point of view of the men of religion. Not only that. The other strata seemed quite enthusiastic that it should be! People had moved out into wider social relations. Insofar as the Learned Families stood for religious knowledge and a Shi'a identity, others were perfectly content and no doubt found it absolutely appropriate that they should play the part of the Imam's army. Insofar, however, as they constituted a locally predominant group of landowners subject to certain externally generated socioeconomic changes, then the peasantry and the shopkeepers were clearly not legitimating any general power or competence in the village for the Learned Families by putting on the play.

Ironically, too, the sheikhs and sayyeds were by now, if I

* Peters, 1968, p. 198.

may put it this way, increasingly being compelled to be religious as other spheres of social life slipped away from them. They were being restricted to their religious competence as a basis only for religious authority, precisely at a moment when their declining control of labor made it more and more difficult for them as a group to live a "religious" and privileged life unsullied by manual labor. Clearly in such a situation internal differentation within the group is of even greater significance for those who can and those who cannot afford to lead the good life, or at least the life of the good.

Yet the drama itself apparently had been both preserved and strengthened in the vividness and intensity of its primary symbols of the community of the elect whose conquerors weep and flagellate themselves in bitter atonement for their ultimate sacrilege. Why should this be so? Why, if the sheikhs were losing their position and people had access to different conceptions of the world and different places in a changed social order, should everyone be so eager to devote their time and money unstintingly to the story of the martyred Imam? For the drama is not compulsory, and many Shi'ite villages and towns do not perform it.

I doubt that we should seek any simple answer to the question. The death of the Imam Hussein can be understood and experienced at different levels by the same person, never mind by the different social strata. There is no one "full" or "correct" interpretation that can be clearly set out, either by them or by sociologists. For it is quite likely that for specific individuals and groups it expressed complex and varying ideas about the world and suffering, the nature of man, the personal biography of each, the profound power of the images of innocence and righteousness slaughtered without mercy. Round this central core we should expect to find a whole constellation of feelings and understandings.

Certainly the sheikhs' view may well have been more specific in its reference than the view of other groups and more particularly centered on their own position. But theirs is by no means the whole story. The entire community may well have been emphasizing its identity specifically as a Shi'ite community because of the great importance that religious confessionalism has in Lebanese politics.

By the late 1950s, however, more and more was at stake

economically and culturally for such villages. It was a time of migration, new possibilities at the same moment as a new relative disprivilege, of which slowly they must have become aware. The play, too closely tied to particular local realities of domination that no longer existed, ceased to be presented. The sheikhs and sayyeds could exercise their specific religious competence, which no one would dream of denying them, and thereby reassert a special position in that dimension of life. But for the community as a whole, its nature so profoundly modified by political shifts and alliances and by the incorporation into economic relations of a different type than that predominating before, the mythological simplicity, concentration, and clarity of the play no longer made the sense it had previously been given.

This does not mean that people ceased to believe that behind the transformations of social life, making sense of all the developments through which they were living, still lay the ever-present reality of the Imam's martyrdom. Equally, there is no reason to suppose that the play might not be revived. In the context of Lebanese confessionalism this dramatic aspect of public Shi'ism could serve the new professionals and businessmen no less well, though in a different way, than it had served the sheikhs.

Points of Contrast

The juxtaposition of these two examples of religious special-ists, both within the Shi'a cultural tradition but on a very different scale and in very different social settings, has brought out several major issues:
1. The Iranian 'ulema in the nineteenth century were located at the heart of a state system and allied with a powerful merchant stratum against the central government. Ideo-logically they embodied learning and the model for imitation against the worldy power of the Qajars. In this way their own role in reproducing the overall social system was symbolically transcended, and they were free to be the people's champions, the liberal constitutionalists against despotism, and the men of religion against the impious.

The Learned Families of south Lebanon show us an

example of a microlevel, peasant community. Initially they were an independent local landowning stratum centered on a given village's subsistence economy. Their control of land, the vital factor of production, coincided with their privileged access to the secrets of salvation in their role of guardians of the traditions. A monopoly of knowledge and literacy and cultural resources associated with religion, in a tradition of Shi'ism, which placed great emphasis on this aspect, cemented their predominance. They were not against a ruling stratum. They were the local, socially dominant group. The fact that learning depended on land and the organization of labor introduces a crucial ambiguity at the heart of their claims to social pre-eminence on religious grounds.

2. Both groups, therefore, were concerned with the preservation of the bases of a privileged position. The Iranian 'ulema, however, could focus resentment against a supposedly oppressive dynasty, and their economic and cultural bases might remain intact. It was perhaps in fact because the dynasty was relatively weak that the 'ulema could assert their independence and at the same time veil the sense in which they themselves were fundamental to the total economic and social order.

The Learned Families, by contrast, were in a far more ideologically and economically exposed position. They had no Qajars against whom they could be seen as defenders of the oppressed. They were a very local group, not in a position to act politically vis-à-vis Lebanese society as a whole. They were not part of a national status group with influence at the center. They had no powerful class allies. The limitations on their position were progressively revealed, and they could not, despite their efforts, have the best of both worlds: the cultural world of suffering and the economic world of local dominance.

3. Both groups were vitally affected by the impact of Western capitalism and or political influence. But it was neither the same type nor the same stage of capitalism in the two cases.

Iranian society in the nineteenth century was exposed to the first wave of European power, which the Qajars were too weak to resist. Western interests and the threat of the destruction of local economic and social forms (for example, of trade and the artisanate) were paramount. Such changes were, moreover, a danger to the commercial and social position of the 'ulema-merchant "bourgeoisie."

In the Lebanon of the 1950s a rather different historical route had been followed. The main impact of the Lyons silk industry during the nineteenth century, which effectively transformed the center of the country and the economic position of the Christian Maronite peasantry, had long since had its effect throughout the wider society. The capital, Beirut, had grown enormously. There was a highly sophisticated service-based economy and a powerful sector of finance and commercial capital. In such transformations the underdeveloped south had become part of the economic and social periphery within Lebanon. Suffering decreasing agricultural production and investment, dominated by large landowners and political bosses through economic controls and patronage, it was excluded from the benefits of development and increasingly pauperized. By the 1950s emigration had become well established. There were new forms of urban employment and unemployment, new possibilities and new impossibilities. The results of capitalist penetration to some of the local population appeared as a breakthrough, out of a declining backwater and into the modern economy. Furthermore, that penetration came in Lebanese guise (not as the predatory activity of foreign merchants) and in a political system that still enshrined religious identity as a key principle of the distribution of power and patronage.

4. The meaning of the passion play, part of the core of the Shi'ite cultural tradition and a key representation of the fundamental symbolic organization of the community, varied enormously in its social implications.

In Iran it presented an image of the world reversed. But this same image dissimulated the fact that the 'ulema were very much part of the dominant strata within the social order the play meant to show to be oppressive. In this sense we might even say that the play did indeed reverse the real order of the world, and a great deal more thoroughly than some of its performers could have imagined! It was part of a powerful armory of ideology and political-economic power that gave the 'ulema wide freedom of action.

In Lebanon it was the world of the Learned Families that was being reversed. They were being forced more and more into a rather limited religious role, ironically enough at a time when religion may have been achieving wider significance to the Lebanese Shi'ite community at large. Not only was *Shi'ite* a confessional label of great importance for political representation and identity, it was also a label under which migrants to the poorer suburbs of Beirut and members of a growing petite bourgeoisie of shopkeepers, traders, and providers of services might come together in clubs for mutual assistance, recreation, and social (political) gatherings with men of influence.

This was not, however, the framework of the Learned Families at the village level. Indeed Shi'ite culture in its local forms, with its ideology of learning and descent, had become for them more a restriction for their own comprehension of, and action within, the new order. To remain economically and politically important one had to leave the village, develop other relationships and bases of influence and social authority. Whereas to be a sheikh, if one wished to make that one's basic social identity, meant that one had to cultivate an ideology that was less and less productive of general social privilege and status. Their special competences and authority became even more confining and confined, at a time when the notion of the community of suffering was being in some senses regenerated and taking on new significances at a wider level.*

* I have drawn extensively on two articles by Emrys L. Peters for the material on south Lebanon: "Aspects of Rank and Status among Muslims in a Lebanese Village" in *Mediterranean Countrymen*, ed. Julian Pitt-Rivers (Paris/La Haye: Mouton, 1963), pp. 159-200; and "Shifts in Power in a Lebanese Village" in *Rural Politics and Social Change in the Middle East*, ed. Richard Antoun and Ilya Harik (Bloomington/London: University of Indiana Press, 1972), pp. 165-97.

CHAPTER 4

The Operations of Grace

One of the key signs of grace and authority, the most concentrated and dramatic for the believer, is those acts of wonder and power that we call miracles. These are the vital proofs, the sudden transfixing moments in which the "ever-present" reveals its otherwise veiled purposes in life, re-establishing the sense of the vividness of the Divine and the power of holy men as well as offering an assuring and triumphant experience of blessing. Now every time the anthropologist sits down in a café and hears these narratives in the company of others who are far more than merely an audience but are really participants, he, too, is an active participant. He, too, is an actor in the drama, because the miracle is performed each time it is retold. He "does" it as much as his friends do, by his acceptance of the account, his presence and interest, his comments and exclamations, his recital of appropriately pious formulas. It does not, therefore, matter whether or not such-and-such happened or what the original miracle was, and if he goes looking for it, he will be chasing himself up a blind alley. There are endless versions and varieties of "the same" miracle. Miracles are made every day in cafés and conversations, and it is there that they are created, reproduced, and transformed.

Such moments may be baffling for the outsider. Deafened by voices eager to retell, and thus relive, these moments of intense contact with the power that orders the universe; present when a dead saint is hailed ecstatically for his extraordinary act; observing the rapt faces as an account of the miracle is given; hearing the (to him) curiously matter-of-fact, even "ordinary" narrative that gives rise to such transcendent enthusiasm, he moves back a little abashed from the table in the Cairo café where this torrent of discussion has been unleashed, until insistent hands pull him back in and friends compete to demonstrate to him the astonishing events that have occurred. "Don't you see? *This* happened!"

He still does not understand. Where is the miracle? Well, obviously the saint made this event happen! No, it was not obvious to him at all, and the fact that all the others immediately grasped the import of the narrative they have heard makes him even more aware than usual of his confusion and distance from their world.

What can he hope to understand of such scenes, which he encounters with disturbing frequency? What significance, theirs and his own, can he find in them?

Gradually he begins to see that miracles have their patterns and their forms. Those unique occurrences also seem to be transformations on themes that slowly emerge and re-emerge in different ways. He even acquires a limited but real capacity to anticipate the miraculous, to look for it in certain settings and certain situations, to "read" events so that he gains some ability to participate in miracles with his friends (where others to whom he retells them see nothing but everyday sequences of incidents), or to deny miracles when they are claimed by certain others. He, too, starts to make connections between events, where previously he had only observed conjunctions in space and time of no particular significance. He shifts his own naive learned inclination to ask "what the person actually did" and "what actually happened" and focuses instead on those who create and re-create the miracles through their perception of the world and in their lives.

Miracles, then, have a very general significance: in the construction of the meaning of experience; in local understandings of the nature and workings of power and knowledge; as a commentary and a challenge to the everyday world and its dominant orders. More specifically, they are proofs to the world, a possibly opposed and skeptical world, of the truth of a holy man's mission. The two aspects are complementary, of course, since it is the idea that a given person is a channel through which the true, concealed linkage between events is revealed that is so important for that person's authority.

Like the holy men, the miracle is always potentially dangerous. Anything that opposes the given order of things, that disrupts causality, that confounds our ordinary expectations, and that, by definition, is not controlled but comes from an external, nonhuman, transcendent source is in essence subversive. It is not simply distinct from the law, the texts, the given and received authority, the suppositions on which the society is based; it is (or can be) their contradiction and negation and thus a tremendous threat.

We need not be surprised that the miracle is so often a weapon or refuge of the dominated, an essential part of the discourse, hopes, expectancies, and creations of the poor. It is no wonder that these miracles must be denied, stigmatized as superstition, and denied authenticity by the powerful. It is no wonder, either, that if the powerful are also claimed to be divine or quasi-divine, they should by all means seek to monopolize the miraculous and guard it as an attribute of their unique position and a legitimation of their dominance. They seek, after all, to establish a correspondence between the divine order, the order of the world, and their own rule of society. Acts that are not by them and (even worse) the people who are held to be vehicles for or performers of those acts are profoundly disturbing. Such miracles destabilize, put into doubt, demonstrate that God has chosen other instruments, contradict a ruler's claims, dramatically verify the alternative reality.

Guardians of the holy law have had to be quick to define the nature of the miraculous. They establish where it may be said to exist and hedge it around with a whole system of restrictions that as far as possible rule out its unauthorized and inconvenient presence. Though in every way it contradicts the rationalizing and "knowable" universe of the 'alim, the latter must nonetheless seek to incorporate it by whatever definitional means into part of his text and within his competence. Miracles are made into the things we say miracles can be and are defined officially according to necessity and the dominant interpretation of those doing the defining.

If necessary, those who claim to have seen (not to mention performed!) such occurrences may risk a whole series of sanctions. Qualified in the ideology of the dominant groups as ignorant or superstitious at best, they may be ultimately denounced as following non-Islamic practices if the threat to social stability develops. But since reality cannot be totally controlled and the Divinity resists the limitations that His guardians seek to put upon Him, miracles, too, resist even the most thorough efforts at control and make their subversive appearance.

There is, moreover, a highly significant shift in the social meaning of miracles. Where in the premodern period there was a general acceptance of a conception of superhuman powers that included the miraculous, there has arisen in the modern period a stress on controlled power, controlled religion (for social and political reasons), and sober, "orthodox," and "correct" beliefs and practices. In traditional society one might compete with miracles in trying to legitimize one group rather than another, but the existence and nature of miracles themselves was unproblematic. A centralizing and highly bureaucratic government, such as that of President Nasser in the 1960s, however, which was strongly nationalist and in many respects concerned to curb religious groupings, might see the invocation of miracles as a basic contradiction of the kind of society the government was trying to create.

Miracles and an Urban Sufi Order

We can begin by looking more closely at the place that miracles have within a specifically religious organization, a Sufi brotherhood in Cairo, and examine the way in which the miraculous varies within it depending on the social stratum of those who are constructing it. By "constructing it" I mean that what people define as miracles, as with all other events in social life, have to be "put together," agreed upon, accepted or rejected as having that status, tested and developed, and handed on to others as authentic and as proofs for particular attributes of different kinds.

Within the Sufi brotherhood that I studied in Egypt in the middle 1960s what was remarkable was both the clarity and the problems that surrounded acts or events that were hailed as "miracles" (mu'gizāt) or as "indications of divine power" (a rather clumsy translation of the word karāmāt).*

The principle itself, to begin there, was absolutely clear. Within the world and beneath the surface reality at which men live out their daily existence (the zāhir) there is the underlying dimension of the hidden reality (the bātin). From this hidden reality, through the mediation of a holy man or the free gift of blessing by God (baraka), flow forces and powers that are witness to the interrelations of God and man and nature.

It is the characteristic of the miracle to break the everyday routine and pattern of things by showing the unseen but "true" form that lies beneath. In this sense we might say that the miracle or the karamag is like a miniature passion play — a dramatic, vivid illumination of what is otherwise concealed but from time to time punctuates and comments on the nature of ordinary worldly reality. They offer a reminder, a basic marker of the "real" essence of the universe.

These signs transform life, if only briefly, by demonstrating that there are in fact significant inward relations between things where apparently there are only the outward routine and unproblematic succession of events in standard sequences whose interconnections are neither important, consciously thought of, nor reflected upon. Those who are regarded as living their lives entirely in the realm of appearances (the zahir) will not, by definition, see the miracle even if it happens under their noses (the anthropologist originally failed to do so, but his Muslim friends understood his blindness and sought to cure it). Thus, those who challenge the miracle that a particular individual or group accepts — and the opposition may come from a neighbor or an 'alim or even the government — show by the very fact of their doubt that

---

* Mu'giza basically means an act or sign that makes it impossible to contest someone's prophetic or saintly claims. It breaks the normal pattern of things and forces opponents to admit their error. The notion of challenge and contest is very strong. Karama indicates the bestowing of divine favor.

they are incapable of seeing the inner and "true" world. Their attempt to discredit it is thus taken as a triumphant demonstration of their own failure, and they are themselves discredited! (Since those who do make the challenge are generally expected to be persons and groups in positions of social, political, or cultural domination, the mutual attempt at discrediting has many implications.) Every denial by the outsider is a proof to the insider that it is really he, helpless or impoverished or disprivileged though he may be, who "knows" and experiences the truth.

So although the principle of miracles is accepted, what you regard as a miracle is very much a problem and an issue. Within our Sufi order many of the members lived in anticipation of those miracles to come and in constant rehearsal of those that were past. Moreover, in the general current of popular religion in Egypt I would guess that most people accept and experience moments or events they regard as signs of divine power or grace. There is a general language and set of shared understandings of the nature of the possibilities within the world, at the center of which are the notions of baraka, karamat, and mu'gizat. Though the miraculous, by definition, is extraordinary, it is also incorporated into the potentials of everyday life. It may happen at any time. People expect and look for it. And when it does occur, they are amazed but not surprised!

Most of the members of the brotherhood were thus prepared to "see," to construct or constitute certain sequences of events as being miraculous. It was part of the way in which they formed the world, part of the symbolic armory with which they were equipped to interpret and express and feel experience. Living lives that suffered greatly from disconnection, they were ready to make connections.

The majority of them were poor. Many were illiterate. Work was uncertain, and one might say that immediate contingencies and short-term coping with the world as it happened to them formed their universe. But insofar as their lives were predominantly controlled by external forces that acted on them in often uncomprehended and mysterious ways, leaving them with little illusion of the power of men to make their own life circumstances, it was striking that the concept of chance or accident was almost entirely absent.

Though things happened *to* them rather than through or by them and their life was a daily series of unpredictable difficulties that centered on the fundamental issues of finding food, clothes, and work, the very unpredictability was a constant; it was assumed to have a pattern, unseen but a pattern nonetheless. Nothing was fortuitous, nothing was accidental. In a universe in which, if we can speak objectively, hazard played a major part because of their structural place in society (their marginal economic role, their almost total lack of access to those institutions that might permit of an active transformation of their life circumstances by themselves), "chance" as a conception or organizing notion played no part.

For such terms as accident, hazard, and chance deny the notion of determination and of purposeful meaning. They suggest an idea of a more everyday contingent causality linking events. The members of the order, on the other hand, lead discontinuous and unpredictable lives that they believe are *not* so. They are sure in the notion of hidden determination and continuity in the secret purposes of the Divinity, itself irregularly but constantly manifested through the direct, immediate, and "visible" action of the divine power, often through a holy man's particular good offices. Such manifestations occur in miracles and acts of grace or blessing (baraka), which show the permanent and determining relations between God and men but appear only when God so wills. Men may hope and pray for them, and there exist all sorts of ways of going about obtaining them through specific individuals at particular places and seasons. But fundamentally they are unpredictable in their occurrence.

The concepts and operations of baraka and miracles therefore closely correspond to certain aspects of the life circumstances of the members of the brotherhood. They are part of a set of notions that surround relations with what is conceived to be the true ruling Power (the Divinity) and that are part of a system of activities directed by and toward that Power, whose purposes are by definition mysterious. So in the everyday world men experience the operations of abstract forces (the market, the political system, the changing nature of work and production and time), which generate and structure what the German sociologist Max Weber called their life chances. There is, of course, a pattern to the forces that mold and delimit their social and economic situation. But it is not visible as such in the everyday world. It can be analyzed at an abstract level by using economic and political theory, but it is experienced in the daily routine of the poor of Cairo by irregularity, unpredictability, uncertainty, and an awareness that one does not produce one's own life circumstances. The minute but crucial fluctuations in income and family needs, the sudden but recurring emergencies of illness, the changes in the prices of bread or tea or sugar that can wreck a household economy until adjustments are made (if indeed they can be made) are only the most immediate and obvious elements. The overall factors that generate these changes and that structure this world remain essentially concealed.

Within the Sufi order of the *Ḥāmidīya Shāzilīya*, which I studied, the forms of baraka and mu'gizat are various and varying. Yet we can say that they are structured and controlled and given a particular focus for the members. For within the group it is most important that the principle of strict organization be not imperiled by the irruptions of "unlicensed" grace. It is crucial that the saintly founder alone be granted the monopoly over such powers. The same problem that in general faces the dominant groups in society occurs on a small scale here. Namely, how do you make sure that access to the miraculous is restricted to those in whose hands it is "safe" and regulated, in this case the dead founder and his living guardians (the officers of the brotherhood).

These latter play a key role. Through their writings and their daily contacts with the members they help to focus the attention on one figure — the saint after whom the group is named. It is he alone who is thought to have been able to act as a channel for God's particular grace through different acts and occurrences; it is he alone who can be accredited with helping to bring about the amazing moment when one comes into contact with the determining purpose that rules the world. The disciples (as we may call the inner core of officers, for many of them are old enough to have known the saint and to have been part of his original band of followers) are therefore crucial in the control of miracles. Just as they restrict the manifestations of ecstasy (that other dangerous and disruptive force that has its place within Sufism), so they act to guard the gates of blessing. They recount the founder's miracles, the perfect model form of his existence, which is itself a constant seamless pattern of grace, and his attributes. They guide the brothers in the way in which they view and apprehend the meaning of being followers of the holy man.

Nonetheless, there are important variations within the group as to when a miracle has taken place, whether the founder alone has the power to bring it about, and what forms the manifestations of grace may assume.

The striking thing for the observer is that for the large majority of members virtually any conjunction of events can be held to demonstrate the workings of the saint, however matter-of-fact such events may seem to be. A suitcase that was left on a bus but is returned by a stranger; a pound note found in a school textbook after some unexpected visitors had caused a sudden and straitening outflow of money; finding a taxi fare in a pocket that before was empty. It was for me, I must confess, a bit of a shock to be present when such incidents were recounted as karamat (grace acts) when my own childhood and religious training had taught me to look for loaves and fishes, for water into wine. The miracles did not initially seem to me miraculous enough!

Equally they did not seem miraculous enough to many other Egyptians to whom I told such narratives. People outside the order but of the same general social position were quite ready to see mere sequence of events where members saw an extraordinary manifestation of the inner reality of things. Within the group itself, however, there was almost a competition in claiming such contacts with the saint, and no cluster of events was so mundane that it might not serve as a proof of his powers and as a living and experienced contact with the founder (and through him, with the Divine).

The difference seems to be therefore not skepticism on the part of those who did not find anything miraculous in the events and credulity on the part of those who did. It depends rather on two things. The first is the fact that within the brotherhood one attends to events, is on the lookout, has a focused interest on the interrelations between acts and occurrences — the crucial link, where the "true" causation is to be found. The saint serves as a kind of lens through which members see. He is also a scheme of interpretation by means of which they explain and apprehend the multiple hazards and changes that play so great a part in their lives. Those who are not associated with the order, however, do not frame their interpretation of life in the same way. They have no necessary interest, no burning motive, to make the connections of grace.

The second factor is related to this. It is simply that membership in the group is something that involves individuals in a constant round of meetings and ritual and socializing with one's brother Sufis in a world in which signs of God's power are everywhere. The constant experience of those signs as active forces is an endless process of experience, reinforced by one's fellow members. Miracles are only one form of a constant and pervasive power, a kind of pulse of energy that shoots out from the center, which is always charged and active. They are also proofs — of the legitimacy of the order, the saintliness of the saint, even therefore the significance of one's own life. If a group is to be successful, if it is anxious to recruit members and develop its organization, the continuation of the saint's acts after death is a crucial element. It is all the more important in the context of government hostility and suspicion of popular Sufism (during the middle 1960s).

I have mentioned the matter-of-factness of many of the narratives, but this needs to be qualified with some care. First of all, many of the members had more startling experiences to tell: One was snatched from a river into which he had fallen and brought to the bank where the saint's voice warned him of the dangers; another was pulled away from the path of a train; a third did not take a particular taxi to Alexandria that later crashed into a ditch killing all the passengers. So on the one hand we see the minutiae of life (the lost suitcase, the money in the pocket where none had been before), and on the other the dramatic intervention. Both are liable to doubt by others: the first on the ground that really nothing has happened at all, the second that rather too much is claimed to have happened!

Such doubts are present within the order itself. Given that there was a kind of competition over miracles, members were not above suggesting that X was getting altogether more than one might reasonably expect or that Y was overdoing it a bit or that Z was at least suffering from pious but wishful thinking. (It would have been interesting to discover how the recently initiated fitted in here, whether they were inclined to experience more or fewer karamat, one of many points that I did not consider at the time.) None of this diminished either the notion of the saint's power or of miracles in any way. If anything, it strengthened both. It was precisely because the issue was so fundamental that such doubts were raised and authentication was so important. The "readiness of mind," the constant attention to grace, the competitive element, gave energy to the whole movement. It inclined people to find proofs of blessing and at the same time to be demanding about the circumstances in which others found it. It ensured the continuance of the charismatic flow.

For the officers of the order, however, it presented certain problems. They were inclined individually and as a group to label rather different phenomena as miraculous: for example, the fact that the saint had had little formal education but is supposed to have had a brilliant and precocious knowledge of math and Persian; or that when challenged by the 'ulema to prove his religious credentials by answering certain extremely difficult theological questions, he replied by setting them a question that none of them could answer. This latter notion of the operation of power is very interesting because it testifies both to the saint's learning and to the fact that although his miracle apparently showed him confounding the 'ulema, the point really is that he does so on their ground. He shows himself even more of an 'alim than any of them can claim to be, even more of a knower of the sacred texts and theology than those specifically trained for it, even more orthodox than the orthodox. It is this form of karama, much commented on by the inner circle of the order and often described, that both defends the dubious principle of miracles by saints (dubious to the 'ulema, who attack what they regard as the questionable nature of popular Sufism) and incorporates the saint into the most respectable and pious ways of religious propriety. The miracle is used as an instrument of incorporation, not challenge; it makes a synthesis of elements that are otherwise often opposed.

The officers of the order, acutely aware of the suspicions with which government and religious establishment view popular Sufism ("superstition," "un-Islamic and ignorant," and so forth) are embarrassed, therefore, if too many claims of too startling a nature are made. Finding suitcases is one thing. Snatching people from rivers is a little too close for comfort to the tradition of moving mountains and asserts a degree of power that, of course, he may have had, but all the same. . . . It is a little dangerous, a little too disturbing to a social order of which they are very conscious and which they are in no position (nor have the wish) to challenge. Mostly made up of teachers and clerks or those in minor but relatively steady occupations in small companies or businesses, all literate and all with a relatively advanced degree of education, they are neither inclined by training, social position, nor rank to be enthusiastic about enthusiasm. Just as they rigorously control the rituals and immediately restrain anyone who gets out of line by going off into his own private ecstasy, so they frown (discreetly but firmly) on the too miraculous act.

They have to cope with another ambiguity that is produced for rather different reasons. That the saint made and makes miracles goes without saying. It is what makes him a saint and legitimizes his status (in fact, it legitimizes the followers, though they do not see it in this light). The successor to the saint (who died in 1939), who was therefore linked to him by the chain of blessing (silsilat al-baraka) was his son, connected to him also by the chain of blood relationship (silsilat ad-damm).* He was thus in the closest possible relation to the founder, and many believed that by virtue of his double participation in the saint's succession he had the powers of blessing at least (baraka) and perhaps also of acts of grace (karamat). Others were uncertain and wavered between acknowledging the possibility and saying that in fact they did not themselves know of events in which they felt he had miraculously acted.

The difference was not only one generated by the nature of his ties with the saint. It also reflected perhaps the different positions in wider social forms occupied by the two men. The first had his small group bound to him only by personal links and convictions of his sanctity, which were founded on his

---

* The son, Sheikh Ibrahim, died in 1975, some time after I had finished my fieldwork. See chapter 10 for the events that followed his death.

life pattern, his teaching, and his baraka. The order did not grow large until late in his career, and the original charismatic impulse, carefully tailored and fitted in the laws (*qānūn*) of the order, was at the center of the claims to adherence of the new members.

Members of the brotherhood continued to need the signs of grace, but the founder's successor was in a different position. He had organization rather than baraka, and the former was for him at this stage a much more predictable and useful instrument. So the two aspects coexisted. The members' access to blessing remained open through the constant activity of the saint, and the successor's control of the order remained stable in a society in which the position of the Sufi orders in general had become more and more precarious and vulnerable to attack. It was the task of the officials to organize the baraka, whereas the situation was seen by members as one in which organization followed and was the mere servant of baraka and of the charismatic flow.

Moreover, it is necessarily the founder and saint who is being continually reproduced and re-created, in relatively complete independence of his "actual" life, personality, and so forth. In fact, the biography of him written by one of the officers of the order who knew him personally for years is entirely (and not at all surprisingly) written in formulaic, generalized, model, conventional, hagiographic terms. What one might think of as biographical particularity or individuality is quite irrelevant to his significance, which is preserved in terms that are virtually indistinguishable from the pious biographies of other saints written a thousand years after their deaths by men who never knew them. This given and apparently depersonalized and frozen form provides the followers with an icon that has all the proper qualities of icons and around which they are free to create miracles. For them he is quite unique as well as being totally within the model of "what saints are." For they experience his uniqueness constantly in their lives and themselves endlessly produce it.

The Blessings of the Poor

In some cases the miraculous, the operations of grace, and the achievement of an ecstatic state are central to a group's being, whereas organization is quite insignificant. We can illustrate the case in which only a very limited role is played by the organizational dimension of a Sufi order in forming the ritual and religious experience of the poor by looking at the Ahmedīya order, whose zikr (Sufi rituals) I observed at Aswan in Upper Egypt. They were a small group of illiterate men, mostly in their twenties and thirties, whose lives were spent in the penumbra of society. They were outside the range of the proletariat, their labor was not bought, they had no way of acquiring either work or skills, they had no education or training. As the town expanded and prospered around them because of the then new High Dam (1965), only a few days here or there wheeling barrows or loitering at the worksite punctuated life and time in an irregular manner. They lived in and around the outer fringes of the town, near the brothels, in huts of tin, fruit boxes, sacking, or stone.

The sheikh of the little group of some fifteen to twenty men took part in the rituals without any special role, and the idea of leadership was vague and specifically played down. "Is not leadership and organization the mark of those who are not real Sufis and therefore have need of such external forms? Are we not all equal? Do we have any need of that kind of authority?" Thus the sheikh said to his unexpected foreign visitor. For even in a small, bare, lantern-lit room amid the filth and misery of the *lumpenproletariat* of Aswan one can claim to have the "right" way, the key to truth, the insight into the mysteries of Divinity.

More, one can experience that truth through the ecstasies of ritual. A man can hurl himself into the walls with strident shrieks of "Allah!" dashing blindly from one end of the room to the other between the two inward-facing lines of the brothers to smash headlong into the stone; a grandfather, so bent as to be almost circular, can hop from foot to foot clutching the hand of his grandson who seems unsure whether he is supporting the old man's ecstasy or experiencing his own; and the one there in the middle, peacefully grinning and spinning around, first on one foot and then on the other, and perpetually knocked over by the man who is still hurling himself from wall to wall. . . . The sheikh looks over at the anthropologist and smiles encouragingly.

In a universe in which daily life is governed by the arbitrary, the mysteries of God's purposes are part of a complex that embraces equally the presence of the *jinn* (spirits); the play of entities of different kinds and orders that are not a system so much as a bundle of semipersonalized forces to be magically manipulated, appeased, cajoled. From some one must be protected, whereas others, such as the saints, can be sought out eagerly. The notion of contact is central. And contact with the mysteries of God comes through the saints and through ecstasy. In the zikr men experience a concentrated power. They call out and chant the Names of God, thrust backward and forward in violent rhythmical movements, give themselves up to forces that seem to come from outside, from the word of the Divinity that reaches down into their nerves, their breathing, their innermost physical and emotional natures. Each man is free to construct his own vivid moment of truth through whirling around, leaping up and down, gasping the Names of God, without any official to reprimand him or any sanctions on his behavior that would in Cairo be so frowned on and so immediately checked.

Baraka and its expectation at this level of society take forms that are determined by social forces, even though it is the emotional and diffuse symbolic notion through which some marginal hold on a marginal life can be taken. It is the exclusion from words and texts, the enforced submission to nonstructure in daily life, the fragmentation of existence and the individual biography, the absence of labor with its cardinal importance in the formation of time and the relations within and between groups, that make baraka assume its particular character among the *lumpenproletariat*. Where, as was the case for so many in Algeria for example, colonial rule and displacement from rural areas were equally linked causal factors in the disruption of the world, the reasons for the production of baraka as a dream form become even more apparent. For, to put it simply, the *lumpenproletariat* produce not, neither do they exchange. Baraka here ceases to be at all founded in a series of transactions and exchanges within the material and symbolic systems of production and becomes indeed merely "the opium of the people."

It fills the symbolic and conceptual vacuum created by the total lack of significance of this social stratum within the political, economic, and cultural order. For the dominant classes everywhere the bidonvilles, which are viewed as centers of agitation and anarchy, are also stigmatized as the domains of superstition and ignorance. This same superstition and ignorance are then cited as *causes* of the situation in which the poor find themselves. The sober forces of "modernism," the austere interpreters of the texts according to the appropriate advanced-technical-state idiom, provide a *religious* explanation and causal pattern for the class situation of the most disprivileged.

We must stress the class nature of the latter's position. For the *lumpenproletariat*, as Max Weber long ago observed, is made up precisely of those who are in the purest and most uniform class situation, being an undifferentiated mass composed of completely unskilled and propertyless individuals depending entirely on irregular employment. At the same time it is the class above all in which class consciousness is most fractionalized and fragmented by the structures that produce their class situation — by their place in systems of production and exchange, their access to the market, their life chances, their exclusion from status, education, or any form of social right or privilege, their dependence on arbitrary, ephemeral favors or patronage for even a temporary occupation. Individual ecstatics and the fantasies of baraka give an irregular, cloudy transcendence of this situation, just as they serve as a proof to the religious specialists and the more privileged classes of the moral and ethical degradation of the lowest level of society. The ideological circle is socially closed again.

In this milieu, therefore, the particular notion of baraka that I have sketched out is at the core of the apprehension of the world in symbolic-conceptual terms. It is held to produce ecstasy, and that same ecstasy is seen as the proof of baraka's presence. It is part of the fundamental idea that the true order of things is concealed from men and is in fact the reverse of the way in which the world is actually lived out in the day-to-day. The presence of saints and holy men provides powerful symbolic experiences of this reversal of daily reality and of the dominant sets of categories and representations that serve within the culture to interpret and structure the world and life within it. As Vincent Crapanzano has shown, a saint's followers often acquire baraka by drinking the holy man's vomit, or the polluted (that is, dirty in the everyday definition) water left when a holy man has washed, which is transformed into purity by the fact of his blessing and holiness. Such systematic symbolic reversals are part of the language of baraka for this stratum. And it is the same power that enables men to attain that extraordinary state of being (the *ḥāl*, or ecstatic condition) that is the very opposite of one's routine, mundane human existence. That at least one can do, that at least serves as a guarantee that one has access to the ultimate Power as much as do the learned men, the ruling orders, the dominant groups who in so many different ways seek to guard its approaches.

Baraka is therefore the key to practices that in a fictive way transform things into their opposite (as do so many miracles) and enable the passage to be made from the ordinary world to the realm of the sacred (even though that passage will only be an ephemeral one for men who are not saints or the descendants of saints). Oppositions are transcended, cures effected, miracles produced, the individual's own biological and emotional nature momentarily dissolved into a "higher" state of being.

Exchange is not entirely absent, however. It is usually the ordinary members of the orders, or those who make pilgrimages to a saint's shrine, who go into ecstasy. They have to constantly seek out baraka while the religiously privileged holy men and their descendants possess it by definition. Seeking out, for the laity, involves not only ecstasy but offerings (money, food, little gifts of all kinds) to the shrine and the shrine's keepers. Among the Hamadsha of Morocco, studied by Crapanzano, the idea that a saint's baraka is inexhaustible allows those who have privileged access to it an equally constant stream of donations that in fact permit them to build up their own material wealth.* The flow of exchange (offerings in exchange for baraka) is blocked by the privileged (for whom the saint is changed into cash by the

* Vincent Crapanzano, *The Hamadsha: A Study in Moroccan Ethnopsychiatry* (Berkeley/Los Angeles/London: University of California Press, 1973), p. 123.

operation of and control over baraka). Baraka here is thus an illusory transformation of the world that is doomed to remain at the level of a symbolic disruption of the dominant modes of organizing society and nature. The only exchange the poor can make — offerings in return for blessing — is turned into false coin and the opposite of what was so dearly sought.

Grace from Peanuts

To take finally an example where baraka is, as it were, pushed to its ultimate as an element in unequal exchange and as an ideological instrument of great political and economic significance, let us consider the Muridiya of Senegal.* Here blessing has gone through a series of metamorphoses over time, as the nature and history of the order has changed. It begins as the charter for a saint and the order that he founds (a perfectly "classical" version) at the end of the nineteenth century. Behind it unite both Muslim peasants and those who had been pagans and bastions of the old political order before it was disrupted by French colonialism, particularly in the 1880s. Where secular military force failed to stop the colonial advance, and it is most important that it did fail as a mode of opposition, the field was left open to the power of God. Baraka, therefore, was the ideological cement of two initially opposed groupings, the peasants and the warriors of the old order — opposed culturally and historically before the coming of the French, but now, in the context of foreign invasion and the military defeat of the indigenous ruling order, synthesized in the new brotherhood of the Muridiya. Behind the typically pure, scholarly unworldliness of the founder, Sheikh Amadu Bamba, a powerful organization was formed that united the former warlords, their staffs of warriors, and the Muslim peasantry.

The brotherhood based itself economically on the growing of peanuts and the exploitation for this form of agriculture

* There are two interesting studies of this order by Donal Cruise O'Brien, *The Mourides of Senegal: The Political and Economic Organisation of an Islamic Brotherhood* (Oxford: Clarendon Press, 1971) and *Saints and Politicians: Essays in the Organisation of a Senegalese Peasant Society* (London/New York/ Cambridge: Cambridge University Press, 1975).

of whole new areas of hitherto uncultivated land. The economic transformation that has resulted, given that peanuts came to dominate the economy of Senegal, not only makes the Muridiya a political power of the first rank in the development of the country, but also places work and production at the center of the organization's activities. Baraka has become part of a driving and mobilizing ethic of obedience to authority and labor for the order. In return for this work, the ordinary members obtain some redistribution of the profits (which are enormous) and the possibility of eventually becoming small landholders themselves. Basically, however, they form a cheap and highly structured work force that accumulates large reserves of capital for the elite. The state founded by the French has, in the words of a leading student of the Muridiya "remained chronically deficient in moral sanctions of any kind." In that context of ideological uncertainty at the center the saint and the order constitute a formidable and religiously legitimated authority.* But again, the opposition of state and brotherhood is often more apparent than real, and the state sometimes even acts as a kind of guarantor for the disciples' own offerings: "The great mosque of Touba, apparently the symbol of the disciples' economic devotion, was in large part financed by the colonial administration and by Leopold Senghor's *Union Progressiste Sénégalaise* (which contributed over one hundred thousand pounds to the mosque construction fund for the 1960 election alone)."†

The proofs of baraka are furnished on the one hand by the state and on the other by signs of an exceedingly worldly kind. Status, being a language of consumption even where the status is religious in its foundation, takes on forms that conspicuously demonstrate the importance and success of the saints who are quite content that their authority should be translated into worldly terms: vast cars, mansions, and sumptuous life-styles, all the followers that wealth can purchase, and idleness, the ultimate evidence of grace in such a context! For, after all, does not all this blessing come freely, without any particular saint having to descend to such mundane matters as work in order to attain it? Work, like the

---

* Cruise O'Brien, *Saints and Politicians*, p. 10.
† Ibid., pp. 76-77.

search for baraka, is what identifies the followers. So blessing is inseparable from display. How very small scale the little miracles of the founder of the Hamidiya Shaziliya seem set beside such a powerful and constant miracle of luxury and power allied with economic development!

CHAPTER 5

Miracles and Worldly Power

LORDS AND SHEIKHS IN NORTH LEBANON

In the case of Sufism among the poor and petite bourgeoisie of Egypt, we saw that the miracle is a source of individual or group satisfaction rather than constituting a weapon against the broader social system. A challenge is there, but only of a very muted kind. For the Ahmediya order in Aswan and the Hamadsha of the Moroccan slums baraka and karamat become a dream in which one finds refuge. In Senegal they bolster a powerful economic and political organization.

In another area in which I worked, however, miracles and grace acts are constituted quite differently and have quite a different social and political sense.

To begin with, in the setting of north Lebanon it was noticeable that the conception of baraka, which, with some Egyptian experience behind me, I spoke of quite naturally and often as a property of men and things or situations, was never referred to at all. This was most confusing, since I had always assumed that karamat and baraka went together like cheese and biscuits, or its Middle Eastern equivalent. They were surely a natural pair? And yet I was alone in the village in speaking of baraka and was clearly not seeing the same universe. So some unlearning had to be done about how the universe is constructed, and a new start had to be made.

Furthermore, it appeared that miracles (karamat) were found quite explicitly in open confrontation with the embodiments of worldly power. What could explain such a fundamental contrast?

The situation in north Lebanon can be briefly characterized as follows: The region was, and to a very large extent still is, dominated by a ruling class who are also described as being in the broadest sense "one family." That is to say, they bear the same family name, though they are based in different areas of the region and split into several major branches. By origin Kurdish, they were probably established in the north around the eighteenth century by the Ottoman government, which then ruled Syria and Lebanon, to guard what was basically an important strategic route constantly menaced by Alaouite (Shi'ite) mountain people from one side and other Shi'a groups in the Lebanese mountain to the south. From this beginning they acquired a more or less total domination over the local political economy. They monopolized the ownership of land, controlled laboring groups who had scarcely better than a serf status, operated an exploitative tax system to their own advantage, and claimed a whole series of rights and dues as lords. Their palaces were, and are, located in Sunni Muslim villages, and it was in these villages that the rule of the bey, or lord, was most direct and most total (the term *bey*, or *bek*, is a Turkish military-aristocratic rank). It was in one such village that I worked.

The legitimating charter for this ruling group has been from the start, therefore, one of force of arms and military control by a "family" of foreign origin. They rule because they were installed to defeat certain other religiously labeled groups (the Shi'ites) and to control the area politically. Power and domination, and, indeed, what is called *zulm* (oppression), were the explicit foundations of the system they established. Violence and the means of destruction became largely their monopoly, and they also employed small family groups as retainers in particular villages in which the beys were based, to run estates, bear arms, put down any resistance, organize labor groups, and generally furnish that vital staff without which the lords could not have maintained themselves.

There was thus a very clear correspondence between the

social-historical bases of the system and its day-to-day realities. Power, which is founded on class domination, was (and is) also personal and direct. Political relations are articulated by favor, violence, the organization of violence and intimidation, and the mobilization of groups by particular leaders who also control the main local factors of production — land, labor, and technology. The laboring class was and is very directly in contact with the dominating groups that produce and reproduce the system.

Opposed to this ideology and reality of power (*sulta*), domination (*masaitra*), and oppression (*zulm*) are the sheikhs. They are the men of learning ('ilm), insight (*ma'rifa*), and authority. They are also in theory of one family, but of local, not foreign origin. These holy men claim to have preceded the beys in the region and to be the indigenous men of authority. They are also concentrated in particular villages and are in theory organized into a Sufi brotherhood (though this has very little practical meaning).

Their position, then, rests on the fact that they are the men of religious learning and illumination, and also the markers of Sunni Muslim identity (again, in the Lebanese setting and given the local mix of religious groups, including both Greek Orthodox and Maronite communities). The sheikhs were always spoken of to me in these terms and as the contradiction of the worldly order embodied by the men of power, the beys.

The contradiction had taken, it appeared, very concrete forms. When I asked questions about the relations of the sheikhs and the lords, I was frequently told of the miracles that the former had performed at the latters' expense. In other words, there were no more incidents of suitcases and pound notes, of extraordinary learning and knowledge of theology; it was sheikhs versus beys, and in the local accounts, to my great interest, the men of religion seemed to win every time. To be sure, most of the figures discussed dated back to the 1930s, but the basic principles of opposition were always stated to be constant.

A particular sheikh who died before World War Two but whose name was locally still very well known was often referred to me as the type case. He was of special importance because his victim was the lord of the village in which I worked for most of the time. The lord, who died in 1958, had been a model of tyranny. Judging by eyewitness accounts and oral evidence, which I was able to compare and evaluate, his violence was by no means mythological or exaggerated but was only too real. He was also perhaps the most powerful man of the entire region, possessing many villages lock, stock, and barrel all across the northern plain and into Syria. He had been the first to see the importance of technology and capital investment for agriculture after World War I. He had collaborated with the French, who furnished his men with arms, which were otherwise strictly controlled during that period (1919-1940), to maintain political order. He had further been the first to put his money into town properties, to buy buildings and urban real estate and small businesses, to buy also a European education for his son, who later became a minister of finance and was murdered by a rival in 1953. With all this he built a splendid little rococo palace full of tiles and brocades, chandeliers and velvets and painted ceilings and all the appurtenances of aristocratic luxury.* Within were received French generals and the world of Lebanese notables; outside was another world, of the laborers and the rural poor.

This same lord, whose relations with the French in the between-war period had been very close, had been able through this connection to secure control of the all-important arms technology that was to be so central in the preservation of power by the ruling stratum. Pistols and rifles replaced those other honorific means of destruction, the lance and the sword. He was said himself to have practiced occasionally by trying out a new rifle on a worker who was constructing a wall or a boy who refused to get water, both incidents for which there were more than one living witness.

Obviously this biography has become "iconic," too, though much richer in historical particularity and personal detail, and far more varied and susceptible to inquiry than our Egyptian saintly iconography, and of rather different moral significance! The picture can be completed by merely adding that he was said to know every single sheep and goat on his domains, something still retold with astonishment, admiration,

---

* We shall discuss the significance of this and other signs of domination in chapter 8.

and regret by his shepherd. Note that the tyranny is much more historically based and far less "mythologized" than that of the Qajars of Iran and that the lord really was in a position to run local affairs much as he pleased. There were and are many other lords and notables, but few have had his wealth, acumen, and local standing.

It was against this formidable figure that our saint carried out his miracles. Clearly it was no small task. What sort of miracles were they?

On one occasion the bey had lost his patience with the sheikh and had roundly cursed him. Shortly afterward the lord's new car broke an axle, crashed into a ditch, and his arm was badly broken (and this in the 1920s when a car, of which there were in any case very few, was *the* symbol of the new order of wealth, machinery, conspicuous consumption, and social status in a region of miserable poverty and exploitation). On a rather similar occasion the bey was punished by the death of his favorite horse. Another time he bent down to tie up his shoelace and could not stand up again until the sheikh appeared and allowed him to. Such events were attributed to the holy man's powers and produced a healthy respect. "The sheikh was the only man whose hand the bey kissed," as it is put locally. This sign of deference and respect was thought of as being forced out of him by the sheikh's power, based on religion, to which his own, based on force, had to submit. Force is compelled to give way to grace, to knowledge, to "sheikhliness" as incarnated in our saint. As the latter's nephew, himself a sheikh who will reappear in these pages, smilingly remarked in answer to my question as to how the saint and the lord had got on together: "Very well, but we had to teach him a lesson first!"

The fact that other miracles were also described that featured other lords, and even French officers who at various times were in charge of the region, only serves to give a more explicitly political and oppositional character to the whole notion of the operations of grace. Though the world may be in daily life and on the surface of things directly dominated by certain almost feudal political forms and an all too visible armature of coercion, the sheikh can vividly demonstrate the other, "underlying" reality by being even more forceful than the lord. A different language of religious power and compulsion is what he uses to teach the man of power a lesson. Through him it is power of a totally other kind that proceeds from God, not from worldly dominion.

The image and conception of sheikhliness is contrary in the most fundamental sense to the nature of the beys was and is, therefore, very strong and is generalized to the notion of opposition of sheikhs to beys on the levels that I have indicated. Let us look a little more closely at the context of this opposition to see how the idea of religious authority versus worldly power is operated on in the everyday world and in the sociopolitical system at large.

We should first remark that on the plain (as distinct from other groups in the mountains and on the borders of the region) we do not find sheikhs in villages dominated by the lords or vice versa. (There is only one exception to this: a village ruled by a lord but with a minor "house" of sheikhs who do not wear the green turban [a few wear white headgear], who work at ordinary jobs and have no marked social status.) There is therefore a spatial separation of the two "opposing" groups. We then find that in their own villages the sheikhs are roughly in the position of those Learned Families of south Lebanon, which we have already discussed. That is to say, they are the dominant landowning groups. Equally they are the biggest single descent groups (i.e. claiming a shared genealogy) in their villages. Such villages, made up of small traders, independent landowning peasant families possessing small plots, sharecroppers, agricultural laborers, and seasonal workers, are also of a familiar pattern. There have been killings and open crises between landowning sheikhs and other groups in at least three of these villages on the plain. However, the villages are still very impoverished, they are not market centers, and by and large they are less changed by migration than the settlement of the Learned Families in the south.

So in their own villages the holy men of the north are the main landholding groups and moreover seem to be very much associated with a repressive political and social order from the point of view of the other strata of the village population. One further discovers that it is very often the beys who are leasing land to the sheikhs at very favorable rates, or even altogether free. It is and was also the beys who provided other opportunities for the men of religion to acquire income through offerings and additional social standing. For at the births, marriages, and deaths of the lordly families, when these occur on the plain or in Tripoli (the main city of the north), where local people are expected to attend the various rituals as a mark of respect and loyalty to the lord, the sheikhs play a very public and often dramatic role. They assemble in little clusters and compete with one another as to who can eat fire, chew live coals, or make a meal out of light bulbs. Respectful young people present separate the contestants, assuring them that no one doubts their holiness and qualities and that no one needs such dramatic and alarming proofs. The competition is then transferred to the more peaceful arena of Sufi ritual (the zikr), in which different sheikhs manifest different extremes and modes of ecstasy (not without a certain ironic gleam in the eye of some observers present, who occasionally tip the anthropologist a disconcerting wink after some particularly deafening cry of one of the Names of God).

The picture that begins to emerge is not exactly the one presented in the miraculous accounts. It becomes even more interesting when we look back to the saint, who so discomfited the great tyrannical lord in their various miracle-producing confrontations. As the bey embodied oppression in his personality and style, as well as in his economic strategies (as we have seen), so the sheikh appears to have been a perfect representation of unworldly holiness. This was by no means a great medieval prelate figure capable of confronting the political arm and maintaining his own high style. Rather he was a quiet, ascetic man of learning and devotion who stayed for the most part in his extremely simple house and there received whoever chose to visit him. The rooms, when I saw them, were bare of all but the merest necessities: a couple of rugs, a mat or two, a portrait of a thin, bearded face staring from an unpainted frame. No brocades and red velvet drapes here but an entirely different symbolic universe, austere and unadorned in the same degree as that of his opposite was rich and decorated. There is no glittering surface, only the courtyard, the whitewashed walls, a few naked lightbulbs, and a Quranic text. It was in such a setting, which in its spatial form so denied the world, that lived the man whose hand the great lord kissed because "he was forced to, whether he liked it or not," because he had been "taught a lesson."

Where the lord held open house for the notables, traveled everywhere in great style, personally supervised the management of all his estates, and occupied himself with both rural and urban investment throughout the crucial period of European impact on the region (between the two World Wars), the saint stayed quietly at home. Yet he too held open house; he too dispensed freely of his hospitality, his food and drink, his room to all who came. The key word is *freely*. Baraka and karamat are above all thought to be qualities freely given by God through specific individuals (or acts or holy places). They drop like manna from heaven, as we might say. No return is necessary, there is no contrast, no notion of exchange. Indeed they are the most radical denial of all that is worldly precisely because they negate the worldly principles of gift and countergift, of calculation, of routine and mundane social reciprocity. Certainly nothing could be more contrary to the lord's hospitality, which is at once an attribute of his status honor, a demonstration of wealth and of political power over men, and an instrument for mobilizing followers — in short, the "generosity" of the powerful.

Through the sheikh pure and free gifts flowed without thought of recompense. Men might eat and drink, learn and listen, pray and meditate, sleep and talk all within his house thanks to his baraka, which was entirely independent of their own labor (upon which, by contrast, the lord's acquisition of wealth depended). The holy man's disinterested distribution of grace is conceived of as being made possible by his sacred qualities and his favor with God. He has no organization and no disciples, he is simply an ascetic and a blessed man (*rajul mabrūk*).

How was this miracle of the endless river of religious bounty maintained? It was in large part funded by the very lord who represents all the principles of which the saint's life is the antithesis.

For it was the lord who sent the sheikh sacks of wheat and grain and seed, even money when necessary, and who leased out land to other members of the family. Nor is this in any way hidden. It certainly does not diminish for many local people the idea of free flow and sanctity. Quite the reverse.

It makes manifest in the most significant way the fact that the unsullied authority of the saint compels the worldly power of the lord to make what almost amounts to tributary offerings of respect. The material base of the holy man's open house, which involves an enormous economic outlay, was therefore secured by the adversary with whom, after the lesson had been taught of course, he had had "excellent relations" (as his nephew also added).

So the cooperation of the two not only reinforces the idea of the saint's power, which is made all the greater by the status of his "opponent," it even bolsters the ideology of the contradiction between religious authority and political power.

Sociologically, there are other interesting dimensions to the signs of power. Clearly it is the lord in this case who frees the saint for religion and helps to produce baraka as a social phenomenon and a reality that men experience. It is the secular power that underwrites and is the foundation for the operations of grace, in an idiom of respect and compulsion by the force of that same baraka which it has made possible (another circle). The rest of the sheikh's descent group, who are the local dominant landowners, can also go about their business of leasing land from the lords and receiving gifts of food and supplies where appropriate without anything troubling the character and position of the saint himself. His virtues may be said to liberate them to get on with the job of being the main village status and economic group. This is by no means an isolated phenomenon, of course. One often finds that the saintly founder or central figure is the very image of solitary purity and is so unworldly that he is quite incompetent (and should be!) in all the questions of administration, the control of finances, and so forth and that the latter are left as an often rich prize for his family and relatives, who do not have to bear the same load of ascetic holiness.

The beys, therefore, supported and support the sheikhs. The latter are in a far stronger position than their equivalents in south Lebanon. They represent the subordinate religious wing of the predominant economic and political power of the region. They have the lords' backing in the most material sense and are not left to fend for themselves, as were the

Learned Families. On the contrary. They are part of an overall regional system of domination. In their own villages, given all the restrictions placed on development in the area, many of the laborers and sharecroppers are dependent on them, and they play the most important role of givers or withholders of work. Sanctity has, always, very practical applications. At the same time they have little corporate group influence outside these specific villages, few connections out into the national economic and political scene, no really independent economic base (no sheikh is given particularly good land or enough of it to make him into a quasi-independent factor).

For the lord, at whose local rituals the holy men officiate, the sheikhs are far more than a mere decorative appendage of power or a nod in the direction of popular religious feeling. At one level they are important allies within the restricted spheres of their own villages and the economy of the plain. They help both directly and indirectly to control the local population and its integration into certain forms of economic relations with the major landholders. At another level the sheikhs have a very concrete *group* interest in the reproduction of the current social system and the preservation of the very oppression to which in miracles they are so opposed.

We might remark in passing that none of the miracles ever tell of peasants being saved from injustice by the saint. They tell of a slight to the saint that is punished in a way that quickly obliges the bey to show his deference. "The equilibrium must not be disturbed" is the real message, and the miracle in a way is as much for the victim's good as for the sheikh's satisfaction: a message to the lord that he had better remember both that religion is *not* his domain and that a proper respect is appropriate (and inexpensive) public behavior. One might also say that the fact that religion is so specifically made the concern of the sheikhs and so clearly is excluded from the nature and political charter of the beys avoids any contradiction in the theory and practice of domination by the rulers. They can hardly be accused of injustice when injustice is one of the elements that defines them! In this respect religion is incorporated in a well-bounded, separated, and subordinated field of authority, with its own guardians, who safely represent the potentially troublesome forces of Islam.

The guardians exercise this function with vigor. The same sheikh (nephew of the saint) to whom I have referred and whom we shall meet again was an enthusiastic defender of the status quo. On several occasions he appeared on a very political mission in the village in which I was working in 1971/72 (not a village with its own sheikhly group, since it had been the local seat of the now dead tyrant). He came to summon the tractor drivers and semiskilled workers, who formed a group traditionally attached as strong-arm men and retainers to the beys, against the "peasants," mostly tied laborers on the plain. His teachings in one of the reception rooms in the village included frequent homilies on the necessity to respect the established order, in which most of his listeners felt they had a firm interest, vis-à-vis those lower in the status order. The peasants were very frequently invoked as sources of trouble and disorder. (The word he used, *fellaheen*, indicates "lowest of the low" in status honor terms rather than any occupational or economic sense.) His audience was actually composed of impoverished agricultural workers at the beck and call of one of the other lords with whom this particular sheikh's lordly patron was constantly at loggerheads. The battle between the two lords was fought out by sending the wretched peasants, who lived in tin shacks on the plain, to plow the land of the opponent and then by waiting for the reaction (usually the shooting or beating up of one or two of the peasants by the other lord's own forces).

The message of the miracles hardly describes, therefore, the true relationship of the two groups, sheikhs and beys. It is most important that it should not do so. Here is an interesting situation. These are acts (and a general ethos) that seem to be the very type case of the political/oppositional gesture: One kind of power, that of God/the saint/authoritative truth, conquers another kind of power, worldly rule/the beys/powerful and illegitimate "falsehood." The principle that divine authority is utterly opposed to worldly power and oppression is grounded in theology and miraculous experience. It is more specifically at the level of social relations that the miracles conceal the link of dependency that is quite contrary to the message that the miracles appear to transmit.

The sheikhs depend upon the lords. They need them to maintain their locally predominant position in their home villages and as providers of land. It is the lords who make the miracles possible, both in the material sense that they provide the wherewithal for the sheikhs to keep up a sheikhly life-style and in the sense that they are the pole of contrast throwing into relief the legitimacy of the men of religion as against that of the men of power. Most significant of all, it was the great tyrant who created, or made possible, the baraka of the saint; that vital, pure, free flow of grace mani-fested in the sheikh's personal poverty and his capacity end-lessly to receive and give the means of sustenance to all comers, his assimilation to the paradigm of what sheikhs are.

The implications of the fact that it was the lord who supplied the saint are perfectly incorporated into the ideo-logical and symbolic scheme by the notion of compulsion (he was "taught a lesson") and respect ("he had to kiss his hand whether he liked it or not") and serve as a proof of the holy man's power.

In return the lords have harnessed the local religious stratum to their rule. They are attended on when necessary by the sheikhs, they can rely on them for support in critical circumstances, such as when the peasants on the plain give trouble, and may even have the pleasure of knowing in some cases that it is their portrait that serves as the main decora-tion of a sheikh's reception room. Indeed it is not at all unusual to see particular sheikhs engaging in straightforward electioneering when their patron is involved in struggles for a seat in the National Assembly.

So our men of religion are in a rather more solid position than the Learned Families of south Lebanon, for reasons that should be clear. We have noted, nonetheless, that there is considerable tension within the overall socioeconomic system of which they are a part. Within their own villages, since land has remained locally very important and they are virtually "guaranteed" by judicious arrangements with the lords to remain the main local landholders and employers in agricul-ture, they are in a relatively stable situation. But they are also very much in opposition to the peasant/sharecropper/laborer strata. Many of the latter are bound to them by economic ties. They depend on the sheikhs for work, and some of the poorest attend on the rituals arranged by a given sheikh (and vote the way he wants!).

The rest have begun to have access to other possibilities. But education has been very, very limited in the area, as have all the main services, such as water and electricity and roads. Administrative jobs are few in number and filled by outsiders from the capital or other regions, so that not many of the lower groups have been able to break out of the local field. And a challenge to a particular sheikh or sheikhs is also a challenge to a regional system of political domination that has strong national connections.

Furthermore, the leading holy men have their sheikhly but impoverished relatives as a private family labor force, whether in the fields or in the reception room serving coffee, performing whatever duties their wealthier and more influential cousins require of them. So although I (and the people locally) have talked about "the sheikhs," they are by no means a uniform group with individually equal positions in the social scale. The green turban and the notion of descent within one family do not disguise the marked internal stratification of the group and the fact that its internal relations are regulated in very worldly terms of who has the goods and who has not (a point to which we shall have to return).

None of the above precludes, of course, a quite genuine respect that a particular lord might have for a particular sheikh nor even the acquisition by certain of the beys of a reputation for considerable scrupulousness in the matter of religious forms. Some of the older lords who had been born and brought up on the plain were notably more attached than were their sons and grandsons to the presence of certain sheikhs at the performance of appropriate rituals at marriages and funerals at which the agricultural laborers would form the bulk of the local audience. Their sons and grandsons appeared more concerned that their Mercedes cars had some difficulty in negotiating the cart tracks across the field to the house, which had long since ceased to be inhabited by their generation and was used strictly as a focal point for local affairs. Some young lords even went so far as to indicate a certain distaste for the rituals of the sheikhs and to express loudly the view on leaving that it had nothing to do with religion and was a complete waste of time. For these beys-become-bourgeois, whose ties to the region were now marginal, whose own life-style and economic base had little to do with the olives and cereals of the remote north, this pandering to "peasant religion" appeared either comic, irrelevant, or offensive. They could see no reason for maintaining what basically seemed to them to be a charade, and indeed they had absolutely no reason for any positive valuation of the local collaboration with the sheikhs. When, at a funeral in Tripoli, the cigarette holder of the saint was produced by one of the minor beys and reverentially handed round to be kissed and exclaimed over as an object of precious value, it was very noticeable and commented on that some of the young lords could not control their derision, however discreetly muffled.

This tiny incident gives a hint of the emergence of a new, more obvious class pattern of local religious forms. For the young lords, engaged in the liberal professions or the political-social careers of better-placed relatives, the local scene is increasingly irrelevant, save at election time. Their fathers, who shared the services of the same religious personnel as the other social strata of their villages and often did not have much more knowledge of theological and holy texts, fitted naturally into a mold that the sons find merely amusing or a demonstration of rural ignorance. This trend is reflected in what I was often told in explanation of the fact that there had been no other outstanding holy man since the death of the saint in the late 1930s: "There are no saints and miracles now." "Why not?" "Well, because there are no beys." And it is true though the lords still made constant appearances in their villages, they are nonresident and carry on politics and the management of their estates (those that have them) from Beirut or Tripoli. More and more the local business is carried out by ill-paid foremen or bodyguards who travel to the capital, get their orders, and return to carry them out. The conspicuous and highly upper bourgeoisie life-style that is at least aimed at by many of the lords further distances them from the local population, though the operations of their power are as immediate and direct as ever.

The Presence and Absence of Grace

The previous discussion may help us in trying to determine why the notion of baraka as an abstract but very real power that manifests itself in a multiplicity of ways was so strangely absent from the north Lebanese world. For though I have described the saint as "having" baraka, that is my rather Egyptian way of putting it. In fact I never heard of any sheikh, however well known, described as "having" or "possessing" baraka, let alone of baraka as a force or power through which men could and did receive blessings from the Divinity. Individual sheikhs (including the saint) were occasionally spoken of as rajul mabruk (roughly meaning a blessed or holy man), but this indicated a general respect for their personal qualities and exemplary natures, not the attribution to them of privileged links to God. This elusive essence, which was so pervasive among those with whom I worked in Egypt, was almost totally absent as a concept in Lebanon, even if the saint had made his miracles.

How can we explain the variations in the nature and operations of baraka within society at large that the different situations we have considered seem to demonstrate?

I am inclined myself to begin looking for the answer in the degree of directness by which people experience the operation of power and determining forces in their lives and those areas that are relatively unstructured in terms of everyday life.

Let us think about the saint-bey relation in north Lebanon with this very general idea in mind. There is a social system in which individuals and groups encounter the dominant forces that produce and reproduce their world in a very immediate and "uncovered" kind of way. The hierarchy of status honor and stratification is public, supported by styles of behavior, modes of interaction, and the presence of different controls and sanctions based ultimately (and often proximately!) on force. The ruling notables (who are allied to the national ruling class through marriage, finance, and position in relation to the market and to production) possess the land and the capital and also have the power to give or withhold access to work, education, and the means of life by using their personal influence through the patronage system. Those who need favors, if they do not see the notable himself, have a face-to-face contact with one of his local link men. Thus contact with those who are at the top of the political and economic heap is direct and relatively unmediated. This does not mean that there are not in fact all kinds of ideological and symbolic schema that express and mystify this power structure: the claims of status honor, the cult of individual force, the idea that the system is really nothing more than the personal contacts by which men are forced to live. All these do actually mediate between the political and economic foundations and the everyday world of men's experience. But the practice of control is known, clear, personal, direct, as are the sanctions that can be brought into play.

Most people in the village had only too vivid memories of work lost, jobs taken, money cut off, threats, the use of the apparatus of strong-arm men and chauffeurs for intimidation. There could be no illusions about any of that. Equally, those who were on the other side of the fence because as members of the staffs they were part of the operations of power (however individually poor and precarious their livelihood might actually be and however dependent on the unpredictable favors of the notable) felt themselves to be on top. The system was their guarantee of status superiority, of the use of a gun, of access to the lord. Their interests seemed to them quite obvious. Finally, it need hardly be repeated, the lords' own ideology was one of force, of conquest as a tradition of two hundred years of "honor".

The only institutional role associated with the possession of baraka, that of sheikh, was safely incorporated into the political and social system by the means already indicated. So that even a sheikh who was thought of as rajul mabruk had his baraka produced by the "respectful" gifts of the lord. In this sense we can say that the latter played a key part in the creation and reproduction of religion in its structural and ideological forms. The secular produces the material bases of the sacred.

As a function of such a pattern of social organization the lines between the social groups and levels were very well drawn. In the village in which I worked, for example, there were only a very few marriages among the descent group (some fifty-six households), some of whom made up the local staffs of various lords, and the "peasants." Such marriages marked the already total poverty and loss of status by the households which had made them. To my knowledge (and it is based only on oral information of an unsystematic kind) the sheikhs' women were not allowed to marry out into other strata. Even declassed lords tended to marry into other and equally declining lords' families. If we add that social interaction between the strata was cast very rigidly in terms of relative status and power, we can see just how complete the definition of social life is.

It appears to me that this degree of ideological and social closure and control and the directness of the workings of power and sanctions explain the absence of the problematic force of baraka, which is so important in our other example.

We can relate this to baraka among the groups discussed in the previous chapter. The Muridiya of Senegal, of course, have it all very well organized and totally integrated into an ideology of "grace equals work," though we have seen what exchanges exist to support such an equation and such an ethic. The hierarchy of the order and the control over production make of baraka a highly structured and directed ideological power, a religious technology, in the hands of the officers of the order and most important to their continued legitimacy in the eyes of the members. In both north Lebanon and Senegal, therefore, we find a high degree of political and economic control that either excludes baraka from the religious and ideological field or harnesses it as basic legitimating concept to an institution that is defined as in essence religious but also constitutes a highly organized political and economic unit.

Baraka is the key ideological transformer in the whole Muridiya operation, the crucial element in the making of money and the control of labor by a particular section of the brotherhood, the pivot of authority. It is a valuable property to be dispensed or earned by the faithful through labor, to the point where in one branch of the *tariqa* (the way, or path, of Islam) work is even put above prayer as a duty. One might almost say that the largest resulting miracle is the peanut export figures! I would be inclined to say that baraka here is the core organizing concept of religious practice in this form of Islam.

We should remark how far control over or possession of baraka extends into the everyday world. For domination over, or monopoly of baraka is also power over the way in which the world is thought of, symbolized, and experienced. It is certainly not too much to say that it has a critical effect in the realm of everyday logic and the construction of a universe, since above all it expresses notions about causation (as do the equally well-guarded miracles). It deals with the relations between events, the relations between persons and the Divinity, and the power that such a relation gives to a particular individual or group (and therefore of the social system within which they and their class or stratum exercise rulership).

In Lebanon this power is conceived of in terms of a principle of opposition to worldly rule by the authority of the religious specialists, but it is in fact produced and maintained largely by the lords. Among the Muridiya the power is constituted in a direct relation of murid [follower, disciple] to sheikh (though the secular government plays a key role also). Both staffs and systems of authority and power work to exclude and to make alternative modes of thought unthinkable. Relations between persons and between events and the ways in which the former are thought to bring about the latter are highly patterned both socially and ideologically. The idea of chance, or of a free-floating baraka, are thus absent from the scene.

In the setting of the Sufi order of Cairo we entered another social world organized in other ways. For most of the members the brotherhood is the most certain, organized, and predictable fact of their lives, though it is by no means a total framework in terms of which all their experience is structured or felt to be structured. At different levels of the order the members are able to create, or "see," or take pious comfort in rather different visions of what constitutes the baraka of their founder and his son and the kinds of miracles that may be produced. The organizers help direct and form the intense readiness and eager looking out for signs of grace into channels that are not only internally within the tariqa but in more general social, political, and theological terms "safe." They do so in a situation in which popular Sufism as a form of religious practice has been subject to 'ulema and government attack and so is vulnerable to certain changes in Egyptian society. The variations in belief and expectations are kept to tolerable limits and the miracles likewise. The variations are wide, but they are part of an everyday way of thought into which grace acts are integrated as an anticipated part of existence.

This readiness for grace is not only a function of membership in the order and of following the saint. The lives of most of the brothers are in major part subject to more mediated, distant, impersonal, and abstract institutions and controls through the social system than the personal-direct experience of north Lebanon. Indeed, it would be easy to find far more unstructured conceptions of the operations of grace and divine power within the same strata of Egyptian society that supply the Hamidiya Shaziliya with its members. Such conceptions center on private and public acts of reverence to saints and the presence at such special occasions as the *mulids* (saints' festivals). As we move into the white-collar levels of the order (which provide the organizers), so baraka as a dramatic force irrupting into daily life becomes more and more organized rather than organizing, more associated with the ascetic and religious attributes of the saint, more a question of a diffuse quality or state of being of events.

Without the forms of closure and definition that the order sets up in ritual, organization, and ideology, baraka could easily become highly disruptive because it has more room to move, if I may use such a phrase, than in the Lebanese and Muridiya examples. Processes of social change in Egyptian society may even help to liberate and produce baraka precisely insofar as for some strata they break down established patterns of life without generating new forms of social, economic, or political coherence or focus.

The picture in our other contexts is in considerable contrast. What characterized the Sufis of the slums of Aswan and the teams and audiences of the bidonvilles of Morocco is a broadly similar position in economic and political structures. It is a position that is almost completely beyond the institutional organization of the dominant interpreters of religion (the 'ulema, the government, the universities and schools in which a certain model of Islam is taught). Here baraka is truly the hope and dream of the poor. The rituals are ecstatic, authority limited, participation relatively open. They are part of a world structured by exclusion, hazard, and disprivilege and shot through with what I am tempted to call a nostalgic expectation, a dream or fantasy of grace that has before and may again suddenly strike.

Irregularity and a sense of suspension, the total abstraction and indirectness of the forces that determine people's life chances and social position make a universe in which *religion* as a term is even more than usually unhelpful. For it is as incoherent as the experience into which it is absorbed and of which it is supposed to make sense. It is the very incoherence of baraka and the fact that it may be integrated and "found" by individuals in any number of ways that meet their personal needs that make it a kind of magnetic pole that clusters events but does not really organize them. For the poor of the urban margins the truth of baraka in life is guaranteed because it fits so completely the disruption and discontinuities of existence.

Its elusive power is sought for in highly concrete phenomena: a cure, disturbances of the body or mind, the attainment of physical ecstasy of an extraordinary violence and intensity. It goes together with protection against the violence of the world and evil through charms, spells, oracles, shrines, the performing teams of the Hamadsha pilgrimages, the mysteries of the written word and talismans, the placation of the *jinn* (demons).

Where else can power be identified? We find a series of personal and group cults that individuals and collectivities construct for themselves with the possibility of systematization reduced by the circumstances of life (so unsystematic in themselves) and yet made all the more vital and yearned for precisely because of that lack of pattern and ordering. These cults and the clustering by significant events of baraka are not the sole mode of building a universe that everything continually conspires to destroy. But their flexibility, the personal freedom of interpretation and commitment, may make them of desperate significance. There is only the free gift of the unseen powers to hope for, since the possibility for this social class of direct incorporation into other relations is so diminished. Contractual relations that are dependent on personal intention and promises of certain kinds of pious behavior in return for some form of saintly baraka are one of the very few acts and contracts men can independently initiate.

Baraka is therefore a vital part of the religious *bricolage* of the poor, part of a cobbling together of all kinds of different events, relations, and persons into a single form that contains objects of many different colors, shapes, and sizes.* Certain particular poles of attraction (shrines, trees, murids, and so on) serve as immediate and concrete foci and sources of access to blessing.

So on the one hand (among the Muridiya of Senegal, for example), baraka is essential to the instrumentalities of power, production, and exchange, it is vital as an organizing and transforming element in the ideology of the total universe the order seeks to construct. On the other hand, blessing is the refuge of those whose lives are most unstructured, or destructured, in terms of immediate experience (however determined they may be by wider forces in the society). It can be the language of domination or of the dominated, but in completely contrasted forms and with very different significance.

---

* The *bricoleur* is one who makes use of whatever he can lay his hands on at the time to accomplish a project. He puts together in *bricolage* a work or form made up of very mixed elements that may have originally been part of quite different objects and relations. See Claude Lévi-Strauss, *The Savage Mind* (London: Weidenfeld and Nicolson, 1966), pp. 16-18.

CHAPTER 6

Sheikhs and the Inner Secrets

Of all the many factors that in different combinations go to make up a sheikh's authority, perhaps the ideological kernel is his knowledge of the inner secret truth, the batin. Behind the vain appearances of the world (the zahir) is that which is real and true and answers to God's hidden purposes (the batin). In north Lebanon the sense of this division of what is merely seen with the eye and what *is* is fundamental to the view that men have of the everyday social world. It is particularly present in dealing with sheikhs, who may be of holy lineages but who individually are known to have only too human qualities. To be regarded as a sheikh in the fullest sense means that the individual has to establish some more personal reputation for knowledge and insight into what the ordinary, lay eye does not see.

There are thus many discussions of what makes a "real" sheikh and what constitutes proof of knowledge of the batin. For it is open to individuals in different communities who are not from sheikhly families to grow their beards, read the Quran, and become a sheikh. And there are sheikhs and sheikhs, after all. So the man who presents himself as a sheikh, and therefore as a man of knowledge of whatever degree from the great to the slight, is the subject of continual and sharp-eyed observation. Nobody is going to accept a beard and a green band round the turban and a few pious phrases (or even a lot of them!) as proof. The matter is far too important for that. There have to be signs of the secret.

The interest for the sociologist here is enormous. For how do you persuade people that you have this knowledge of the secret when it cannot be told or revealed? Given that its essence is to be hidden, how is the batin nonetheless practiced and understood in everyday life? How does it make its appearance? If it is the key to the sheikh's reputation for sheikhliness with a particular group, we must explain how he comes to be credited with it by that group.

My first reaction to such problems was earnestly to ask a sheikh whose reputation was well established with a particular group in the Lebanese village in which I worked the simple and stupid question: "What is the batin?" He, and my friends, were far too polite to say: "What on earth do you mean? The question is nonsense. Can you be sitting there asking for the hidden purposes of God?" He sat silent. Blindly I persisted, despite the sheikh's murmured pious phrases designed to cover for my stupidity. Finally, since I seemed to insist on an answer to my unaskable question, the holy man replied: "The batin is the future (al-mustaqbil)." I at last fell silent, no doubt to everyone's relief.

Despite my naiveté the sociological point of the question persisted. What indeed is the batin, and how is it realized and taken to have been demonstrated in social relations, symbols, and values?

Since I have defined it as the core of the sheikh's identity and as being *the* secret, let us look for its social meaning at the core area of individual and group life: sexuality and reproduction.* Here is *the* realm of secrecy in social life, of purity and pollution, danger and security. It is central to every member of the society at the level of personal identity, as member of a social group, and of a whole culture that formulates and prescribes certain strict conceptions of rules and sanctions for sexual behavior and for the reproduction of society through its "proper" conduct.

It is therefore not sociologically fanciful to start our search

* I should emphasize that I am certainly not suggesting that sexuality, reproduction, and pollution are always the foundation of the social logic of the batin.

for the meaning of the batin and sheikhly authority in what at first glance seems the totally separate dimension of sexuality and the closely associated realms of purity and pollution. In a society such as that of north Lebanon both batin and sexuality are in the realm of power and the conceptions of power in the symbolic and social systems. Who marries whom, who has sexual relations with whom, the constraints on both and the choices involved are major issues for group structure and relations. Moreover, infringement of the rules of conduct, of the ideologically dominant code of honor and shame, the pollution of individual and family name by female sexuality outside the bounds of marriage, pose a terrible threat to the whole conception of the meaning of relations between the male and female worlds and among males. Honor and shame, purity and pollution, are vital concerns in life.

Now in our discussions in the village of how you *know* a real sheikh who has real authority and insight in the batin, one theme recurred again and again, though without my paying too much attention to it at first. "Sheikh X was a real sheikh. Don't you remember the time when old so-and-so was getting ready to pray in the mosque, and the sheikh said to him: 'Have you carried out the ritual washing?' And he hadn't of course, even though he had just urinated [that is, he was in a state of pollution and unfit to pray]!" Or again: "The sheikh just looked over at Y, who realized that he had not performed the ritual ablutions after sexual relations with his wife that afternoon and had to go out to do them."

In other words, the real sheikh knew when you were in an impure condition, both in the sense that you had failed a ritual duty of ablutions and more specifically that you had masturbated or had sexual relations with someone, or that you were indulging in some illicit sexual relationship. It would be courting disaster to be in the holy man's presence or to join the prayer or a zikr ritual if you were in such a state because some form of discomfiture was sure to follow. It could pursue you quite a way as well. Take the case of one young man's amorous entanglements with a woman in the south, an affair that had become well known to his friends. When one of them, in the middle of some very relaxed banter, suddenly said to me with great earnestness: "Of course, he hasn't actually slept with her," I assumed that this was an attempt to preserve a correct image of the young man concerned in my eyes and out of respect for a person (myself) in front of whom sexual joking might be inappropriate. Not a bit of it. "Oh no," said the young man concerned, in considerable and evident alarm, "I wouldn't have dared. The sheikh would have known. It would have been 'hot' for me in there. I daren't."

The theme of sexuality, pollution, and knowledge began to develop more clearly. It took on another variation when one adolescent who had become part of the sheikh's regular following in the village, participating in the rituals of the zikr and praying with great regularity, gradually withdrew from the circle, seemed almost to avoid the sheikh, and stopped praying. He would hover inconspicuously by the door or even outside if the sheikh was in someone's reception room. I was puzzled for days at this and at his obvious, but controlled, disquiet.

Then one evening the sheikh, as he left a ritual meeting in one of the houses, stopped next to me and greeted the teen-ager, who was in the doorway. "Are you praying, Muhammed?" he asked with a slight smile. The boy was reduced to complete confusion and muttered only: "Sometimes, sidna."* "What?" said the sheikh gently, "Will you add lying to your other sins?" With a quiet chuckle and a pat on the shoulder he moved on, leaving a pale and frightened young man leaning against the door. Famous among his peers for self-possession, aggressiveness, and verbal dexterity, the boy was almost speechless. Then, looking at me, he whispered simply: "He knows." It emerged that he had started an affair with a girl and had withdrawn from prayer and the sheikh's presence because of it and his fear of the sheikh's capacity for insight into the realm of the secret. Yet at the same time he felt drawn to the rituals and to the circle of followers of which he had been a part. Suddenly, in his eyes, he had been unmasked, and he attributed knowledge of his most private and guarded world to the sheikh.

The miracle, once more, had happened in front of my eyes. "He *knows*" — about illicit sexuality, secret encounters,

---

* Literally "our Lord" or "our Master": An expression of high respect, regularly employed when addressing men of high prestige and particularly holy men.

and the state of pollution. His knowledge induces fear, changes action, compels avoidance if possible from his dangerous presence. Here was "proof" of authority and another variation on the sexual theme that showed very concretely the kind of situations and action that could be involved. It tied the sheikh very explicitly to the most veiled, concealed, and potentially dangerous elements of individual and group life upon which honor and family depend.

We can now see how potent and significant in this particular society are the manifestations of sheikhliness, its "proofs," that indicate impurity and pollution. What had appeared to be two quite separate symbolic and social dimensions (religious knowledge and sexuality) are now revealed as intimately linked. The "real" sheikh is the one who has knowledge of this most dangerous and vital force. His knowledge is a sanction on the sexual behavior of all those who are in some sense attached to him or acknowledge his insight and interpret his remarks ("Will you add lying to your other sins?"), or a glance, or what seems to be a veiled hint or allusion, as a direct comment or even a challenge.

The Sheikh and the Young Men

The account of the young man's confounding points us toward more specific social implications of the sheikh's role. In this village, and I suspect in many other villages and towns of the Muslim world, the sheikhs are associated informally with what might be viewed as an extended rite of passage for those in transition to full adult male status. That is to say, those who tend to make up the bulk of their followers or attendants, who go to the rituals, and sit in their reception rooms are very often the unmarried (or only recently married) young men. My suggestion is, and it is only speculative, that the sheikhs were, and in our case still are, often most important for providing a moral and ritual framework and sanction for a group that for many different reasons is central to the problems and ambiguities of sexuality and honor in such societies.

What is the situation of this stratum of the young men? Until they are married, the adolescents and young men present and are presented with certain major problems. The ideology of absolute paternal authority, the dominance of the notion of family and lineage and honor, says that they are subordinate, without status as a group. On the other hand, they are internally stratified, with the elder brother taking precedence, and strict respect between siblings in order of seniority is mandatory in public. In a traditional setting, such as the Lebanese village (and within the world of the members of the Cairo Sufi order also), they sit in the lowest-ranking seats near the door, run errands, speak when spoken to, sit up, do not smoke before the older generation, and act as servants for the family and for any visitors.

At the same time, however, they are the guarantee of the future of the family and the ever-present force to maintain its place and its honor in quarrels, feuds, and displays of solidarity. In Lebanon they have a major role in the organization of violence and quasi-military activity, in which they are potentially "heroic" warrior figures who snatch up arms to defend religion, family, and village. In this latter case they bear a huge burden, but in other respects they are cast as nonsignificant in status terms, nonresponsible, and always potentially irresponsible. They are also a threat to the social order because they are unmarried and not caught up in the full obligations of mature adulthood.

The hierarchy in which they are placed and the ideology of subordination to higher authority (older brother, the father, senior relatives, family, and village notables) obscure what is in fact a most interesting but not formally defined and instituted role. This centers precisely on the area where they are supposed to be most at danger and to have their own choices determined by others — namely, sexuality and marriage and group relations through women.

There are two main aspects here: the sanctioning of morally dubious behavior and a significant degree of influence over marriage patterns and therefore links between groups. Anthropologists and historians have often noted how in Mediterranean societies at many different periods in history up to the present, it is the young men who — by their joking, mockery, bawdy songs of an often brutal directness, and tacitly licensed attacks on particular figures in a given community who have broken the moral standards (for example, by adultery or publicly visible unchastity) — defend and reinforce the dominant code. Their role is in practice a conservative one, even though the code they conserve is the same one that ensures their own social subordination at that period of their lives. Despite the image of threat to sexual purity and honor, they are vital to the preservation of both.

It is *because* they have only limited status significance that they can come and go and move around the community far more freely than the older men, who supposedly regulate affairs and who are normatively set up as the figures of authority. The young men (the *shebāb*) idling on the corner, in a little group clustered round the shop, drifting into an aunt's or a married sister's house, moving about the village singly or in twos or threes in the early hours of the morning when all good men are asleep, see, talk, observe, gossip, keep silent, plan, spy, share secrets, confer, organize, pass on messages. They build up their own store of "secret knowledge," which is part of a kind of underlife culture and a covert challenge to authority ("we know what *really* goes on here, whatever the adult men say or do, and we play a much more active part than they can ever know"). It is necessarily the basis for internal differentiation within this stratum, for some "know" much more than others and can and will use that knowledge. They form a dense network of relations and information and in doing so a means by which families can keep in touch with the crucial minutiae of daily life in a way that would be quite impossible for the family heads.*

Being "irresponsible" liberates the young men to a highly active role in the production and diffusion of information in male-female relations and marriage. They know, for example, which boy has his eye on which girl (and vice versa). All kinds of unspoken negotiations, jockeyings, and manoeuvers go on to define just who is linked with whom; looks and glances that the others choose not to see set up elaborate unspoken dialogues. Outsiders who may otherwise be on good terms with the young men or a descent group come up against a wall of exclusion of even violence if they make any serious move in the direction of women to whom they have no claim in the eyes of the family's young men. Furthermore,

* We shall see further elaborations on this theme in the discussion of the position of women and children in chapter 8.

association in jobs, or in school, *or as followers of the sheikh* gives them contacts with those from different families and lineages to which their fathers may even be opposed or with which their own families simply have no social access at all.

It is therefore most important that it is the young men who make up the bulk of the sheikh's following, who organize (in the Lebanese case) prayer and study groups, who set out to learn all the exact regulations for the prayer, the Sunna (orthodox practice) of the different rituals, the alternating rhythms of the chanting of the Names of God in the zikr, the laws on fasting and divorce, and many other topics. Younger brothers, often only five or six years old, make up their own little groups, imitating their elders in the prayer and zikr movements and the hymn singing, hanging around when their seniors solemnly rehearse the ritual prescriptions. The sheikh's role as religious educator is thus often widened and per- formed by his young followers over a much broader social and age range than the sheikh himself possesses. Through the young men it reaches also the sisters and mothers of the house, whom the sheikh himself may on occasion be invited to bless, since he is the sole category of stranger permitted to pierce the boundaries and restrictions that hedge the women's position.

Through their attachment to the sheikh the young men therefore come to exercise an important religious function, and this key period of their lives before marriage may be greatly influenced by his personality and their conception of his knowledge and authority. Since we can now appreciate better the nature and scale of their true role in sexual and family relations, we can also grasp the importance of the link between his insight into the batin (and pollution) and the partial identification of that insight with sexuality and states of purity and pollution.

It is defined as socially appropriate for the young men to be followers of the sheikh, just as it is appropriate that older men who are being displaced by their middle-aged sons from their once central position in the family go on a pilgrimage, read the Quran during Ramadan, discuss points of theology and hadith with the sheikh and among themselves. In between these two ends of the male social spectrum the fathers and family heads get on with the business of adult life: questions of politics, marriage, and status; living, existing, and subsisting; and being the formally defined "responsible" figures of the community.

Stages of Crisis and Ultimate Salvation

All our present themes of sexuality, social control, and holiness can best be illustrated by considering the emergence of a serious crisis that threatened to bring about social disruption in a community and the destruction of an individual. We shall watch it pass through a series of stages of an increasingly critical intensity to culminate in an unexpected way after the failure of the young men to produce an acceptable solution.

The account of events will be given through the eyes of a stranger (myself), who, after some months in this particular Lebanese community, had his own role to play: stranger/intimate, distant/close, outsider/insider, teacher, man of prestige yet also one whose existence ultimately was in a kind of limbo or cocoon.

The stranger gradually became aware that two cousins (paternal first cousins in fact, an ideologically close relationship) who worked in the same group in Beirut and formed a joking and horseplay partnership were no longer speaking to each other. To be more accurate, A was no longer speaking to B despite B's attempts to carry on as though nothing had happened. Whenever the latter greeted his relative and erstwhile friend, the reply was silence and a turned back or averted gaze — a silence which has all the impact of a hurricane warning.

None of this was initially too disturbing. Young A (about twenty-one years old) was known after all as contentious, shifting in his mood, argumentative, and forceful, all the characteristics of his very senior father and his three elder brothers in fact. As the youngest son of his family and very junior within the work group in age and experience, he was both a fit junior partner for several others in fooling around and was licensed as an all-around provider of facetious remarks, light relief, and verbal and physical play.

He had established a dominant-subordinate relationship

with the only other individual who was lower on the pecking order, his very quiet and socially clumsy cousin B. The latter, also the youngest member of a well-known family, could not have been more different. He had no verbal gifts, no obvious forceful public personality, no individual claims to make, though his brothers and father were very well respected and had a healthy reputation as men of independent views well able to look after themselves. A tractor accident had left him with a slight limp and he thus, by the cruelty of fate, only too well mirrored in his halting walk his social position.

The drama unfolded as follows: A began to ignore B on one of the periodic returns of the work group from Beirut to the village. For a day or two the situation continued at this level, despite the occasional lighthearted remarks by others and the casual queries as to the nature of the problem. A refused to respond at this level and explained his behavior by saying that there was nothing at all wrong and that he did not want to talk about it. This, of course, in effect defined the situation as too serious and irreversibly set in motion for it to be changed by the informal chat and encouragement of his peers.

Since the casual remarks, mild teasing, and "unfocused" efforts of members of the young men's group served no purpose and A continued in his behavior, they had to try another tack. One or two of his peers together and separately tried to chat to him about it in a more formal and deliberate way, only to be greeted with the same response.

Highly discreet speculation began as to the possible cause. Since A declined to speak, it was assumed to be within the most "secret" and private realm. This realm was not named. I think that it was tacitly communicated by friend to friend by looks and mute assumptions. The casual joking gradually ceased, and no one referred publicly to the issue, thus acknowledging it as serious by the group silence on the subject. This pattern followed the lines of practical social logic. The refusal to speak and the consequent assumption of the most private nature of the issue could only mean one thing: sexuality.

Sexuality, in any condition where it may threaten the reputation, honor, and identity of the group, where it may pollute and desecrate a family and an individual, is hedged around with a barrier of silence. It is a silence that no one can break. Because if it is broken, then the act of breaking immediately produces enormous crisis, shame, challenge, and possibly death. The sanctions on guarding silence are therefore very heavy ones. The trouble is that if people outside become intrigued and do start asking questions, the very evasiveness that ensues and the denials of any problem also shows that something is being covered up. The silence then becomes a sign. A's declining to speak was just such a sign.

This forced us all into a third stage, and even those of us (such as the visitor) who had regarded the whole thing as merely a storm in a not particularly large teacup began to be disquieted. The situation now required some more formal and institutional means of negotiation. Too many people were getting to know about it, thus widening the dangers that those not really in the group of young men would stir things up, spread gossip, shame or humiliate group members, and make it all public. No one knew, or claimed to at least, whether the older brothers of A and B were already aware of events and merely playing the game that nothing is wrong or whether they simply knew nothing. The possibility was already on the horizon that they would be forced in when the issue became public and have to line up against one another in any number of different ways, with enormous potential for political and personal disruption. I have said that A and B were related through their fathers. Their families formed part of the same factional bloc within the descent group as a whole, lived within the socially defined distance of the neighborhood as well, had intermarried, and each had its own networks of kin and connections. The patriarchs of both families, moreover, were both leading figures of great prestige and public respect, and both were highly insistent on the code of honor and shame.

So a deliberate attempt at mediation and conciliation was made by a couple of the young men who were within the group of friends/relatives/workmates, and it was set up as a peace mission. It failed completely. Young A refused this most solemn invoking of their friendship and association with him and clearly rejected them as not having the weight to put in the scales against the conflict. This he did simply by saying that there was no need for mediation because there was nothing to mediate.

Increasing alarm and a sense of alternatives being rapidly used up filled the group. Each stage further restricted the range of possible compromise or tactics. And each stage seemed to bring them closer to a public face-off that might involve not only the families of A and B but all the notables of the wider descent group to which the families belonged. By this time there was the unspoken conviction that there must have been something extremely shameful for A to have kept it going and to have kept it so hidden when he had had plenty of chance to issue clarifying denunciations, comments, barbed remarks, and so forth (the normal course in disputes).

The young men decided to employ the stranger. One young and newly married man came to my house alone and with great discretion. He explained the seriousness of the situation, though both of us maintained a tacit understanding that the real cause was a mystery — who knew what it might be? — and in any case the question was bringing A and B together and not worrying about whatever might have been the original problem. He gave an excellent sociological analysis of why and how present means were exhausted, what the dangers were, and why it would be impossible to use the family heads and notables. The latter would be polarized between the families of A and B, and there was no one who would have the standing to mediate between them. However, there was the grave possibility that they would be dragged in, like it or not. The crisis would become public, formal, official, and defined in the terms of the code of personal and family honor that puts a premium on violence and allows for little flexibility of action when people are forced to confront situations in which they are directly challenged.

Hence the importance of the stranger in their midst. He had links with both sides, was received in both houses, was senior to the young men, and had a publicly established status with the notables, to whose level he was publicly assimilated, that gave him authority over the young men.

The visitor nervously exercised his authority and ideological appeals to family unity, his own personal status with A's father, and whatever other instruments of influence he could conjure up. A bowed to this pressure in a private interview and was formally reconciled with B at the visitor's house.

Cousin B immediately followed up by inviting the peace-maker (as I had now become) every day to his house in the early morning, to sit in front of it in the very small courtyard that gave on to the public road smoking an elaborately prepared hubble-bubble pipe (*nargileh*) — a ritual mark of seniority and standing — and drinking coffee. He attended on his benefactor (for he made it very clear that he felt that I had done him a great service), who was put publicly on show as a social-symbolic guarantee that all was well. His position was thus sanctioned by the honored guest's authority. This was not a totally adequate relationship, however. For a start, the visitor already had an attendant, the man whose family cooked for him and who was also a kind of bodyguard. In the second place, he could not extend his symbolic protection every morning and all the time, since he could not be permanently involved with one household or, by implication, with a person of very inferior standing and age. Both would be totally inappropriate, and a semipermanent association would be quite incongruous. Therefore, for various reasons, the stranger was a good umbrella in the short term, but in the longer view he had to withdraw from too specific a relationship with B.

So in a week or so B was alone again. The mediation process had gone through many stages and was apparently finally successful, since A replied to greetings in the appropriate formal manner. And yet ... Clearly things were not back to normal overnight. The momentum of the whole affair had produced intense but very private and coded speculation over the real cause. Such speculation and imagined knowledge as to what must have happened for it to be so disastrous and so secret could not be forgotten. Knowledge is always there, however well controlled. It feeds insidiously into status, personality, gesture, speech, and silence.

The danger therefore remained. The unfortunate B was slowly being relegated to a position of disregard (not mere nonregard) and isolation. Whispers still passed from one to another. The stranger's intervention had arrested the pace of what had become a galloping crisis, but when he withdrew from constant attendance at B's house, the problems were still there. One day there might be a direct reference, an insult, a sneer, a deliberate forcing of the issue by someone whose own factional role would be well filled by bringing the two families involved into open division.

So what was B to do? Suicide? Leave for Beirut at least, if not for overseas? The choice seemed to be close between death (he was virtually socially dead as it was) or removal from the community. He had to become "invisible" by whatever means and at whatever price. The stranger puzzled over this and could see no other alternatives. What else could the boy do?

He became a disciple to the sheikh.

He grew a beard and put on a small white cap, both ritual signs of publicly taking on a religious role. He invited the sheikh into his house several times (where the sheikh had never previously been), prayed regularly, followed the holy man around on his visits, and joined in every zikr circle.

A kind of explosion of piety followed. There was a rash of religious meetings and celebrations (mulids) as individuals discovered long-held intentions to honor the Prophet Muhammed, to listen to the local hymn singer, and to join in the zikr. The sheikh's range of contacts in the village was increased as different sections of the descent group either attended his ritual and teaching sessions at B's house (that is to say, the house of B's father, for though the young men were often the instigators of such meetings, the hosts were their fathers and elder brothers) or, not to be outdone, invited him themselves. In his new religious garb B became "invisible". All talk and speculation ceased. Beneath the sheikh's umbrella he was safe. He had a role that no one could attack, and his marginality was transposed into the religious idiom, where it became positively valued and accepted as he was socially neutralized. Ritual assimilation to the holy man made the social and moral problems of which he was the center unseen and unknown. Though I had assumed that one cannot "not know" something that one knows, within the active social force of the sacred even that is possible! This evocation of the ultimate criteria of truth and power on which the world is "really" based enabled him to claim sanctuary and a stereotyped identity as disciple of the sheikh. He was saved.

I hope the reader's patience has not been tried by this drama. The denouement is very much a product of the whole previous process I have given in some detail, because it shows in a very concrete way the operation of religious authority in a situation that passes through various levels of crisis. We should note that the sheikh made no move at official arbitration. It was more than sufficient simply for B to give the signs of the religious role (the beard, the white cap, the constant attendance at, and encouragement of, prayer and other rituals, the invitations to the sheikh). By doing so at a moment of ultimate peril he achieved social salvation. He acquired an acceptable and unassailable self that was established on different bases from the social identity and personality of the other young men. He attained a kind of religious anonymity that removed his status to a different dimension of life. The past was made irrelevant, not a matter of attention or account, and positively dangerous as a reference, given that the sheikh's hand had protected him and might be presumed to strike anyone foolish enough to tempt heaven by attacking the new disciple. He was not less marginal, but marginal in a different way, since attending on the sheikh put him outside the criticism, values, and concern of the everyday world.*

The sheikh, who by definition knows all secrets, thus dealt with an issue whose real cause was secret but that threatened to become public and caught up in the rigid and inflexible codes of honor, shame, and status. No one had defined the issue. Both A and B treated it as unmentionable so that what it was could not serve as a center for argument at the various levels of mediation. As I have said, this convention of unmentionability in fact led to the assumption that the problem actually lay in the most private area of all. That area was sexual morality and behavior. We assumed some sexual immorality and behavior. We assumed some sexual suggestion

---

* It is worth noting again that both the young men were at that stage of their lives marginal in local social terms. They were the youngest in their respective families, subject to constant ordering around by their elder brothers (who were all married), junior on the work team, and, as noted, very much fit objects of joking and ritualized horseplay. But this does not in any way diminish their importance in such a case because it was their membership of a family and of a group and the collective honor of brothers that was at stake.

or offence or hint or imagined allusion or invitation between the cousins *because* no one would name the cause publicly. Silence spoke louder than words, and all the dangers of dishonor and pollution of the family name were increasingly present. The formal regulative processes of the young men all broke down. The formal power figures of the family heads could only act as a last resort and would have been trapped in the requirements of the honor code (which might well have led to the expulsion or even killing of B by his own brothers, or to violence between the two families involved).

Where the dangerous and secret force of sexuality and shame was involved, only the sheikh's authority offered a way out. B became totally identified as a disciple of the holy man and not merely just one of the young men who respected him and attended his evening sessions. The title of sheikh was by courtesy extended to B, as it was to the two or three others who had taken this step of attaching themselves specifically to the religious identity.

Now it is tempting to say that our narrative reveals a hierarchy of the sacred in the community: that the sacred and fundamental code of personal and status and sexual honor was transcended by the sacred discourse of Islam, as represented by the authoritative figure of the sheikh. For various reasons, which will become clearer in a later section, I am not totally persuaded by this idea. The main point seems to me to be that it was rather because the case involved the young men (lacking public status, authority, significance), because of the association of the sheikh with them and the links between sexuality and his knowledge of the batin, and because the issue had not yet become defined as public and significant for the family heads, that B's move under the wing of the sheikh brought his salvation. I am certain that had the problem become a public one, B's taking on of the disciple's part would not have saved him. Moreover, the sheikh would never have tried to use his authority because he would have tacitly recognized that in such matters of public family honor he had far more limited standing. It was his social and symbolic relationship with the marginal young men that enabled his authority to operate on an issue restricted to that group after a whole series of increasingly formal attempts at mediation by them had failed. Had the notables been brought in then, the religious figure would have remained on the sidelines, carefully aware of the limitations of his competence.

When Sanctity Fails

It may seem curious at this stage to say that the sacred is precarious for those who represent it when we have just seen how effective it is. Surely a sheikh is a sheikh is a sheikh? If one gives all the right signs, is arrayed in all the right symbols (the turban, the beard, the long outer garment, or whatever is taken locally as signifying a sheikh in manner and dress), and knows all the sacred texts and truths it is appropriate for a sheikh to know, then one's identity as such is presumably not a matter for debate.

Well, it is not and it is. I have already indicated that the knowledge of the batin is a rather problematic thing. It depends on giving "proofs" of such insight, and it depends on others accepting or interpreting certain words, gestures, expressions, or performances as being demonstrations of the powerful authoritative knowledge. The 'alim, as we have seen, is the product of training and examination in 'ilm; the religious specialist who has no such training and is rather a member of a Sufi order or a holy family or is simply a prestigious individual bases his authority on what I have called illumination (ma'rifa). That is where the problems start. For, as my Lebanese friends somewhat brutally put it, "Any fool can grow a beard!" They were very much on the watch for any sign that one who made himself out to be a sheikh lacked true illumination, not out of ingrained skepticism or a keenly ironical eye (both of which they abundantly possessed) but because it is so desperately important. One may really have to know whether such and such a person wearing a green-banded turban and a beard and murmuring his pious formulas is what he seems to be and exactly what degree of knowledge and power he possesses.

It is perfectly possible, therefore, for someone who actively claims to be a sheikh and seeks to live out a sheikh's role on whatever basis to fail to establish himself as authentic with those who form his social context. The reasons for such failure vary enormously, of course, and any number of political, economic, and cultural factors may be involved. Whole families of sheikhly origin may be forced out of the religious economy. I want to give here a more individual example to show how the religious symbols an individual uses can, in certain circumstances, be turned against him; how one can employ all the appropriate religious language and signs only to be interpreted as being illegitimate and not a true sheikh.

In the same village in north Lebanon that we have discussed in the case of the crisis among the young men, there was no major sheikhly family. As I have explained, it was the local seat of a descent group of great lords who "respected," and supported, certain sheikhs from outside the community. There was one holy man who had established himself as a welcome and important visitor in a certain section of the village. For one thing, since he was a relative of the famous saint of the 1930s, he came from a religious family well known in the entire region and possessed the blessings of descent. Also he was related by marriage to the village mayor's family. It was naturally in this family's house that he was usually seen and there that he stayed on his visits. The youngest brother of the mayor acted as his particular attendant and disciple in the house. (The most junior son of some thirteen children of the now dead father, he was newly married, about twenty years old, and occasionally employed as watchman or agricultural worker or armed retainer for a political notable.)

A group of young related males clustered around the sheikh on his visits. They learned the proper form of prayer, the zikr ritual, his opinion on certain questions of holy law, and the form and model of behavior that were contained in the term *Muslim* and locally embodied in the sheikh. Older men from this family attended the prayers and zikr, too, and in their presence the young men were relegated to the back of the room. But it was they who escorted the visitor around, went to see him in his own village or on his land on the plain, announced his movements and arranged introductions, and most enthusiastically hurled themselves into the rhythm and ecstacies of the Sufi ritual.

The link was thus built up initially on the basis of kinship with the mayor's family, on the prestige of the sheikh's descent (to which the mayor's circle often referred, of course), and on the fact that the sheikh was not in his home context. For in that context he was a landowner and part of a dominant (sheikhly) group that had very ambivalent relations with the peasant stratum. In our village he was the stranger-guest-relative with a purely religious significance, with no embarrassing internal social relations of dominance. His range of social acknowledgment and religious influence was quite limited, and many in the village were barely aware of his existence. But within the extended family of the mayor, he was an established and authoritative figure. He had been coming to the village for several years and possessed considerable knowledge of the character, relationships, and biographies of his congregation.

Into this small and undisturbed pond a stone was dropped.

One evening another sheikh (from Syria) arrived in the village with a companion and was directed automatically to the reception room of the mayor, in which all strangers were received. Our sheikh, as we shall call him, was also there, and both holy men were seated at the head of the room in the place of honor. As news of the unexpected arrival went around the quarter of the village in which the house stands, the reception room quickly filled up. Those present were some of the senior men of the family and a mass of young men, adolescents, and children, including members of other related families who were only rarely at the mayor's house save for local problems. Our sheikh took his place behind the visitor as a sign of honor for the guest, who thus acted as prayer leader. After the prayer the man most well known in the community for the beauty of his voice and his repertoire of hymns sang in the praise of the Prophet Muhammed. Everyone uttered complimentary phrases, rocked back and forth in rhythm, and joined in the refrains. Our sheikh appeared deeply moved and wept, shaking with intense feeling. and gave deafening cries of "Allah!" as the spirit moved him.

The visitor sat silent and unmoving.

At length the singer ceased and our visitor's companion took up the hymns in a different style. The Syrian sheikh then suffered the same exquisite pangs of ecstacy our sheikh had undergone: loud and pained weeping and uncontrollable jerks of the shoulder as the "ecstatic condition" (the hal) overwhelmed him.

Our sheikh then stood for the zikr and led the performers in his customary gentle and controlled rhythms, himself standing at the center of the circle and turning slowly around, bowing back and forth in time as the assembly chanted the Names of God. The Syrian sheikh suddenly interrupted the chanting and began to show us a totally different rhythm and movements of a very quick and complicated kind that swiftly threw everyone off balance. The ritual disintegrated because of the participants' failure to keep in unison.

When our sheikh left the room to sleep, the guest commenced a vigorous campaign of proselytization to the crowded little assembly. Our sheikh, he said, was certainly a very worthy man but not effective because he did not teach. Perhaps he was too old to instruct the young men. Whatever the case, they should have a spiritual guide, and they were left in no doubt as to where that guide might be found. He was before them, seated on the white sheepskin rug and gesturing abruptly and peremptorily to emphasize the importance of his words. It was his "way" (his tariqa or path) that they should take.

One of the group then stepped forward and shyly asked to make the oath of membership, and obedience to the tariqa. At this point, though our visitor did not realize it, all was lost. For the "convert" who so piously knelt before the sheikh, almost doubling over his immensely tall frame in religious humility, was one of the leading jokers of the community. He had very early in life lost both his father through sudden illness and his acres of olive trees through eagerly encouraged generosity that swiftly exhausted all the resources of the then teenager.

He was left with nothing, he had become known as a performer, an actor, a discreditor, someone who had made it his business to know the gossip and personal underlife of the village. Small wonder, then, if the spectacle of our friend in the posture of a new disciple radiating an expression of eager faith produced a series of glances and barely suppressed looks of complicity and amusement.

He left the room to make the ritual ablutions and a certain number of prayers as commanded by the Syrian sheikh. In his absence the visitor claimed insight into the batin. There was no need for any examination of the character of the new convert, he said in reply to a question, because he could see into the heart, which would in any case be purified by the conversion itself.

Our friend returned to the room and took the oath to the visiting sheikh.

After much sermonizing, accounts of miracles he had performed, and ascribing his violent bodily jerking during the hymn singing to the descent of the spirit of the Prophet Muhammed upon him, the visitor went off to sleep, presumably well satisfied with the evening's reception.

Had his insight into what is hidden been functioning, he would have been disturbed at the roars of laughter of his "convert" and the revelation that, far from washing and praying, our friend had been eating heartily throughout all the sounds of piety we had heard from the next room. Moreover *he* (the disciple) *had had sexual relations with his wife that afternoon and had not carried out the ritual washing afterward.* In addition to the specific point that the visitor had not seen into the joker's real purposes in coming forward was the fact that the latter was in a state of pollution following sexual relations, which a true sheikh would have known.* As it was, the stranger was presented by the pseudo-disciple as a fraud who possessed none of the insight to which he pretended.

The following day the unfortunate visitor found, when he made his rounds of the houses expecting pious offerings, that no money was forthcoming, the family heads were unavailable, and no one was at home. He and his companion left the village empty-handed.

Now what does this comedy tell us about the way that the sacred is worked out in daily life?

To me, in what was an extraordinarily dramatic and at times even farcical performance, very important themes were revealed in a way far more concentrated than in the rituals I had attended with our sheikh. For the drama revealed so many of the underlying assumptions and practices that are veiled in "unproblematic" situations. First of all I had witnessed the discrediting of someone who presented himself

* A return to the area I emphasized at the beginning of this chapter.

as a man who possessed sacred knowledge and power. Not only had he displayed the proper religious form and model in body and demeanor (the beard, the manner of sitting, the style of gesture and regard), in clothing (the green-banded turban, the flowing outer garment), but he also used to the full the discourse of religion (miracles, pious sayings, quotations from Quran and hadith, the hymns of his companion). Yet his authenticity was denied and his attempted appropriation of sanctity collapsed in front of his own unseeing eyes.

Clearly, for the performance of our joker to take place at all he had to feel sure of two things: first, that the visitor was not a real sheikh and that therefore it would not be dangerous to engage in this charade of piety; and, second, that a tacit consensus had been established among us during the course of the evening up to the moment of his stepping forward as a disciple so that we all read the situation the same way and could be relied upon to play along with his performance. On both counts he was correct, and it is not difficult to see why.

In the specifically religious sphere the stranger had presented all the model traits required. But he had also claimed insight into the batin (as well as the right way to do the zikr, the capacity to teach people, the working of miracles, the contact with the spirit of the Prophet Muhammed). He put himself up for testing by claiming as his something that in cultural terms only God can give, and sociologically only men can award, to the individual. Insight is to be demonstrated, not claimed. It is not for a man to say he sees into the secret purposes of God, that he *knows*. Once the visitor had done this, he was inviting trouble in the social realm, where he was in fact *bound* to be incompetent. The audience-participants were almost all from the same extended family. They all had intimate knowledge of one another's lives. He knew no one at all in the village and was therefore at a total disadvantage when the supposed disciple came forward, since he had no context in which to place him or to interpret his behavior other than at its face value (it is precisely face value that a real sheikh sees behind).

Moreover, he had challenged our sheikh, after the latter had gone off to sleep, by saying that he was not a true teacher. His claims were thus competitively directed against our sheikh — a man who was credited with insight into the secret, who was related to the mayor and the family and who shed a religious prestige over the latter's reception room by his presence, and who had become firmly established with the young men. Our sheikh knew, no one questioned that. And it is absolutely certain that had he stayed in the room, the joker would never have dared to carry out his act for fear of our sheikh's displeasure at his mockery of a religious personage and guest.

The high comedy in fact demonstrates the extreme seriousness and significance of sheikhliness, the batin, and dealing with the sacred in face-to-face encounters with its representatives. Our pretended disciple was profoundly convinced of the knowledge and authority of our sheikh and was in considerable awe of him. His destruction of the other holy man by showing that he did not know was a defense of belief and sanctity by an attack on a false pretender to it, not at all the mockery of religion that it might at first have seemed. It was a statement of conviction, a support of the symbols and meanings of Islam in practice in that setting, by someone whose own status as disreputable, dishonest, and unimportant was central to the success of the unmasking.

Like so many in his position, our joker was profoundly conservative. His private shafts against the actions of others (and they had to be private and in malicious gossip, since he had not the social standing or backing to make them public) were always in the name of the "true" code of honor and conduct, which these others, he would say, pretended to uphold while in fact they were just as disreputable as he was, only he did not claim to be anything else, did he?

The visiting sheikh was thus a glittering and rare chance for him to play his role publicly, with tacit approbation, by subverting pretensions to a vital identity — that of being a sheikh. It is the marginal man here who knows all the discreditable things and has no status, who discredits by his lying performance one who offers himself as an embodiment of truth and authority. The audience was mainly composed of young men who backed up their ally during and after the comedy, who went around rehearsing and making huge play with the event for days afterward. The family heads and senior men played no obvious part; they shook their heads and smiled over the joker's cunning. But tacitly he also made possible what they themselves could never have done. It would have been unthinkable for any one of them to play out such a part. It was the young men who operated as the guardians of religion against fraud, the marginal man who defended the central truths.

Conclusion

The principle that things are not what they seem necessitates in this society that a great deal of energy go into discovering or deciding just what things really are. The notion of batin and zahir, far from being the subject of metaphysical debate among experts with no relevance to daily life, is here the stuff of daily existence. It plays a significant part in the discourse and practice of everyday life, for the elective affinity between this Islamic set of terms and the social world of north Lebanon, with its heavy emphasis on show, appearances, the manipulations of the surface, and the acquisition of knowledge of what intentions lie behind it, gives an enormous resonance to the distinction between that which is visible and that which is invisible. This sets the tone of life and runs like a theme through any number of different relations, rather like baraka does in other settings. The puzzle has been to try to discover what meanings these conceptions have in this society and how they come to have those meanings in practice.

Certain dimensions of life, as we have seen, are particularly related to a conception of inner, hidden reality in this community. Sexuality, with all its elaboration in the code of honor and shame, the purity of women, pollution, and danger, forms a field of activity that may affect all others. It is most to be hidden, whether by those who are guarding their families' good name or by those who have in fact infringed on the purity of others by illicit sexual contact of whatever kind.

Then there are the rules of purity and pollution that apply to specifically religious occasions, such as the prayer or the zikr ceremony. One must be in a purified state and have performed the correct ritual ablutions. But beyond that, and less explicitly defined, is the notion of one's intention in performing the particular religious ritual and one's general state of being with regard to practices that are forbidden (*ḥarām*) or frowned upon.

Anyone who knows about these complex and dangerous areas of others' most intimate lives is himself potentially threatening. Such knowledge means access to the secret and guarded core of a family's world. It means broken boundaries. It means a possible use of any act that might be construed as shameful against the family. A factor of enormous and constant uncertainty is introduced into everyday life by this play of secrets and knowledge.

Sheikhs as a category are held to know the batin, but a particular sheikh cannot in fact rely on the outward signs, as the comedy of unmasking so clearly showed. It takes time, the construction of relationships with a whole range of persons, including the apparently marginal young men, for a holy man to take on the full implications and powers of that identity.

Insight into God's secret purposes is the ultimate secret with which he can be credited, and it is referred to as the basis for the respect paid to him and as the ground on which it is assumed he knows about sexuality and pollution. But we have seen that determining how a given figure comes to be treated as having such knowledge is very problematic. This is so not least because the indicators of his knowing — words, gestures, looks — are often so indirect, so seemingly non-specific, so elusive and unrelated to any particular issue or event. People decode a remark as having devastating implications, when all the outsider hears is an inquiry as to whether a person is still praying. They see relations between events (as in the case of miracles), where perhaps no one else makes any connection at all.

The sheikh becomes, as it were, a conscience. It is an interior shame or self-denunciation, within the batin of the self, that occurs in saying: "He knows." For, in as much as I could tell, it was extremely difficult for anyone else to tell what it was that he might know. And that sort of empirical-minded question is not very relevant. The field of interpretation is wide and flexible. The signs of knowledge, precisely because they are so nonspecific and do not, or rarely, publicly name any act or event or offender, can be taken to have a host of references from the most general to the most precise.

At the same time, since they are both said and unsaid, one is not openly discovered or one's secrets revealed. In a given instance, you know that he knows, but others will be blissfully ignorant, you are therefore not exposed to public risk, whereas in the case of anybody else's knowing, you might well be. But you are exposed to that glance, look, or word of the holy man that strikes you as a bolt from the blue.

Though he obviously has his channels of information from relationships through kinship connections and his followers, the social processes in which he is caught up are not the same as those in which knowledge comes into being and is used by other members of society. If I, as an ordinary person, know things about you, there will be no great mystery about how I come to know them because you find out about me by just the same means. With the sheikh, on the other hand, not only is he taken to know, in a general and diffuse sense, what lies behind all the world's appearances because he sees the batin, but you do not even comprehend how he knows. He just does. That is the qualitative difference between him and others, and it is the double mystery of his authority.

CHAPTER 7

Everywhere and Nowhere

FORMS OF ISLAM IN NORTH AFRICA

In effect the essential thing is to gather into groups this people which is everywhere and nowhere; the essential thing is to make them something we can seize hold of. When we have them in our hands, we will then be able to do many things which are quite impossible for us today and which will perhaps allow us to capture their souls after we have captured their bodies.

Captain Charles Richard*

Captain Richard's report on a revolt in mid-nineteenth-century Algeria sheds a cold light on the mechanics of French colonial power. They were confronted with societies in which tribal groupings that were often composed of nomadic and peasant elements were of enormous and sometimes paramount importance. The problem was to fix, to group, to pin down in space, to define within boundaries of law, property, territory, and symbolic classification these elusive social groups. Then, once the bodies were captured, the same means could be used to extend control even over the esprit, the inner

---

* From his *Etude sur l'insurrection du Dahra* (1845-1846), quoted in Pierre Bourdieu and Abdelmalek Sayad, *Le déracinement* (Paris: Les éditions de minuit, 1964), p. 15, (my translation).

world or spirit. For ultimately power would be incomplete unless that final domain were also taken over and permeated with a new set of conceptions, beliefs, apprehensions, attitudes, and evaluations. As long as it too remained "everywhere and nowhere," total control, such as the French came to seek in their policy of a colonial absorption of Algeria, would elude those who sought it.

That the realm of esprit might be peculiarly vital as generating powerful forces of revolt was certainly clear to Captain Richard himself. For he had experience and knowledge of Algerian apocalyptic traditions of Mahdism, which took on concrete historical significance again in the first decades of the French conquest.* A student of these movements, Peter von Sivers, has examined four such revolts that took place in southeastern Algeria in 1849, 1858, 1860 and 1879.† All of them featured the annunciation of the coming of the deputy (khalīfa) of the Mahdi or the Mahdi himself. All of them were framed by the conviction of an ultimate crisis of the community, an ultimate crisis of the end of time, beyond everyday time, just as action to confront it would transcend everyday action and its rationalities. Vivid signs were given that became increasingly organized and coherent in the sequence of revolts, from strange dreams and the tinge of the holy color green in the khalifa's body to an elaborated discourse of triumphalist prophecy and miracles and a reiterated intense "call" (da'wa, frequently translated as "propaganda," though I feel this term to be too loaded in contemporary Western usage to be quite satisfactory).

All of these movements failed, not only in the mere fact of military defeat and disintegration. They all failed to resolve the contradictions inherent in attempts to achieve both a permanent revolutionary state or condition outside time, in which mundane actualities are irrelevant if indeed not treated as nonexistent, and at the same time to act in the world by subordinating it through the force of the apocalyptic vision, which must take on physical, military form yet which at root anticipates that it is the vision itself that will guarantee the

* The *Mahdi* is a member of the Prophet's family who will return at the end of time to establish the reign of social justice on earth and to purify religion.

† In *Humaniora Islamica* 1 (1973): 47-60. I have leaned very heavily on von Sivers's work here and on personal discussions with him, for which I am most grateful.

destruction of the unbelievers.

Clearly such movements draw on deep cultural wellsprings. Sufi *zawiyas* (lodges) were the centers of organization and authority that preserved or acted as a seedbed for the tradition of the apocalypse and its authentic signs. Men drew back from the world into asceticism, and withdrawal from the wickedness of those who called themselves Muslims was once again an imperative of preparation for the moment when the signs would come and the true khalifa would appear. (We shall meet this set of themes and practices again in discussing contemporary Egypt. The paradigm of the Prophet Muhammed's own foundation of the original community is here a powerful, lasting model and warrant.) What von Sivers calls "the vision of an imminent realm of justice" is built on a logic and practice that is *not* that of movements of rebellion or resistance, which also occurred in the same period against the French, but of something that is experienced by the participants as transcendental. The whole world must be purged by forces coming from beyond it, not merely of the presence of the French but of the corrupt Muslims and the false prophets as well.

Captain Richard had and was to have, therefore, plenty of reason to plan the capturing of the esprit of these people of everywhere and nowhere. He and his fellow officers were equally right in identifying part of that elusive esprit as being the political and economic organization of the society. Such identities had to be broken down, not only by the process of conquest but more subtly by wider means: by cadastral surveys and land registration and by the institution of private property in land. As another French colonial officer, Captain Vaissière, put it in 1863 when referring to the land policy: "It is in effect the most efficient war machine that can be imagined against the indigenous social condition and it is the most powerful and fruitful instrument which can be put in the hands of our colonists."* That the defeated only too well appreciated the nature of such a policy is also clear from the words of an elder of one such tribal grouping, the Ouled Rechaich, who lamented that though they might recover from military defeat, "the constitution of individual property and the authorisation given to everyone to sell lands which

* Bourdieu and Sayad, *Le déracinement*, p. 16, n. 1.

are given to him as shares is the death warrant of the tribe."*

Such land policies reach for the heart of society because they contribute to the dislocation of a whole series of relations and practices of production and property rights that are the basis of social life. As one instrument among many of a new colonial social order, they combine to transform life in different ways and different rates and rhythms, sometimes with brutal suddenness, sometimes in modes that are not immediately directly perceived but, as it were, creep up on a society, setting in train processes whose nature and outcome neither colonizer nor colonized can grasp.

Bourdieu and Sayad's work on Algeria shows how the sense of time and the control over time are transformed in a slow and uneven process as a tribal and peasant society is broken down and reintegrated into an economy dominated by a capitalist metropole and what in this case was a large population of colonizers. Work and the calculation of the relationship between work, time, energy, wages, and product gradually develop as part of different kinds of consciousness among the different classes and strata — rural *lumpenproletariat*, agricultural workers on colonizers' estates, land-owning peasants themselves existing in very varied contexts and conditions, and many others.

Moreover, with the disaggregation of the traditional society comes a shift in patterns of hierarchy and authority. Work and money become the criteria for authority in the family, and the young men who are wage earners often begin to take a far more important family role, even to the point of becoming the senior and commanding voices. There thus develops a strong generational element that produces a reversal of the authority of older over younger, with its complex of ritual, stratification, and family organization and decision making.

In any colonized society the esprit of the colonized and of the colonizer is profoundly affected by the outworkings of the system of exploitation and domination. But in Algeria, which more than any other Arab country was subjected to a global control and the implantation of a large population of French colonists as farmers and estate owners from the 1870s on, the experience was peculiarly deep. To both sides everything was at issue, not only military and political power

* Ibid., p. 34, n. 2 (my translation).

145

but the interior identity of individuals, groups, and society as a whole.

At the authoritative center of that identity was Islam, but Islam in forms and modes that changed in very interesting ways over the long course of colonial Algerian history.

In the first phases of French expansion, from 1830 to the 1860s, when the tribal groupings, which often included both transhumant and agricultural elements, were the most significant in the society in political and economic terms, certain Sufi orders assumed a crucial organizing and mobilizing role in opposition.* In one sense there was nothing at all new in this. Sufi orders have often in history transcended particularistic loyalties and group boundaries to bring together against a wider threat units that might otherwise be opposed and interests that in everyday terms were conflicting or contradictory.

They had also been part of the political strategy of empires and states. The Turks, who at least in theory ruled Algeria prior to the French, might support one order against another in a pattern of alliances that needed constant adjustment and sensitivity to local power issues in a context in which power was diffused rather than concentrated in an easily definable set of institutions. The apparently chameleonlike character of the orders, taking on the color of their local, regional, and class settings and an often far wider context of political and trade relations had an elasticity and flexibility that enabled a wide range of functions to be filled and relations to be made.

Like the maraboutic [or holy] families to whom they were sometimes but not always linked, they might be the means of guaranteeing peace and a certain degree of security, which the Turks themselves could not ensure. They might be able to keep open trade routes and lines of commerce and markets, which would otherwise be threatened. As distinct from being nested within given specific social groups, as so many maraboutic families were in a semiclient or "resident holy men" position, the *turuq* (Sufi orders) crossed social bounds.

It is, however, important not to exaggerate this element of the degree to which the orders transcended other groupings

---

* A very useful article for students on religious and political movements in Algeria is Fanny Colonna, "Cultural Resistance and Religious Legitimacy in Colonial Algeria," *Economy and Society* 3 (no. 3, 1976): 233-52.

and local identities. A tariqa might be dominated by a particular family, which had its own particular political and economic interests; it might be closely allied with the Turks in attempting to extract a surplus from the rural population through taxation and levies or outright seizure; it might in a particular area or city be intimately linked with the interests of one class or tribe against others, thus entering very directly into the play of those relations as one factor among others and not by any means as an overarching or umbrella-like association.

Yet the principles of being a tariqa, of "the way," of the linked notions of baraka and a chain of descent and authority that is other than those by which people in the world conceive of and order their relations (name, kinship, descent, history, and so on) mean a constant potential at least for such a social transcendence, even if it was not always actualized. These principles relate to modes of power, divine power, that both underlies and interlinks constantly with worldly action yet is conceptually and symbolically separate. Relations to such power have to be brought about and always renewed through prayer, through prescribed ritual duties, through contact with the holy. They cannot be assumed. The orders were a major channel in the formation of such relations. They were concerned with the transmission of religious culture, with law, with teaching, with authority. So however closely identified a tariqa might locally be with very practical worldly interests, those interests would not at all be the sole determinant of the way in which the tariqa was socially perceived. Orders were in the world, but they also symbolically articulated the world with the divine schema that underlay it and gave it meaning, a meaning hidden from ordinary men and seen only by those of religious insight and illumination.

In the framework of tribal resistance to the French the orders were able to be political agents of mobilization and to make of the resistance a religious struggle. The esprit of the society was indeed at stake, more than was initially evident in the first phase of French expansion before the latter had aimed at or achieved the level of control enabling them to reorganize colonial Algeria in their image of what a French Algeria would be. That esprit was represented through the relations between groups that were threaded on the string of the turuq. Given the weakness and limited development of the bourgeoisie and the easy subjugation of the towns, the Sufi orders became, as Fanny Colonna has pointed out, a critical organizing factor in the first period of resistance.

While the territorial and collective integrity of tribal and peasant groupings was intact, a traditional form of armed action through the turuq was effective in evoking and articulating relations among different groups. Sufism during this period was a frame for opposition to the emerging political and military forms of colonialism. In this sense it was part of what the French officers meant by the esprit of the society and crystallized the symbolic and ideological force of religion in that struggle. It did not, and could not, transform a series of social units whose character was defined by internal opposition and particularistic patterns of rights, identities, and allegiancies into a unified social movement capable both of defeating the French and of grasping the full nature of colonialism and its outworkings (which were in any case not part of some simple French master plan but emerged over a period of some forty years). The political and economic structures of European colonialism were far from the political struggles of precapitalist Algeria. For that transformation to happen, an equally different Algerian social order had painfully to emerge outside the tribal organization, one with different bases and internal relations, one that grew from a complex interaction with colonial power. Moreover, it was to be a social order that could no longer be contained within the limitations of traditional Sufi organization and practice and its images of human experience; it had to transcend those limitations.

So we find that as French colonial power was consolidated and Algeria was made more and more a part of the European colonial and capitalist system, the orders played a diminishing role. The increasing rationalization and coherence of French control in administration (to which I have referred) mark a second phase, dating roughly from the 1870s. It is a phase in which the dominant social form of Islam begins to shift away from the turuq and the zawiyas as the major centers of social, political, and economic networks, away from generally shared conceptualizations and images of the world that had at their heart baraka, personal authority, and illumination. Sufism was slowly displaced from the core of Islam in the practical social life of the colonized society. Baraka itself, as I have suggested in chapter 4, separated from a Sufi frame and became more a part of class conceptions and ideologies.

What developed has many parallels but occurred with particular intensity in Algeria, in part because of the high level of colonial control and the massive presence of colonists as farm and estate owners dominating agriculture and rural relations of production and exchange. Not only were tribal structures broken down, but different class relations arose within what is often rather too generally called the peasantry as production and labor organization was changed and collective rights partially or in some case wholly disintegrated. This pattern is full of variation and unevenness in scale, too. Between different regions there were considerable differences in the nature and measure of incorporation into the colonial economy, and in the resistance of local social and cultural structures and groups. Certain areas were reduced to the pauperization of a large proportion of the argricultural working population; others were dominated by wage labor on colonial estates yet might retain small independently cultivated and owned landholdings; yet other regions were characterized by migration to the towns by what became a *lumpenproletariat*, and by varied sharecropping arrangements. Unemployment emerged as a significant experience and a new way of being compelled to think about life in the capitalist economy, a way that had not existed in traditional society in which the notion of "job" or "employment" were absent and irrelevant as organizing notions.

The disaggregation of social units was not one unified and total experience throughout society. But it can be said, globally, to have produced a new Algerian society quite distinct from that which the Sufi orders had helped to articulate at the time of the conquest.

This process and the war to capture both body and esprit reached its most crystallized and extreme point at the end of the 1950s in the forced resettlement of an enormous percentage of the entire rural population in villages established under the surveillance and military control of the French. Here, in a grotesque yet "rational" vision of a perfect

colonial universe and of a perfect native space within that
universe, was an ultimate, almost surrealistic extension of
the great principles of the colonizers—rationality, linearity,
order, visibility, uniformity—that were to ensure the final
seizure of these people of "everywhere and nowhere."

As Bourdieu and Sayad put it:

> The [French] officers ... begin by disciplining space as
> if, through this means, they were hoping to discipline
> men .... Through a deliberate or unconscious ignorance
> of social realities, the local authorities generally impose an
> absolute foreign order on the "regroupés," an order for
> which they are not made and which is not made for
> them .... The officers apply without nuance the uncon-
> scious schemas of organization which might belong to the
> essence of every attempt at total and systematic domina-
> tion .... The reorganisation of inhabited space is thus
> obscurely understood as a decisive way of making a
> tabula rasa of the past by imposing a new framework of
> existence at the same time as stamping on the land the
> sign of taking possession of it.*

Now it is not easy to say what religion comes to mean
in the various levels of a population experiencing such an
imposition. Bourdieu and Sayad stress the devaluation of
traditional, agriculturally based life as a deculturation that
creates a kind of "regressive traditionalism," a tradition of
despair in which an impoverished religious practice becomes
ever more bound to a new magical formalism and empty
ecstatics. In this argument many of those whose lives depended on agricultural work for the colonizer farmers
were trapped between an archaic world of a collective social
order that was disintegrating and a colonial conceptual and
symbolic universe for which no means existed to make it
either commensurable or compatible with the workers own
universe of experience and meaning, save through the operations of power and violence.

This inescapable contradiction led some at these class
levels to support for the nationalist struggle; it led others
to take refuge or to refuse to confront their subordinated

* Le déracinement pp. 26-27.

position in "regressive traditionalism," regressive in the sense that it both harked back to nonexistent conditions whose bases were destroyed and at the same time blocked comprehension of practical schemes of action and ideology with which to transform the present.

At the same time, if religious practice did become less rich and anchored in a collective form of life, it may have become more important as the basis of an obscurely felt negation of the contradiction created in the colonial order or as a mode of otherness that was fundamentally inviolable to the colonials and which they could neither "see," control, nor practice. But in and of itself it could not lead to any historical resolution of that contradiction. That came with armed resistance, and we should note that such a form of traditionalism might prove an obstacle to mobilizing for armed resistance, since it itself had to be broken if a new mode of action and thought was to be possible.

The effects on religious practice and conception and its place in the consciousness of different rural classes are therefore not easy to elucidate. They are somewhat clearer to see when we look at another level of Algerian society that I have so far ignored: the urban middle classes, where a very specific religious trajectory was traced out.

An Austere and Militant Islam

Part of whatever clarity there is derives, I must admit, from the brevity and simplification with which the subject will be treated. With this as a warning I will go on immediately to say that the appeal of Islamic "modernism" or "reformism," which in Algeria is associated very closely with the name of Sheikh Ben Badis, has a social location that we can pick out in part because of its deliberate opposition to the worlds of the turuq and the marabouts. For one characteristic of the broad movement known as the *Salafiya** is the rejection of

---

* It is always difficult to know what term to use to qualify a phenomenon such as the Salafiya. I have chosen the word *movement*, but that should not be taken in too formal a sense. There were many who were influenced by it to a greater or lesser extent all over the Muslim world, and there were different tendencies within it. The political and economic interests associated with those influenced by Salafiya ideology also varied in local settings.

what was identified as the tribal and peasant universe of religion and belief: saint worship, and magical and superstitious practices (including claims to Mahdism), which were neither part of Islam nor brought any credit upon religion. And this was a critical time, for Islam confronted colonial and Christian powers who embodied, too, a profound cultural and symbolic threat. Having made this separation of religious universes, the positive identification of the Salafiya was with the authoritative, original practice of the righteous forefathers of the Muslim community. That at least was the charter for a program of reform that their Egyptian journal defined as "a triple unification of dogma, law and morality."

The inspiration came from Egypt in the person of the celebrated modernist thinker, Sheikh Muhammed 'Abduh, who had been a founder of the movement in Paris in 1883.* It was to 'Abduh's exile in Algeria from Egypt that much of the stimulus for the Salafiya was owed. But the lesson here is really that throughout the Muslim world reformism was becoming an organizing and organized form of religious, legal, and social practice by the late nineteenth century. It expresses in many different ways an attempt to distinguish what is at the core of religion, partly hidden and sullied by what were regarded as superstitious accretions and un-Islamic forms. It was also in opposition to the sterile, ossified conservatism of some of the 'ulema in the institutions of Islamic learning,

The idea of a purification of Islam was very powerful in the Salafiya, but not the purification of the apocalypse preached by Mahdist movements. Rather, it was to be a theological and philosophical attempt to recapture the trust of Islam, to reinvigorate the religious response to internal and external threat, to break out of the intellectual and ideological blockage of a religious tradition viewed as having become arthritic and moribund at one end and uncontrollably magical at the other.

Such a movement drew a wide audience and following in Algeria. At its core were many of the urban educated, predominantly middle class but including also those from the artisan stratum, merchants and traders, and members of the

---

* Perhaps the best study of the place of Muhammad 'Abduh in the intellectual tradition of modern Islam is A.H. Hourani's *Arabic Thought in the Liberal Age*. 1798-1939 Oxford: The Clarendon Press, 1962.

newly important bureaucracy. It was also popular, as Fanny Colonna points out, in the townships established under colonization, and she speaks of a semirural and semi-urban clientele as one of the defining traits of its constituency. It was radical, but its radicalism was not that of the funda-mentalist movements that were to develop later among the petite bourgeoisie in so many countries (for example, the Muslim Brothers of Egypt — of whom more later — whose founder once characterized his movement as in part "a salafi way") with a more militant and populist organization and message. Though there were profound implications in the movement's aim of revealing the "true" Islam once again as a religion for this world and in its assertion of the inviolability of religion, members often became socially conservative in their views and largely indifferent to the wider political questions of power and the relations with the new world system in which Algeria was progressively enmeshed.

Others, however, saw a purified Islam as a necessary underpinning to nationalism and feared the secularist pro-grams of nationalist parties that attracted many members of the middle classes. In Algeria there was a particular problem in this regard. For there were those who had become absorbed through the French educational system as French speakers and in complex and highly ambiguous ways as bearers of a certain kind of outsider's version of French culture. The battle for the esprit had been partly waged on the ground of language as an instrument of domination and control. The Salafiya, basing themselves in the Arabic language of the Quran (which was taken in itself to be a miracle), were both resisting this attempt at establishing French cultural hegemony by hacking at the root of the Muslim identity, and presenting a critique of the whole existence of those who were called, depending on the viewpoint, either scathingly, patronizingly, or in praise, the évolués. The cultural core was to be de-fended through language and the miraculous signs of the Holy Book. Assimilation, that many-edged weapon of mod-ern colonialism, was to be rejected.

Colonna has suggested that the Salafiya movement never conquered social and economic power but that it did both appropriate and define the field of religious legitimacy.

It became the arbiter of "true Islam." It fixed the boundaries of religion in a way that had not previously been possible in Algerian history, and in this sense their version became the established version. It has certainly been the greatest influence in the understanding of Islam characteristic of independent Algeria, to the point that it can be spoken of as the official interpretation of the religion of the state.

The *Avant-Projet* (Preliminary Plan) of the National Charter in 1976 puts the place of Islam in a context of socialism and the consolidation of national independence:

The Algerian people is a Muslim people.

Socialism is not a new religion, it is a theoretical and strategic weapon which takes account of the reality of all peoples. Based on science, it is . . . the enemy of all dogmatics and scholasticism.

Islam as an integral part of our historical personality reveals itself as one of the most powerful defenses against all the attempts at depersonalization. It is in a militant, austere Islam, stirred by the sense of justice and equality that the Algerian people took shelter at the worst hours of colonial domination and from which it drew that moral energy and that spirituality which have preserved it from despair and permitted it to triumph.

The Algerian revolution and the socialism preached by its leaders are, of course, part of the new phase in the dialectics of "modernist" Islam. There is also another element, part of the same movement and process. Now identified with the state and with the operations of power, this vision of Islam may become in its turn challenged by different groups and classes who oppose some aspect of state policy or who wish to call the state to account for failing to evolve according to its own socialist program and promises. The fascinating debate launched by the late President Boumedienne all across Algeria in 1976 to discuss the new National Charter contained several hints at possible currents of unease directed at the dominant reformist model and its assimilation with a specific class or political stratum.

A worker in a factory in Bejaia was quoted as saying:

Until now Islam has been perverted, chiefly by the bourgeoisie who have interpreted the sacred texts, deforming both the content and even the essence, on the pretext that religion supported their acts. The working masses have been duped. This is why I ask that we expand the teaching of an austere and militant Islam that is based on social justice in the centers of instruction and even at the level of economic enterprises.*

Here is a worker's vision that accuses the bourgeoisie of distorting Islam, the very charge that the bourgeoisie, through the Salafiya, leveled at the marabouts and the Sufi brotherhoods. But note that where the Salafiya presented the argument as one of *religious* dogma and purification, the worker casts his accusation in terms of *class interest*. This relates partly to a use of the discourse of the state on socialism. "Austere and militant" is very much a vision of society that develops in the revolution and is central to state ideology. It is now used to express, however, a class hostility, which might also embrace the bureaucrats and managers and entrepreneurs who have assumed such an important role in the Algerian economy and whose life-styles are not specifically "austere and militant" viewed from a factory in Bejaia. Finally, at another level of discourse, to a Muslim audience it instantly evokes the Quran itself and the accusations of the Holy Book that make perversion and distortion one of the chief sins of the Christian and Jewish clergy, who are held to have willfully changed and misinterpreted God's Revelations that were previously sent down to their respective communities, thus necessitating the sending down of the final Revelation of the Quran. The defenders of the purity of the "true" Islam thus find themselves arraigned for one of the worst and most un-Islamic practices — perverting the Word of God. The Word must be reappropriated from its self-appointed guardians, who have used it for the interests of their own class.

This fascinating, many-layered text presents a new set of relations that make up a new form of ideological and political language in which Islam is a major element. Such a language is perhaps peculiarly likely to arise in Algeria. But in my view

* *Al-Mujahid*, May 15, 1976, p. 5.

it could be read in many different settings across the Islamic world and would be locally meaningful because it encapsulates the experience, or one element of the experience, of "the working masses." So there is here a more universal set of messages than might initially be imagined. As the Salafiya had its impact at a particular global juncture of the world capitalist system, from Morocco to Indonesia, from India to Egypt, so the implications of this accusation resonate through the same space at a different stage of the relations of these societies to the dominant powers in that system and originating from a different social level.

Besides this we must note a certain alarm expressed over the continued role of the zawiyas, which were uniformly presented in the correspondence in *al-Mujahid* as havens of charlatanism and exploitation. One blazing attack put it as follows:

> In the past, some of them [the zawiyas] assisted the colonizer; today they alienate minds, corrupt our officials, challenge the Islam which is our religion. From the fact that they have a very large audience, these leaders of zawiyas have enriched themselves without sweat and without making the least contribution to the country [in taxes], have organized campaigns of denigration against the agricultural revolution [since their interests were at stake].... We cannot say that they will disappear when the level of education of our people is raised ... for it is indeed sad to see men of culture, in the proper sense of the term, frequenting the zawiyas assiduously and belonging to them wholeheartedly.... Without the radical repression of these zawiyas the whole Revolution will be condemned to blockage, for they are the best schools of counter-Revolution and corruption.*

This blast from the same debate could hardly be stronger, and it seems that there is virtually no fault for which the zawiyas are not responsible! And this after years of ideological criticism and attack from the dominant sectors of Algerian society. Now, laments the polemicist, even the cultivated have joined them....

* Ibid.

It is striking that this hostility and unease seem to characterize all the references to the zawiyas that are made in the newspaper's columns and that it should be so violent. Assisting the colonizer, exploitation and self-enrichment, reaction and counterrevolution, falsification of Islam, corruption of belief and politics — this is a formidable list of images and political vocabularies to picture the sinister powers that have begun to ensnare, though it is not clear why or how, even the official bearers of the revolution and the educated.

It is also hardly the kind of accusation one makes unless the zawiyas are showing greater rootedness and social resilience than the austere and militant might expect, or be able to explain, given their hostility to what they regard as perversions and unorthodox practice as well as to forces blocking the revolution.

There is a fascinating vision recorded here. At one pole we must oppose the Islam of the bourgeoisie, who have falsified it in their own class interest. At the other, there are the zawiyas, which not only continue their old subversion but which are also beginning to attract the cultured and the officials (cadres). And there is, in fact, no a priori reason why some of the cadres might not regard themselves as good technocratic servants of a socialist Algeria, impeccably orthodox believers, *and* members of a zawiya!

An Austere and Militant Sufism

That in actuality Sufi orders have also been the bearers in the modern period of an austere and militant Islam is not too difficult to show. Sufism is not, of course, either in theory or practice necessarily ecstatic, nor are ecstatics its main traits in any case, save in very specific circumstances.*

Certainly there was no question of the orthodoxy and militancy of the Sanusi order, which in the nineteenth century had lodges on trade routes and in areas from Cyrenaica in northeastern Libya as far south as Senegal and

---

* Frequently in the zikr rituals of the repetition of certain of the Names of God only the elite of the brotherhood is even allowed, never mind encouraged, to enter the state of hal, as what we very clumsily translate as "ecstacy" is called in Arabic. It is a very structured and hierarchically framed experience in many orders.

which in the twentieth century became the framework for the independent kingdom of Libya. Although the Sanusi are famous as the ideological and to some extent organizational framework of resistence to the savage and brutal Italian colonial conquest of Libya (which began in 1911), we have to remember that their whole history was intertwined with that of Western incursion into Africa. Indeed, the fact that we think of them as the Sanusi of Libya is a reflection of the fact that during their confrontation with the French in the late nineteenth century they were pushed inexorably back into Libya up the trade routes down which they had not long before expanded into Saharan and sub-Saharan Africa.

This also emphasizes the international character of the order. It had its links in Arabia, where the founder (the Grand Sanusi, as he came to be known, born in Algeria in 1787) lived and studied for many years, Egypt, Algeria, French Equatorial Africa, and French West Africa. Learning, information, and world politics were almost as significant across this network as was the passage of trade goods. It was the advances of the French in Algeria that forced the Grand Sanusi to abandon his project of going to that country and to stop instead in Bengazi. Opposed to the east both by Muhammed 'Ali in Egypt and by the religious and political authorities of the holy places of the Hejaz, and in the west and south by the growing encroachment of colonial power, he made his base in the "betwixt and between" zone of Libya.

The mother lodge, as Evans-Pritchard calls it in his *The Sanusi of Cyrenaica*, was established in 1843. Until the late nineteenth century the order was able to develop its web of zawiyas. Sometimes they were established at the junctions of important trade and pilgrimage routes, or in major oases into which the Sanusi were invited by the dominant tribes, who gave them palms and water as an offering and inducement for a zawiya; or there might be a personal link, as when the prince of the Saharan territory of Wadai, who had been a student of the Grand Sanusi in Mecca, requested the foundation of a center of the order in his region.

Onto this pre-existing network of widely flung relations European power grafted a second dimension of political, economic, and ideological conflict from the late eighteenth century onward. And it may be this that helps to give the order both its strong internal dynamic in missionary work, its emphasis on ascetic and sober orthodoxy, its constant ramifying out of the zawiya complex, and its significance to those who invited its representatives among them. For not only did the Sanusi stand for a kind of institution with which the tribes were traditionally familiar — the Sufi order with its chains of authority, its baraka, its learning and knowledge, its regulation of violence, making of peace, provision of sanctuary, and a host of other services — but it also created an additional set of linkages that in the context of European penetration was given a more intense vitality than usual.

At the moment of its widest distribution, then, the Sanusiya had an enormous social and geographical range and had become an organization of considerable economic and political importance. A large income of offerings and donations in kind and in labor services was generated from the communities where the brothers settled. Stock raising, agriculture, trade, transport, and customs dues were all central to the maintenance of the lodges of scholar-missionary-ascetics who came, classically, as outsiders to the tribal groupings among which they played so important a role.

Learning and Islamic culture flourished in the desert, not for the first time, and there is nothing ironical in the fact that a townsman and scholar such as the Grand Sanusi should achieve his greatest institutional impact in the complex of peasant and tribal societies that became the ocean in which the Sanusi swam. If the Bedu themselves were not well versed in ritual and theology — no better than the average townsman of the period, say — they provided the most fertile of soils for the order to grow in. They protected it and enabled it to generate a level of unity and organization that very few orders of the urban centers were able to achieve. A weak Turkish administration and the fact that, as in Algeria, the towns were relatively insignificant and did not dominate the political and economic networks were other factors creating the space in which the Sanusi could move.

That said, we must not force a heavily institutional interpretation onto the order. Flexibility and relative local autonomy were in any case a structural advantage in such a setting. I differ a little with Evans-Pritchard when he suggests as a source of weakness the fact that the Sanusi had a "crude" economic and political organization for so vast an area. Given precisely the nature and scale of the entire region in which the Sanusi were established, such a crudity seems to me rather a source of strength. If one set of lodges were destroyed or neutralized by the French, there was no structural blow to the order itself, since the level of organizational and functional interdependence was relatively limited. Human and economic resources were distributed over wide areas, difficult to subdue and "fix" à la Captain Richard, and mobile to a degree.

The point is made by Evans-Pritchard that the structural strength of the order was in its particular form of adaptation to tribal structure. Lodges were often established on the boundaries between the territories of tribal sections, as well as at key points on caravan routes. This separation is socially and ideologically an important element in the sanctity of the holy outsiders. They are the people of the potentially dangerous and shifting boundaries between groups. They draw their powers from God and the respect accorded to those whose baraka demonstrates their special position (a familiar circle) and not from violence and the reserve of manpower and flocks that a particular group may possess. Their relation with the tribal and peasant groups is articulated through offerings and sacrifice. They are unarmed. Their settlements are holy places where no blood may be shed. The peace they alone can guarantee by appeal to God and because of the transcendent authority to which they are linked comes in part from this marginal and interstitial position.

It also comes from the relationship of the zawiyas to the dominant clans and sections of the territories within which they were located. I cannot here go into the vexed questions of the possible modes of accumulating power and wealth in societies such as these, societies in which stock raising, agriculture, and trade all play such important parts. There is often an ideological discourse of equality of individuals and groups. The links of the different genealogical sections are often "expressed" (Evans-Pritchard's word) in terms of formal balance and equivalence. Evans-Pritchard himself saw the lineages at each of the different levels of the genealogy as all replicating the structure of the whole system, though he implied that the lower-level, on-the-ground units were more kin-based camps, while at the higher levels one was dealing with more political aggregates.

Now there are two rather different orders of unit and relations involved. Furthermore, critics have suggested that the "segmentary lineage system" is a representation, a set of organizing terms and a way of thinking that is indeed locally used to sort out relations of social inclusion and exclusion in a genealogical idiom but that in any case is neither locally the only idiom nor taken to be a total representation of the whole social field. Nor, furthermore, should it be accepted as a sociological or analytical account of the structure of the society.

One problem this still leaves us with is that of how power is constituted and what its operations are. We know that part of the ideological tradition was of the superiority of the "free" tribes over the associated or client groups. Some of the latter were holy families (*marabtin b'il baraka* — linked by baraka) who made no payments to the free tribes but were settled among them, performed services that on a very small scale were similar to those performed by the Sanusi, and had no wider organization. The relative importance of such a family would depend on local factors, but the range of their significance would be limited. Many from families of such marabtin would play no "holy" role at all and would be indistinguishable from the tribesmen or peasants. Other groups were called "clients of the fee" (*sadqan* is usually translated as fee), who had no religious status and paid dues to their patron free group.

The terminology included, therefore, the notion of the attachment of groups to other groups and the inferiority of some groups to others. It does not explain the actual forms of power and influence, however, because we know that some groups with marabtin status among the pastoralists in fact became very influential and important in some of the leading sections of the free tribes, far more important than many of free status. On the Cyrenaican plateau to the north, where agriculture predominated, Evans-Pritchard suggests that the groups were more often fragmented and owed both fee and labor services to the free tribes.

Though many writers emphasize the precariousness of

personal authority in such settings and suggest that the balanced opposition of segments acts against it, Evans-Pritchard also refers to the need for leaders (sheikhs) to be rich and to the fact that the position is often quasi-hereditary in the same family. Such factors, together with the importance of trade and pilgrimage route traffic, would seem to indicate the presence of groups who established dominance, greater wealth, and the dependancy of others upon them (whether or not those others had the explicit public status of marabtin). They could invite the zawiya in and supply the labor resources necessary to sustain it in herding and agriculture from those who had lost their own rights in land or stock and had become shepherds, dependents, and workers for others. Such links may have been of great significance in the building up of the complex network of economic and political ties the order constructed. The spread of European commercial and military power may have accelerated this process.

If these links were as I have suggested, we can see how important they would be in the struggle against the Italians, a struggle that was only defeated ultimately by massive repression and slaughter. We can also see why, in the wake of Italian withdrawal following World War Two, the Sanusi order and the Sanusi family seemed to be the sole institutions able to act as the framework of a state in a still severely disrupted society. Connections with leading tribal sections and descent groups and a web of relations that extended throughout eastern and southern Libya and had developed over a period of more than one hundred years gave them the political and economic weight to become the new rulers of the kingdom of Libya.

The religious power that becomes the embodiment of state power, however, is placed in a quite different structural position from that of the Sufi order in tribal society. When the Sanusis are displaced by revolution, it is by a revolution in the name of an austere and militant Islam allied with Nasserism and Arab socialism. A new discourse is created by this amalgam of forces − anti-imperialism, the economic explosion of oil revenues, the dynamic, activist religious ideology of young army officers whose model, Nasser, seemed in the early 1960s to embody all that was progressive and independently powerful in the Arab nation as a whole.

What the regime of President Qaddafi has done, or sought to do, ever since is to maintain a state of permanent revolution that will preserve and maintain its force and pristine quality through a new reading of an austere and militant Islam, liberated from its erstwhile champions, the Sanusis.

This attempt constantly to renew, constantly to remodel, constantly to break up and start again, to be everywhere, to produce schemes, definitions, practices, a new society is a radical effort to follow out the logic of religion in this total conception. It seeks to pre-empt internal developments and processes that might lead in turn to its own displacement and destruction by others who may come to see the holders of power again as tainted and corrupted and following class interest in the name of religion.

CHAPTER 8

Forming and Transforming Space

We saw in the last chapter the lengths to which the French were prepared to go in "disciplining space" as part of the establishment of systematic domination. Such disciplining was not only a mark of colonialism and of imposition by outside forces. There were always local, indigenous patterns of inscribing hierarchy in space, and the interplay of the local and the external forms became a vital element in culture and practice even in village communities. I want now to take the discussion farther by looking in more detail at some of the manifold relations of power, ideology, and the sacred in space, beginning with the village and feudal system of north Lebanon, to which I have already referred.

What is immediately striking about this village is that its physical form makes a very public statement of hierarchy and social domination. The lords' large fortress palaces, built of massive blocks of stone, are up on the hill to the left. Before each one is a space set out for receiving guests during the summer evenings. To the side are the reception rooms.* The external walls have rings bolted into the stone where the horses, symbols of feudal privilege and rule, would be tied up. Outside the stables there are now likely to be the Buicks

* The *maglis* (pl. *magālis*).

and Peugeots that are equally symbolic of power, wealth, and prestige in a modern idiom. The stranger will be impressed by the size, by the sheer heaviness of the solidly built fortress houses, and by their distance from all other dwellings, but he will not be able to judge anything of their internal space from their external appearance. He will not be able to see into the inner courtyard, with rooms giving off it on all sides in which members of the lord's family live — sons, daughters, relatives by marriage, aunts and uncles, retainers, an entire household. That is all shut off and enclosed.

Just below this cluster of baronial halls, and equally close together in space and set apart from other dwellings, is an area that even to the ignorant naked eye constitutes a "quarter." Here, in smaller houses also made of large-cut stone, live the families making up the descent group that was for so long attached to the lords as strong-arm men, bailiffs, and attendants. They are drawn up in straight lines and often connected one to the other (as brothers have built side by side and adjoining their father's house). The windows are well above the head of any passerby, only stables and storage rooms being at street level. Entry is usually up a narrow stairway, with the reception room, if the family maintains one, facing it across the small courtyard at the top. Even from above the quarter on the hill behind, one will not be able to see into the houses. The boundaries, even the visual boundaries, are firmly drawn in order to set off the public from the private, nonfamily from family, outside from inside.

Here, then, are two hierarchical social levels clearly set in stone and form. The third level is away on the hill to the right, where the stranger notices a large huddle of roofs, narrow twisting paths, walls, and buildings that are so tightly crammed together that he can hardly sort out one from another. They are all of one storey, each path between turning so often that the stranger cannot tell how many houses there are or which are separate dwellings. Though many are now built in concrete and breeze blocks, there are still some that are cobbled together of mud and barely shaped stones. They nearly all seem small and impoverished, though again his eyes cannot see inside, and beyond their poverty they give nothing away about their inhabitants or their internal house plan. No windows give on to the alleys. There are no signs or direction markers. The stranger would need to find not only someone to take him to the house of a person he might be seeking but someone who had the right to take him there. This is the quarter of the peasants, but that it is in turn divided into separate family clusters will not be immediately apparent to him. Where each descent group of lords has its own independently sited house, clearly separated off from all others, and where the dwellings of the *aghawāt* (as the retainer stratum is called) are in distinct lines and clusters, the peasant quarter impresses by its seemingly jumbled, undifferentiated, almost haphazard arrangement in space.

The visitor reaches the peasant quarter by what has been for fifteen years a road but what was before a dirt track through a cemetery that takes up a barren and rocky part of the hillside. The distance between laborer and lord that is thus expressed and given form in space is clearly far greater than the mere one hundred meters the visitor's European mind may have noted, and it exists in several dimensions. The organization of space that makes up "the village" insists on *dis*continuities, separations, opposed categorizations. It makes one immediately aware of hierarchy and class. On one side of the cemetery are lords and retainers, status honor, social order, power, precedence, and wealth; on the other side are agricultural laborers, dependency, exclusion from status, service, powerlessness.

Between these two major spatial divisions of the village there are two mosques. The one below, where the road comes up from the plain, is a low rectangular building, dwarfed by an enormous tree that spreads its branches completely over it. Just at the foot of the tree, some ten meters away perhaps, a spring of water gushes out from the hillside. Under the low-arched colonnades of the mosque facade is a plain, unvarnished table that the stranger will later discover is used for washing the dead. By the side, propped up so that its lidless top and shape clearly show its function, is the coffin in which all the bodies of the dead are carried to their burial place on the hill behind, and from which they are lifted before being placed in the graves. In front of this small mosque, which has no minaret (the call to prayer being made from in front of the door), is a space where people sit in the shade of the tree, wash and carry out the ritual ablutions at the spring (without which the prayers would be invalid), pass the time, exchange information and gossip — a public, visible, collective space. It is a place where strangers will first arrive at the village and first be seen coming up the approach road, a place where even the police and army will wait if they come on business because to move from it is to move into the village, a right that must, as it were, be granted if they are not to risk what would be seen as a violation of collective space.

The nature of this public zone needs a little further qualification. To begin with, because it is a public space in which by definition everything is visible and seen, it is within the sphere of the men. Women do not gather at the spring, nor do they enter the mosque or cross the area in front of it. The sacred in its collective, public, and social sense excludes them in this society. So the groups of women at the well, which is so important a meeting point for them where it is located outside a village or in an area defined as "invisible," or set apart and not entered by adult males, are not seen here.

As we might expect, for the public prayer on Fridays a congregation gathers at the lower mosque from all parts of the village. Not everyone will be there, however. There will be no women present. Moreover, someone who knows the village will also know that a history of blood feud between one section of the aghawat family and a family of peasants bars the presence of either from this most public and social of spaces where they would *have* to "see" each other and could not "pretend not to notice." They avoid each other, and the village mosque does not serve as a ground on which unreconciled enemies may meet in safety. It is a sacred space and a socially central space, and the requirements of these two dimensions are sometimes in tension. It does not, therefore, negate the world or in some simple sense stand opposed to profane or secular space and activity. Men at certain times enter it in a state of ritual purity for ritual purposes, as Muslims and part of the congregation of Islam rather than as lord, retainer, or peasant. But this is not its only dimension of meaning and practice. Though feuding parties avoid, therefore, attending the collective Friday prayers and say that the mosque is holy and no blood must be shed there, they both know of incidents of ambush and killing at prayer. So the mosque is only a sanctuary in the sense that those who might well violate it if they attended actually keep away from public prayers in the same way that they avoid all public occasions at which they might meet; the public prayer is but the most collectively important.

At the upper boundary of the cemetery is another mosque, but of a rather different form and significance. Built in marble and carefully cut stone, it has not only a large dome but also a very tall and slender minaret, both features lacking in the lower mosque. The prayer hall inside is large and colonnaded around all the sides. Crystal chandeliers hang from the roof, the direction mark (*mihrab*) or niche that indicates the direction to Mecca (the *qibla*) is elaborately carved. The stranger will notice that there is no meeting place before it and that the site and shape seem chosen more because of its visibility for miles around and its domination of its surrounding space than for some organic relation with village structure. It does not seem to articulate space, as does the lower mosque. The latter lies at the nodal point of lord, retainer, and peasant quarters: It is over the water spring where all animals are watered. (The association of water spring, tree, and holy place indeed recurs again and again in the region and obviously has pre-Islamic roots. The lower mosque is, as it were, a transformation of an older pattern and site of sanctity.) It is flanked by the washing table and the coffin, to which everyone in the world must come.

The upper mosque, therefore, though it seems from afar to be central and certainly the dominating mark of the village's existence, is in fact spatially peripheral and unrelated to the social, spatial, and architectural forms around it. What it does relate to and represent, as one might guess from its place and design, is the power of the major lord of the village (now dead). It is his mosque. He built it and is buried next to it in a special enclosure; the upper mosque stands as a public symbol of worldly rule quite as much as of religious assembly and links with the Divinity. Its isolation in space and its total disregard of other patterns and forms over which it towers but with which it has no relation are a flat statement of the lord's appropriation of religion to a worldly system of power and control as an attribute of his position. The meaning of the space and the construction is therefore quite the opposite of that of the lower mosque and is, by comparison, quite one-dimensional. Its essence, at least in conception, lies exactly in its appearance rather than in its function or the religious significance of elements, such as the dome or prayer hall. There are thus two symbolic levels here: One is that of qibla, dome, minaret; the other, which seems to me to be more fundamental, is that of domination and *non*integration into village space.

Now, the same lord also created a secular equivalent to this ostentatious mosque. On almost exactly the same level as the latter, but close to the fortress houses of the ruling families, is what in fact is the first modern transformation of the old fortress forms: a kind of Franco-Italian château, with elaborate stucco work, entirely European in design, plan, and decoration, huge windows opening out the facade, with a staircase that is built to set off the grandeur of the frontage rather than to be a narrow entry to a closed and private world. The whole building is clearly facing onto, and oriented toward, the world. It is the absolute antithesis of village space, form, and representation. Though so different from the old houses of the lords, it is a new coding of the one basic dimension of social relations — the domination of the rulers, their monopoly of wealth, their separateness and distinction in status from all other strata. The new coding, however, is worth looking at for the changes we can read from it.

Instead of the inward-turned, massive-stoned, fortresslike seat of power in which the functional and the coercive are blended in a severe ascetic form, there is in the château the primary importance of facade, of appearance, of show. Glass and highly ornamented stucco set up a completely new aesthetic of power in which domination and display, "style" and luxury based on entirely nonindigenous models, are crucial. The entryway is designed for its pattern and architectural complementarity to the highly decorative facade rather than for its function; the most important things about it are its lines, curving and graceful, and the fact that it is made of marble. The furnishings were imported — I say were imported, for only wreckage remains, following the lord's death in 1958 — from Europe: tasselled brocaded curtains, red velvet chairs, large mirrors in ornate gilt frames, tiled floors with rich carpets, and a plan of rooms that in shape, interrelations, and purpose owed nothing to traditional local models but everything to the French nineteenth century. Clearly their importance was that they totally rejected all local models, even down to the materials used. Mirrors, chairs, and curtains were unused in village houses until recently but established an image of status to which the lord wished to assimilate himself in the colonial period.

Next to the château is the enormous country house of the lord's assassinated son. Never completed, it represents the second generation's transformation of the fortress type. Where the father's château is a kind of deliberately antique form that reaches back in time to foreign images of elegance and insists on a complete rupture with Lebanese time and history as well as space, the son's palace is quite distinct. It is far closer to a kind of urban mansion, with enormous pitched roof (tiles from Marseilles) and concrete throughout. Its location is more central and dominating than the château, which is veiled with trees to give a sort of European notion of a pastoral setting and gracious living and of a time and space cut off from the vulgar and impoverished realities of the village.

We can begin to see that village space, even at this level of first impressions, is a complex phenomenon full of different patterns, disjunctions, and relations. I have already suggested that the place of sacred spaces in these configurations is obviously more complicated than it appears. It would be misleading to say that social space is predominantly articulated by the sacred (either in local perceptions or to the anthropologist). The dimension of the sacred is in any case only one aspect of the zone around the lower mosque, for example. In some ways we might best regard the lower mosque area as an island, a point at once of rest from and relationship between three clearly demarcated spatial complexes (of lords, retainers, and peasants), which in themselves are ordered according to different principles. It is central, and it is obviously particularly crucial in a social setting where boundaries of family, group membership, and social stratification are so tightly organized in space and so overtly expressed that there are very few relatively unbounded, open areas.

I mean by this that at almost all other points in the village one is in a zone that is identified as the space of either oneself or another. It is interesting that over the past ten years or so, as a few shops have begun to open in the village, that a space that has come in practice to be tacitly accepted as "the space before a shop" is also relatively open and unrestricted. People may meet and chat there without being in a socially highly defined zone. They are in what they refer to as a *sāba* ("open" space, in both the literal and the social senses). The commercial transaction creates a situation in which social interactions on a more flexible and chance level may occur. Less multidimensional than the lower mosque space, such zones are nonetheless important in the overall configuration of the village, since they offer the possibilities of transient contact on neutral ground.

In a social context such as this, in which hierarchy and stratification and group identity are regarded as the basis of the social order and the ideology of status honor, we find a preponderance of spatial settings in which relative degrees of closure, exclusion, visibility, or invisibility to all save those who have the right to see are primary. Open spaces are rare. A man's presence in a particular location is taken as indicating either a very specific purpose and relationship to a given individual or group or a recognized right to be present and seen there. Space means relationship. The only way of escaping this kind of constant social definition is either to be within the zones of the shops or the lower mosque or to go outside what are regarded as the boundaries of the village altogether.

In such a highly structured space there is always the question, moreover, of who "sees" whom, because "seeing" is a socially determined act and not a question merely of images on the retina and physiological process. Just as an insult can be negated or avoided if one can affect not to "see" it and if anyone else present at the time is also willing to go along, so potentially problematic situations can be neutralized by not "seeing."

Take a very simple but absolutely crucial example. Women are the center of a family's sacred identity. For the males of the family the women are both the embodiment of purity and also a source of danger and defilement. Their sexuality, which their natures can never totally control, may bring dishonor and destruction unless father or husband or brother jealously guards the shrine. Women may only exist in the private domain, in socially closed space. They have no public and open life. They may only be legitimately seen by very specific categories of males, for contact with any others touches the sacred in the family.

How, then, do they cope with public space? The paths and narrow streets of the village are clearly more public and socially unrestricted than most other spaces, though they are still territorially defined and part of quarter or descent group's zone. Women, when they walk down such a path, are in the literal sense of the word visible. But they are not "seen." That is to say, the path itself has zones of open and closed. Men walk down the middle, women cling to the sides and walk fast. Neither gives any sign of seeing the other at all. The women are socially and for all practical purposes invisible. They must be. For to give any indication in front of witnesses always alive to the merest glance or flickering momentary look or flash of recognition is to change, possibly in the most dangerous ways, the nature of the moment. It may become socially defined as an encounter with possibly critical meanings if witnesses decide in turn to acknowledge that they have seen something, as distinct from tacitly colluding with the pretense that there was nothing to see.

In fact women engage in an enormous amount of visiting to and fro and are quite central in the exchange of information, arrangement of marriages, and so forth, but this is only possible because of the powerful convention, sanctioned ultimately by violence, that none "see" them. They are publicly "not there" *because* they are so significant.

We can complicate matters a little further. "Seeing" is partly a function of position in terms of class, status, and social group. The poor may depend on wives, sisters, and daughters either for labor on their own or rented plots of land or as casual laborers for others during times of agricultural necessity. Such families are caught in a vicious circle. Peasant families are outside the honor scale, as far as those above them are concerned, because they are peasants. If they conceal their women, as "honorable" families do, they lose labor and income and may be taken to demonstrate ideas above their station and what is in terms of social logic a nonsensical pretension. If they send the women to work, then, that is typical of the sort of life you expect peasants to lead. Their women are "seen," and this is one of the most important marks and practices of their overall inferior social status.

Public Spaces: Market and Mosque

It should be clear that space that is nearer to the open and public end of the continuum than to the closed and private nonetheless presents considerable problems. It is not unstructured, free, and neutral, nor is it profane as opposed to sacred. Our observations on the area in front of the old mosque of the village indicate that. In a face-to-face community particularly, when most individuals actually know who most other individuals are, where the marks of group identity are extremely clear, and where there is pronounced social inequality and status differentation, the most public places are very much stages for the divisions and separations between people and groups.

They are also, in a society in which honor and power and individual prestige are so significant, not "merely" stages for the acting of preordained parts; they are rather potentially "fields of force," highly charged and full of social energy. It is above all in such a space that a man's honor, his capacity to challenge or accept a challenge whether verbal or physical, is at stake. In this sense the male's most sacred self is most at risk in public, has to be most jealously maintained by constant awareness of others' behavior. Everyone is on show in such a setting. What is more, there are the largest numbers of participants from different groups in different relations each to the other. So the possibility of "not seeing" something that may be highly embarrassing or socially disruptive, such as a remark that could be taken as a challenge to a verbal duel or worse, is much reduced. (The chance encounter is also most likely.) One might even say, indeed, that such areas are ultimately preferred and privileged zones for confrontation precisely because the audience is at its largest and the risks at their greatest. At the same time, there is a very strong collective interest that public space should in some sense be controlled and not anarchic so that it is not constantly under threat of disturbances and violence whose courses no one can with certainty predict.

This is one of the dimensions that makes the market so significant. For it is the public space *par excellence*. One of the most striking things to notice, therefore, is how often the market is under some kind of religious guarantee or authority (particularly in societies without strong state powers and policing). It frequently occupies an area adjacent to a mosque. Or it may be under the authority of a holy family of religious specialists, whose presence makes of the area a *haram* (a forbidden and sacred place in which no weapons may be carried and no blood spilled). Arms are often left outside the market area. This is of more significance than simply an avoidance of bloodshed. It changes the status of men in the space of the market. For in societies in which competing tribal groupings are significant and opposition between tribal segments is one of the structural principles of society, arms are one of the primary symbols of male identity and freeborn status. Traditionally, to be without a gun or a dagger is to be socially a dependent, a client or a slave, less than a man, without a full social persona and status. The only category of persons who went without arms as a positive aspect of their social and religious position were the holy families and men of religion. The giving up of arms is therefore an acceptance of a particular and unusual state, which is not highly shameful and degrading only because it is in obedience to religious imperatives and under religious guarantees. It recognizes, in ideal terms, a subordination of the sacredness of honor to the sacredness of the divinely established order.

Men may therefore shrink from acting in ways they might consider obligatory outside such an area because of respect for the men of religion, and they are not thereby dishonored. Quite the reverse. Such respect is absolutely required as a living acknowledgment of divine power. But at the same time, they cannot be absolutely sure that an enemy will not violate and profane the market and kill them in public. Such an enemy, or whoever he has hired for the task, may thus doubly defile the victim's group. For he not only desecrates them by the killing but by the deliberate flouting of the religious code that brought them to the market unarmed. The risk is never totally absent.

This close link between the place of exchange — of goods, services, information — and religion seems to me to connect to the demands of a socioeconomic system of pastoralist and peasant groups in which markets are a central institution. They are places in which groups, which may in other circumstances be at feud or without institutionalized relationships, must deal with one another. It is no accident that the holy towns one finds throughout the Middle East, for example, are also often the sites of major regional markets and caravan route stopping points. Religion and economy here link tightly and those who are sanctified men of peace, perhaps descendants of the Prophet, guarantee the functioning of the social system of the men of honor and violence. They extend a symbolic canopy of religious sanctions and symbols over the market and impose, at least in theory, a qualitatively different order and code upon those who come together there.

Such a guarantee is part of a whole complex of relations of exchange that go well beyond the narrowly economic. If the holy men guard the market, as it were, they may also make of the settlement itself — whether it is a village or oasis — a sacred area. The space thus formed is a world apart, even though activities within it may be of a very worldly and practical nature. If, in symbolic terms, it rests on opposed principles to that of the zone beyond its boundaries, it is also most intimately linked to that region beyond. The making of peace at this kind of sacred site is only one of the highly important ways in which such islands of sanctuary are connected to the wider universe.

In sacred space things become possible, even prescribed, that may be uncertain and problematic outside. There is protection — of goods, of persons, of collective and individual property. There is teaching and knowledge transmitted by the religious specialists, perhaps also a shrine and the occasion to acquire blessing and aid from its always active saint. There is the exchange of information — on rainfall and pasture, herds, the harvest, marriages, deaths, politics — and the making of new exchange relations. Offerings to the holy men of sacrifices at the shrine, of animals and products or even money, constitute a symbolic as well as material capital for the sheikhs, which is repaid by a multiplicity of functions and acts that only they can fulfill.

Under these conditions public space has a complex range of meanings. These meanings are not socially neutral or vaguely defined but rather make a field in which certain social forms and relationships that are vital to the identity of groups in the ordinary world are neutralized by forces defined as religious. And this is especially true of the space of the mosque itself. For the mosque is public in the sense that within it men form a congregation as Muslims that ideally dissolves the specifics of self and family and group into what is taken as the basic, fundamental identity of membership in the community of the faithful. It does, in this way, oppose the social definitions of space and its significances that operate in the everyday world. Within it men may sleep, talk, pray, study, but they do so (or rather, in part, they *can* do so) free of their ordinary social marks of rank and relationship, at least in terms of the ideal. Even where the mosque is specifically associated with a community, or an urban quarter, or a particular social grouping, that association is transcended by a wider identity.

In practice, such an egalitarian transformation may well be more an ideal conception than an experienced reality. Tomas Gerholm, whose book on a highly stratified Yemeni town is so perceptive in its analysis of space and ideology, has noted how often the way in which the congregation actually forms in line for prayer replicates the social hierarchy. He goes further, seeing the prayer in the Friday mosque (the major public collective space) as a kind of extension of the market:

> While the small mosques usually do not keep their visitors for longer time than is required for the prayer itself, the Friday mosques are places where it is tempting to stay on, perhaps reading the Koran but probably just talking to friends and watching people pass by. For those who use the mosque in this fashion, it may lose some of its singularly religious quality and become more an extension of the life in the adjacent *suq* [market]. Social intercourse within the precincts of the mosque do not appear very different from sitting on the steps to a mill in the Grain Market exchanging jokes and rumors with one's friends. While thus assuming a more central role in one's social

life, the activities in the mosque also become less distinct from those going on outside.*

The same point might be put from the other side — namely by saying that the suq seldom ever has a singularly economic quality and that it rather might be seen in its turn as an extension of life in the adjacent mosque. For village and tribal markets at least are not just arenas into which everyone leaps, economic fists at the ready for battle, where anything goes in terms of bargaining, self-interest, profit calculation, and getting as much out of the other fellow as possible. The suq is intensely personal and social. Relations of honor and good faith are as crucial there as are the niceties of local forms of accounting. Transactions are marked by language in which reiterations of pious formulas and the swearing of religious oaths on the Quran and by the Prophet are an integral part. The fact that they are conventional, are formulas, are constantly and automatically produced is testimony to their absorption into life and not to a superficiality or insignificance.

This kind of incorporation of the mosque into the social life of communities is one that we must emphasize. For most people a visit to the main, central mosque (often called the great or Friday Mosque because it is there that men attend the communal Friday prayers and listen to the sermon) is a once-a-week event only. Other prayers may be in any one of the small local mosques. Many of these will have neither the dome nor minaret that are so often regarded by non-Muslims as necessary elements by which a mosque is identified (for example, the lower mosque in the Lebanese village had neither of these two elements, whereas the upper mosque made them the dominant and most visible aspects of its entire form because they are most obviously attention claiming and inexorably draw the gaze). They may be small buildings, scarcely noticeable from the street and easily passed, unlike the saints' shrines, which stand out from their surroundings by their characteristic of having a dome upon a square base.

Such local mosques are rarely part of those large complexes

* *Market, Mosque and Mafraj* (Stockholm: Stockholm University Press, 1977), p. 174.

of buildings and spaces that are associated with Friday mosques — the mosque itself flanked by perhaps a decorative water fountain, baths, *medreses* (religious schools), a saint's shrine, a market, an old caravanserai, a government administrative center. Only rarely do they establish a commanding physical presence in a sense that geographically orients space and defines it. Yet they are vital signifiers of the identity of a particular community in a particular place. Such a mosque is more than the frame within which that community as a congregation of Muslims meets. It is a sign of the constitution of a number of people as a community and not merely as an agglomeration of individuals that has neither corporate existence nor claims to it.

Here, too, politics and the local structures of power and authority play their part. The establishment of mosques has very often in Islamic history been the task of the ruler, administrators, or notables. It therefore represents a legitimate order of the community and its rulers. Equally, the absence of a mosque may reflect a refusal of legitimacy to a community, a negation of its claims to be a group. A modern illustration of this principle can be taken from north Lebanon. Some of the feudal lords of the plain of Akkar, precisely those lords who still lived in fortress buildings and relied on more traditional means of sanctions and coercion for their maintenance, were dependent on laborers brought in to work as semiserfs on their land. As part of the lords' domination of the laborers the latter were refused either a mosque or a cemetery.* They were landless agricultural workers; they were defined as being without a social territory or space, without a communal identity in that spot. The denial of a mosque was a radical imposition of power by the lords, who wished to refuse any indication that the laborers existed as anything more than a fragmented agglomeration, completely alienated from the setting in which they stayed, as it were, only temporarily and as dominated objects. (The laborers' shacks were spoken of as shelters, not houses, and they owned neither draft animals nor tools. It is hardly surprising that throughout the early 1970s there was persistent "trouble" for the lords on the plain.)

* I am speaking of conditions prevailing up to and during my fieldwork in 1971/72.

Whether a mosque exists or not, however, a Muslim can construct a sacred space set apart for prayer in any place — in his own or another's house or outside in the street if he wishes. He must only direct himself toward Mecca and make the proper ritual ablutions to purify himself in order to pray. We should realize that even in a crowded mosque each worshipper has an invisible but highly defined zone around him that constitutes "his" sacred space. It may be literally marked out, often by his shoes carefully placed in front of him sole to sole so that they do not tread on holy ground. It may be a prayer mat of some kind that serves the same purpose. The identification of a prayer mat as necessary to prayer, however, is mistaken. It is the space that it delimits that is significant normally, not the fact that a mat is used.*

Whether a mat is used or not, the personal sacred space of prayer exists. A stranger will quickly notice that anyone walking in front of a person praying will do so at a certain distance beyond the invisible but real barriers. We are not particularly dealing here with law and theology, though it is actually a matter of prescription by some of the Islamic legal schools who hold that if someone does step into the sacred zone, the worshipper's prayer is invalid and must be recommenced. Rather, we are dealing with a matter of people's everyday experience of constituting certain kinds of space around themselves. The boundaries of this space protect against intrusion by external forces at a key moment for the individual, the moment of the direct approach to the Divinity. These forces may be nonhuman, too, for the devil (*shaitān*) or evil spirits may attack the believer unless he is guarded by the invisible boundaries surrounding him. Just as in Sufi rituals the members of the Sufi orders regard the outer rank of worshippers as a barrier keeping out dangerous powers, so in prayer the person is protected by this zone, which is not

* Where a rug or small carpet is used, it frequently has notions of spiritual or social hierarchy and precedence attached to it. Religious figures of prestige and authority, such as locally known sheikhs, may use such a rug, and when they do, it becomes a powerful symbol and even instrument of holiness. It is a sacred mark of power, *has* power and baraka in it, and represents the gifts that are associated with the particular sheikh. In certain societies, such as Egypt, the rug, or *sigada*, becomes a term that is identified with the leadership of a Sufi order. The possession of the sigada is an indication of the sheikh's legitimate claim to succession as head of the order and at ritual meetings he will usually be seated upon it.

conceived of as symbolically standing for something but as a real force that repels alien presences. All contact with the Divinity, as with all kinds of nonhuman or superhuman powers, is hedged around with dangers, ambiguities, elements that are by definition beyond human control. In prayer man is vulnerable. At the moment when he is most stripped of his worldly identities, most alone with the God of the community of Muslims, the space around him is an active field that must be controlled if the prayer itself is not to be disrupted. The mosque is one such space. But more than the mosque, which is still socially linked, there is this final individual space that clothes him at his most naked and unadorned.

Changing Space: From Maglis to Salon

When changes occur in the construction of spatial relationships, they may do so not only in the rearrangement of particular, already existing forms but by the creation of new forms that mark a major break with all others and with the social principles upon which those existing forms have been based.

We have already remarked for our Lebanese village on the transformations represented by the château and the country house (if we may so term a building that is determinedly urban in its model). They crystallize a separation between what is now identified as traditional and what is seen as modern by the dominant classes. Unlike the fortress houses, the two new palaces (built in the 1920s and the late 1940s, respectively) were clearly intended as splendid rural seats for men whose center of economic and political operations was shifting to Beirut and the national level. They were no longer limited to the village and the northern plains and hills, though they needed to maintain local domination. Their palaces are both a display — architecture as conspicuous consumption and as cultural and political signs of a shared life-style to visiting members of the ruling classes — and a rupture with the regional setting that had been their unique social and power base.

These two buildings therefore translate the phases of the new and more comprehensive kind of domination under which the peasantry and retainers have fallen since the 1920s: They are living not only under a continuing semifeudal system, but also under the more abstract forces of an integration of the region into the overall economic system of a Lebanon that has emerged as a great commercial and financial center of international significance. To the commercial and financial upper classes (to which the successful lords belong) *traditional* is a word synonymous with *backward*, unless it is the purely decorative pseudotraditionalism of "folkloric" dances and charming costumes. Tradition in this sense is something that is constructed by the ruling classes over a very precise historical period, and it has this double aspect. On the one hand, *tradition* labels the way of life of the rural poor, the sharecroppers and smallholding owners, the casual laborers (upon whose labor many of the lords still depend, of course). On the other hand, *tradition* refers to a purely surface, prettified form of what in England would be called "olde worlde." But *tradition* in a third sense — of a generally accepted code of legitimations, activities, rhythms, and sanctions and as a model for social life with a very important religious component — is firmly set aside. For it is no longer a model in the economic and political system of twentieth-century Lebanon as far as the ruling groups are concerned. The fortresses themselves have undergone a sea change. Only the least successful of the lords' families live in them all year round. For actually to reside permanently in such a fortress, the traditional homes of the lords, is now a mark of precariousness, not of power, of economic decline and marginality, an inability to keep up with the enormous increase in consumption expenditure to stay in the political competition at the top. A fortress for the successful is now a charming summer residence, a place in the country for those who operate in Tripoli or Beirut, whereas their poor cousins remain in their "traditional" home because they are indebted and on the way out.

This process of transformation reaches in the social heart of the house, the reception room (*maglis*). This is the crucial space in which the family and all the different degrees of outsiders meet. It is there that the forms and significances of space have been changed in ways that have had a great impact on domestic and public life. And because it is also pre-eminently the space where model behaviors and strict observation of the sacred and hierarchical relationships between people occur, such changes are fundamental for our understanding of the shifting role of religion.

The maglis is a key zone in the symbolic and social world. It may be used for prayer, the men lining up behind the prayer leader facing Mecca, while those not praying remain seated behind or to the side of them, but not in front, for that would impinge on the space of the worshippers and might invalidate the prayer. On all other ritual and general social occasions, such as funerals and marriages, food will be served there to guests. The reader will chant the Quran from the place of honor in the maglis, and if a family wishes to hold a mulid (services in honor of the Prophet Muhammad), that is where it will be performed.

The room is characterized by the wide range of transformations that can occur within it. It is usually a space of extreme simplicity of appearance: cushions, mats, or low divans are placed all around the walls facing inward. There may be a place for making coffee in one corner, and the hubble-bubble pipes to be offered to senior men will be standing on a shelf. The setting is austere. Everything within this uncluttered space is functional and draws no attention to itself. It can be made to serve many purposes, and within it can be created many social patterns of meaning. In relation with the outside the maglis is sacred. On entering, men take off their shoes, from the right foot first as they cross the threshold. Once inside, they are within the sacred space of their host, under his charge and protection. Their presence does him honor.

Strangers and guests may sleep there, or members of the family may temporarily or permanently use the maglis for sleeping. Social evenings of conversation, card playing, and joking are held there and so are vital negotiations over the settlement of disputes or blood money. When a guest comes to the house, it is here that he will be entertained, and anyone entering the maglis will sit in a fairly precise order of locally recognized seniority and precedence. The most senior and high-ranking will be seated along the wall that is farthest from the door (that is, the most "inside" area of the room). Someone who is accorded particular honor may be seated on a sheepskin. Everyone has his place, and a glance around will reveal to the knowing eye a whole scale of ranking in the places in which different individuals are sitting relative to the guest or most important visitors.

While this kind of public occasion is in progress, junior members of the family, particularly unmarried males, will be sitting by the door, at the most remote point from the guests; they only enter their space as servants in order to bring coffee or refreshments. But as soon as those defined as nonfamily (and whose presence has therefore made the occasion instantly into a public one) leave the maglis, the young men of the family will move forward and seat themselves at the sides of the room but away from the space of their fathers, uncles, or elder brothers. Family hierarchy is spatially as marked as public ranking.

Women will never appear there when any kind of public event is going on. It is not that a woman's presence pollutes the room. It is rather the nature of the occasion that determines her presence or absence. As soon as the maglis reverts to "private" use, then it is part of the "inside" again and thus belongs to her realm, too. In this space, where inside and outside meet, where nonfamily enters into the one setting in the house into which they may enter without violation or profaning of the basic sacredness of family space, the women remain within the closed and nonvisible space to which no stranger may penetrate.

The maglis can be the scene both of the most important of religious and ritual ceremonials and of purely family activity. It is multidimensional, but the different dimensions are clearly differentiated. Interaction is carried out through precise and appropriate verbal conventions of discourse that will frame and fill the occasion in the proper ways and will mark out the different boundaries and relations of those present. Each new entrant must symbolically mark that entry with the correct religious formulas: *"As-Salaam 'aleikum"* (peace be upon you), to be answered with *"Wa 'aleikum as-salaam"* (and upon you be peace). If the man is of no social account, that suffices as greeting. If he does have, or claims to have, some social position, then he will go all around the room greeting each person in turn, and all will stand for him. There is an immense range of nuance for the location of individuals through posture, speech, and etiquette on a social scale of influence, prestige, family links, age, seniority, and so forth.

Such a space is still found (the local mayor maintains one of this kind, as does another local political notable anxious to maintain a consciously "Arab" dimension). But increasingly this space is being defined as old and traditional, and a new kind of space is being introduced. This is what is called the salon.

A stronger contrast in virtually all dimensions with the maglis would be difficult to imagine. The model for it, of course, is originally French, but here it is rather local perceptions of what a "real" salon should be, perceptions derived from visits to the houses of notables in Beirut or Tripoli. They in turn are based on the Lebanese-French model evolved out of the commercially based *haute bourgeoisie* as the acme of taste and style. Indeed, the display of the particular family's wealth and taste is quite central to the nature of the salon, in which the visitor finds himself in a kind of dazzling display case like one beautiful object among others. Everything scintillates, everything reflects. Everything *is* its surface, its appearance. The chairs are usually high off the ground (unlike the mats and low divans of the maglis). All the wood is covered in gold paint or gilt. The seats and backs are in shining real or imitation silk. The walls are covered with mirrors — gilt-framed — and if they have on them, in ornamental calligraphy, verses from the Quran or the Names of God, then the calligraphy is also executed in glittering material set out in the most elaborate and, again, of course, gilt frames. The lighting is through crystal or plastic chandeliers that hang down low into the room and dominate the middle and upper space. The tables are in polished marble, as is the floor. All around there are knickknacks — pieces of china, ornate and highly colored vases, decorative baubles of one kind or another, ornamental hubble-bubble pipes, a riot of reflecting surfaces. Perched high on his chair, the visitor catches endless reflections of himself from all angles and a thousand glittering sources. The image is all.

We might express the change from maglis to salon by saying that things have been turned inside out. Just as the château opens to the world and sets up relations of inside to outside that is quite the opposite of the fortress, so the salon is a transformation of the maglis that contradicts all the principles of the latter. In the salon the surface is the message. The display, the furniture (in itself an idea or concept that has no reference to the maglis and does not exist as a category in that universe), fills the room and defines it. Indeed, it *is* the room. So in a sense we might say that the salon empties out the meaning or the range of possible meanings that the maglis has. The salon is one-dimensional, full of objects rather than significations, desacralized — shoes are kept on; carpets show wealth and taste and are not for sitting on or for prayer; the Quranic verses on the walls are decorations rather than powerful signs.

Whereas anyone can have a maglis, a salon can only be assembled by those who have the money for this conspicuous and dazzling display. It becomes merely an expression of its owner's wealth, whereas it is the people in the maglis who are an expression at many levels of its owner's social position and relationships. The rococo, impersonal glitter of the one is in stark contrast to the multidimensional personal richness of the other.

The salon is therefore a "cold" space: neutral, empty, neither really in nor of the house, a consumption object that is no more than the sum of its parts, an agglomeration of expensive, shining surfaces. You do not sleep, play, joke, sprawl, meet, eat, or pray there. All these things are made impossible by this form of space, which has been imported by the dominant commercial bourgeoisie as an image of their foreign masters and models. In that way the salon does indeed faithfully reflect (suitable word!) the significance of very basic social changes throughout the Middle East.

The salon does more than reflect. It is a model for others. It devalues the maglis, much as the château and the country house do the space and house forms of the village. It is a reference symbol for those of the lower strata who aspire to demonstrate their worldly position in a social system increasingly dominated by monetary value, an individual's market position, and purely economic differentiations as vital to a man's standing in the community. Such people who wish to assert their own capacity to have a salon as well create imitations of imitations — their own versions of the dominant groups' version of the space of the nineteenth-century European bourgeoisie. But they are poor. What is crystal and silk in the salons of the Lebanese middle and upper classes is plastic and cheap cotton in the rooms of the few peasants who pretend to a minute but crucial economic advance over the others. The walls become an exhibition of their conception of display and of appropriate images of social status: not elaborate gilt mirrors and pictures, but photos, pious texts in cheap ornate frames, calendar pictures of Swiss mountains, ballet dancers, stags at bay in the Highlands of Scotland — a kind of patchwork stitched together almost at random by the individual as his own newly assembled collection of icons that is "on show" along with the rest of the room.

For the villagers, however, the space thus created presents considerable problems and confusions in practice and logic. What sort of space is it? What is possible within it and what is unthinkable? No one is quite sure. Fuzzy logic becomes uncertainty, nonlogic, incoherence. So some people remove their shoes on entry, and some do not. If anyone wishes to pray there, the room has to be emptied of the imitation marble tables and standing ashtrays and reorganized. Most people end up praying outside in the yard. When friends want to play cards on the long winter evenings, they automatically move down off the chairs to the ground, where the specifically "play" and joking relations of cards may occur (including tremendous mock ferocity, highly obscene language, ritualized insults, and a suspension of all the conventions of rank and respect). When one is seated up off the ground, it is culturally difficult to play cards and perform such highly regularized informality.

Only one group, as a group, seems to resist the salon's challenge and to insist on preserving the austere and now traditional maglis. That group is the sheikhs. The men of religion in north Lebanon who play a public role, have disciples, act politically sometimes for the lords, or are respected by some for their piety, protect the image of the asceticism of the maglis. Here the space becomes even more consciously a model of a moral order — unostentatious, unworldly, full of inner, not outward meanings (though cynical villagers, if they are hostile to a particular sheikh, will quickly hint at the kind of show that apparent piety makes).

The receiving of strangers, hospitality as a religious duty, offerings and prayer, mulids celebrating the honor of the Prophet Muhammad, and Sufi rituals are dominant activities. In such a specific universe of symbol, belief, and practice the maglis opposes the salon as much as, in terms of certain aspects of local ideology, the sheikh opposes the lord. The two opposing spaces are images of the sacred and the profane, of inner meaning against outward appearance.

As the dominance of the commercial bourgeoisie grows ever greater in the Lebanese setting, this opposition of maglis to salon becomes more acute, not less. The moral economy that it represents resists the devaluation that the salon implies. So there is a kind of active challenge here, too. Where the salons of those villagers who try to create them are an uneasy and confusing combination of symbolic, cultural, and social forms, the maglis of the sheikh is more and more seen as a pure type of religious, moral, and social space that the salons, characteristically created by the lords, cannot negate.

Space, Power, and Tradition

Space is not a kind of pure, given form but is a set of structures and relations that have to be learned, absorbed into what is taken for granted, and constantly acquired in everyday life. These structures and relations may be highly codified and defined very strictly in social terms, or very flexibly, or both at different times and seasons. As the rhythms and activities of a society change through the day and the year, so the use and meanings of space that are appropriate for a given phase or moment shift as well.

Space is crucial in thinking about culture and ideology because it is where ideology and culture take on physical existence and representations. These material forms embody, reinforce, and order universes of power and belief. People learn them, absorb them as part of the "as it is," everyday nature of things. Definitions of those universes may also be imposed and maintained by certain groups over others, and those groups will therefore have quite different experiences and apprehensions of space.

The point is that these different experiences and meanings — sometimes complementary and at other times even contradictory — are the essence of cultural systems. People have different purposes, group and individual interests, and networks of social relations. They are placed in different areas of social space, with different activities, appropriate behaviors, and values that may be either closely controlled or relatively open. So even a system of high control and definition, as north Lebanon, in fact contains all kinds of "as if" areas: "as if" men do not see women, "as if" children are not there, "as if" such and such an insult had not occurred because nobody "saw" it. The practices that actually form social life thus operate on what Pierre Bourdieu calls a "more or less" fashion according to a "fuzzy" logic.

At points in the social setting where groups with distinct perspectives and interests and experiences must meet, some sort of practical coherence and order has to exist if a relationship is to be possible. In north Lebanon much of that coherence comes from the imposition of certain patterns of economic, political, and ideological relations through the lords and their dependents-allies.

At other points that coherence is maintained by "as if" conventions and by the separation in space and time of persons whose activities cannot be socially united: Women do not go to the water spring at the village center, they walk in the unseen zone of the paths, are socially invisible whether or not they are physically veiled. Moreover, the significance of the central domain of women, the house, shifts according to the particular perspective of males and females. There is no rigid, logical, and symbolic scheme that fundamentally opposes the house, with all its sacred values to the outside world of varying kinds of outsiders. Bourdieu, who has extensively studied the meaning of the Berber house, expresses the shift in this way:

> The house, for example, is globally defined as female, damp, etc. when considered from outside, from the male point of view, i.e. in opposition to the external world, but it can be divided into a male-female part and a female part when it ceases to be seen by reference to a universe of practice coextensive with *the* universe, and is treated

instead as a universe (of practice and discourse) in its own right, which for the women it indeed is.*

These brief reflections on the various dimensions involved in analyzing space may show something of their complexity. The part played by specifically Islamic forms and institutions is always interrelated with other forms and always in a particular context. As mosque and market are often linked, so are the code of honor (the sacred identity of the individual and the family) and the countervailing forces of divine authority placed in sacred areas, and through shrines and holy men being transmitted to others. What I have stressed are the distinctions and tensions, sometimes even contradictions, that are generated and the ways in which they are expressed in space.

Even mosques, as we have seen, can have very contrary ideological and social significance. Their enormous symbolic and practical importance makes them both signs of community and also fit signs of the prestige and power of the rulers. We noted that there is often a tension between their separations from ordinary social space and their intimate relations to the world. The two mosques of the village can be viewed as models of different aspects of the relationship between religion and society. The lower mosque is part of the same universe as the maglis and the order that prevailed before a new economic and political system transformed Lebanese society. At its side are three qualitatively different kinds of space: that of the lords (the fortresses, and, later, the château and the country house) above, that of the aghawat just below them, and quite to the other side, across the space of the dead (the cemetery), the clustered, tightly jammed together apparent confusion of the peasant dwellings. The old mosque is the meeting point, the only possible meeting point, of this highly stratified community.

The new mosque speaks a different language — that of the salon and the château. Its symbolic reference is apparently to traditional Islam in its flamboyant use of the minaret (from which the call to prayer is seldom made in this case) and the dome and colonnades. But in fact it is an outward form of

* *Outline of a Theory of Practice* (Cambridge: Cambridge University Press, 1977), p. 110.

Islam, an appearance, that suits the old feudal lords turning bourgeoisie. In fact it expresses very much a bourgeois conception of Islam. It is a showpiece of worldly prestige and expenditure that is quite alien in its chandeliered and carpeted grandeur to the local peasantry and quite familiar to the ruling elite.

Most important, it is above all the other buildings, as are the fortresses and palaces. This theme of being above, looking over or down on others (literally as well as figuratively), is a very powerful symbolic element in this culture. It relates closely to the constant concern over "seeing," who sees whom, when, and where. Seeing without being seen is knowledge, perhaps even power. Houses are so built, windows so sited, entryways so constructed that no one can see in. Not being seen save by the privileged and authorized few is one of the things that separates out the most sacred and dangerous in life — the women in the house, the secret, inner knowledge of things that only the sheikh can see. In public places the very publicness, the "being seen," is both a guarantee and a risk. Around the lower mosque anyone may go: It is no one's space, it is communal. But that openness means the ever-present possibility of an attack on a man's sacred honor, his identity, his self. At the mosque and in the market powerful religious sanctions hedge round with prescriptions and taboos this uncertain zone into which anyone may come and where the symbolic game of "seeing" is at its most intense. So to look down on others, while, of course, they cannot do the same to you and cannot even see you and may not know when they are literally "under observation," is of cardinal importance.

Yet there have always been very strong forces that have found in Islam a defense and an attack against precisely this new kind of domination. As it has grown since the 1960s particularly, the movement of traditionalism (of different versions) has been eagerly adopted by those who do not participate in or who challenge the social models of those who "look down." The maglis becomes more powerfully a symbol of the sheikhly, religious, authentic life in north Lebanon, for example. It is a moral setting, reflects a local and universalist conception of space that is identified as real as opposed to the show of the lords' salons. At the same time, it acquires political significance. To keep a maglis is to declare an allegiance, usually a highly self-conscious one, to Arab identity, Muslim identity, a rooted historical identity. I have mentioned the local politician who scrupulously preserves the spatial and ritual forms of the maglis. He does so as a sign of rejection of outside, nonindigenous forces, as an appeal to nationalism. Yet it is as highly self-conscious as the attempts by others in the village to create their own versions of the salon in poor imitation of their masters. The place in the house which is set apart to be seen in becomes more and more problematic. The reasons for that go very deep and touch the daily practice of religion. In doing so, of course, they also touch very profoundly peoples' experience of the material, physical, and constructed world of space.

CHAPTER 9

The Sacred in the City

A Touch of the East

Minarets in Dalston and a daily chant to the faithful. Now that should cause tongues to wag overtime in the days ahead.

There will inevitably be those who see the proposal as yet another step away from the traditional British scene and an unwelcome intrusion of an alien influence.

Others will doubtless be more accommodating, seeing the plan more as an exotic addition to the otherwise boring skyline of Hackney and as a natural development in a nation that has long been mongrelised.

Others will probably not care a jot either way so long as the scheme does not interfere unduly with the fabric of their everyday lives.

Thought about logically, there can be no real objection to the minarets.

Britain's architecture has been influenced for many centuries by the style of buildings admired in other countries. Almost every building of note, from St. Paul's cathedral down, has owed a great deal to architecture seen and admired elsewhere in Europe or even farther afield.

Likely to be less popular or defensible is the proposal to amplify the five-times-daily chant to Muslims of the area.

It is perfectly true that we accept and enjoy the ringing of church bells that are a great deal more noisy, and that we tolerate the incessant shriek of sirens from police, ambulance and fire vehicles.

And the chant could well become a useful means of checking the time for those not in the Muslim faith.

It will be interesting to see how neighbours of the mosque will greet the proposal, and how Hackney Council will ultimately deal with it.

But provided the noise level is not too high for comfort, there seems no great grounds for opposition. The minaret could even become a focal point of interest in the years ahead; one of the points of interest in a landscape that is becoming increasingly stark and unimaginative.

Hackney Gazette (November 29, 1977)

Dalston is a largely impoverished area of the northeast London borough of Hackney. It is a "deprived area," in the dead, modern terminology that hides so much reality. Its population is a complex ethnic mixture, predominantly poor and lower working class with a large immigrant population. Small shops and businesses come and go, and the employment possibilities and tax base become more and more precarious as firms fold up or leave. An apparently odd place to begin an inquiry into the forms of Islam in the city!

Hackney will serve our purposes here, nonetheless, because it has recently had to face a symbolic and material intrusion of Islam that is disconcerting to its English and non-Muslim residents.

The five-thousand-strong community of Turkish Cypriot immigrants (who are all Sunni Muslims) want to put minarets on the mosque (a converted synagogue, just to add piquancy to the story) they have instituted. Under three banner headlines — *"Turks seek daily prayer chants — Minarets planned for Moslems' Dalston mosque — They also hope for dome on former synagogue"* — the local weekly paper, the *Hackney Gazette* tried to come to terms with a phenomenon that clearly more than slightly baffled, even embarrassed its editorialist.

The uneasy tone, the uncertain balancing of those who resent the *immigré* presence (the borough has its share of racist groups and tensions) and those who don't mind a bit of the "exotic" in an already "mongrelised" nation, of the noise of the prayer call with the police siren and the benefits of telling the time (it won't help at all, of course, since the call to prayer goes by the sun, not by fixed hours), and the final doubting yet hopeful rationalization of the minaret as a "focal point of interest" all illustrate the difficulty of making sense of this new form.

For the Turkish community, of course, the mosque is an outward and visible sign of presence, community, self-definition, installation — a separate universe and a center of another form of social life under a different symbolic canopy. It is also a symbol and expression of "being here" (as is the vast mosque built on the high-prestige and high-visibility site of the north side of Regents Park in one of London's most fashionable areas, though in a much more ostentatious and luxurious and powerful sense). It costs, moreover, fifty-five thousand pounds. For these are not *immigrés* from many different regions and countries trapped in the position reserved for them in the European economic universe as *Gastarbeiter* ("guest worker"), economically within but politically and socially outside society, living a fragmented and atomized existence in dormitories, crowded lodgings, isolated slums, or shantytowns on the fringes of the industrial cities. On the contrary, the Turks here are from a relatively small and homogeneous community of origin in Cyprus, and they have built up, through the restaurant and catering trades, electrical shops, garages, and other small service centers, an economic base to which the increasing number of social clubs and cafés also bears witness. They have reached a point where a large, public, imposing building can be created. They do not need to efface themselves, nor are they social invisibles or spatially isolated, as are so many bidonville dwellers. Minarets can be planned to rise above the "stark and unimaginative" landscape of working-class Dalston, and newspaper writers can be left to struggle anxiously to provide some rationalization of this new and unique intrusion that will make sense to the public.

For, of course, even though it is only a simple, isolated

building, it is an intrusion and an imposition on the land-scape. It does jar, does stand out, disconcert, throw a bit off balance, require an editorial. It doesn't fit. Mosques are all right in books, and minarets are a cliché of the "Arabian Nights." But in Dalston? Then it becomes a question of unknown meanings, messages we cannot all understand, separateness and distinctions, a civilization and a history, even a kind of power that the media increasingly speak of as "the resurgence of Islam."

Imagine — and it is very difficult for those who have not experienced the world of the colonized — the effect that outside forces, over a relatively short period of time, can have on the transformation of the *whole* of the relations that make up urban space, including its sacred geography and unquestioned givens of the way things are in cities. Imagine, not only one building being constructed on an alien model, but an entire system of urban life in its economic, political, and symbolic-cultural forms being imposed upon already existing towns and cities that have been organized on quite different bases. Think of the disorganization and disarticula-tion of meaning and practical life, and of the power that bringing about such a change must entail.

If we can get even some inkling of the impact and intensity of such a process, which is precisely a process that has affected so many Third World societies, we shall be on the way to understanding a very important dimension of our relations with those societies.

The Impact of Colonialism

I want to suggest some of the ways in which the form and practice of the colonial city have affected the cultural and social life of the modern inhabitants of Middle Eastern towns and cities. As ever, Islam in its various guises is only one dimension in the transformations that have occurred. But its symbolic importance has been highlighted because in the clash with the colonial powers it became for so many groups in so many distinct ways a banner and definition of what was and is being fought for. The cultural representations of the city, and of the relations of the city with the village and the desert, have all developed and changed in complex ways in the colonial and postcolonial periods. Islam and the practices and conceptions of Islam have undergone a sometimes quite radical evolution linked to these mutations of the social and, more particularly here, urban order.

One mark of this impact of the colonial relationship is the fact that Middle Eastern cities are often thought of as, and seem to the casual visitor to be, divided into a kind of dualistic universe between Western and non-Western, modern and traditional. Scholars have frequently tended to define the indigenous forms by a contrast with Western towns. The latter are taken as a kind of measuring gauge or benchmark. In this perspective, the so-called traditional and "Islamic" cities are almost inevitably viewed negatively, as lacking certain key institutions present in the West, as being non-functional and an obstacle to the needs of the modern economy and social organization.

They have also been experienced by colonial administrators, travelers, and tourists as exotic, confusing, even threatening. How often we read that the stranger feels lost in the unnumbered and unnamed streets and passages that turn and twist in an apparent contradiction of organization and orientation. One's whole sense of direction is suddenly, perhaps frighteningly, completely irrelevant. One cannot use it to order this apparently orderless urban universe because the principles and practices on which it is based are quite different.

The traditional city or quarter is seen as not part of an urban system at all. The actual social logic of its relations and forms escapes the outsider. It is confusing, a jumble of incomprehensible messages, a noise, a mystery, the antithesis of our natural attitude to the city and what we unthinkingly know the city to be.

This powerful sense of alienation and of something that escapes one's comprehension and control reflects a real contrast. But at the same time it hides the true basis and nature of that contrast and the interdependence and relations between the seemingly divided traditional and modern urban worlds. It also conceals the meaning and development of this notion of the traditional city, which has come to play a very interesting ideological role.

The material, cultural, and symbolic transformations of urban space go back most specifically to the nineteenth century. It is then that we find city space being produced and controlled in new ways. In the Middle East, as elsewhere in the colonized world, this transformation was under the commercial and frequently political and/or military domination of capitalist European nations. In many cases colonial powers acted directly, taking over and constructing their own capitals, new towns and quarters and administrative centers that they saw as totally distinguished from the indigenous urban world.

Even where local rulers remained politically independent, not dissimilar processes were set in train. Those figures who, like the Pasha Muhammad 'Ali of Egypt, attempted to strengthen their independence from both the Ottoman Empire and encroaching Europe by borrowing European models of science, engineering, education, administration, and military organization also saw a need to reform and rebuild the urban center of power.

In 1843 the French writer Gérard de Nerval was already ironically lamenting that the Paris Opera in Cairo contained more of the true Nile, the real Egypt, than the Egypt he saw before his eyes. The city he had dreamed of and read about "lies under dust and ashes; the modern spirit and its exigencies have triumphed over it like death. In ten years time European streets will have cut the dusty and dumb old town at right angles. . . . What glitters and expands is the quarter of the Franks, the town of the English, the Maltese and the Marseilles French."

The "dumbness" of the old town is in fact rather de Nerval's own deafness. He no more could understand the inner world of what was rapidly becoming indeed "the old town" than any other outsider of the period. What he sees is a form of French culture being absorbed by the dominant class and imposed on the city.

The new palaces of Muhammad Ali are built like barracks, furnished in the style of provincial social circles, with mahogany couches and armchairs . . . and portraits in oils of his [Muhammed 'Ali's] sons dressed in artillery officers uniform. The whole ideal of the country bourgeois! You

speak of the citadel. . . . I have found a vast square construction rather like a corn exchange dominating the town
which is supposed to be a mosque when it is finished.
Actually, it's a mosque about as much as the Madeleine
[the famous church in Paris that was completed by
Napoleon as a *temple de la Gloire* dedicated to the Grand
Army] is a church. Modern governments always take the
precaution of building habitations for God which can later
serve another purpose when no one believes in Him any
more!*

Though he merely refers to "the modern spirit and its
exigencies" (that modern spirit of which he was in the sphere
of literature so interesting an example), there is a hint that he
is aware of a transformation of the spatial form of the city
being produced by a set of new relations of dependence and
power. There is a social dynamic that he presents as set in
motion by the ruling class and an inevitable European
domination, before which the old city is "dumb" and helpless. A new social, economic, and political order is taking
hold of the city and fashioning it by force. Even the great
new mosque seems in spirit to be entirely of this emerging
order.

Since the models (including those of prestigious domestic
arrangements and dress) are entirely European, the difference
between direct construction of the city as part of the colonial
enterprise and the changes wrought by growingly dependent
rulers during this period is much less than we might have
expected. As economic, commercial, and political dependency
on the West expanded through the nineteenth century in
Egypt (as elsewhere in the Islamic world), so an even more
radical and thoroughgoing change in urban forms occurred,
which explicitly contradicted and was superimposed upon
the previously established structures and logic.

The new social, military, and political center of Cairo
became a testimony to the kind of architecture and urban
planning associated with the name of Baron Haussman and
nineteenth-century Paris. Wide boulevards meet at *étoiles*,
sweeping in a kind of linear grandiloquence straight through

* Gérard de Nerval, "Correspondance" in *Oeuvres*, eds. Albert Béguin and Jean
Richter (Paris: Gallimard, 1952), pp. 895-96.

old quarters, dominating them and making the government control of the town (and particularly the popular quarters) much easier. An imposing spatial rhetoric was produced of European gardens, European squares and arcades, European (predominantly French and Italian) houses and facades and furnishings. There were the great prestige constructions — palaces, villas, embassies, public monuments. In the late nineteenth century Cairo became, or rather parts of Cairo became, an accumulation of signs of the investment by Europe in the Middle Eastern urban universe. Elements of different styles, periods, functions, and meanings were jumbled together in what would have been in Europe itself a totally incongruous, not to say incoherent, way.

For Cairo, and so many other towns similarly appropriated, was *not* passing through the same stages of a unilinear sequence of development that Europe had already passed through on the way to capitalism. It was *not* becoming a great industrial capitalist urban center, or moving from tradition to modernity, or taking on a new urban coherence and homogeneity. Rather it was being made into a dependent local metropolis through which a society might be administered and dominated. The spatial forms grew out of a relationship based on force and a world economic order in which in this case Britain played the crucial role.

The city was becoming, in material ways, a world that had its own sacred forms and relations from which indigenous sacred forms were by definition excluded. Open squares, wide boulevards lined with prestigious and ostentatious buildings, the great social colonial institutions of the hotels and the club, the Anglican cathedral towering on the banks of the Nile, next to the British army barracks with its huge parade ground, with the residence of the English proconsuls a stone's throw away. . . . Religion, arms, and politics together creating a center for a colonial city quite *unlike* the great nineteenth-century cities of Europe, for all the elements of polyglot borrowing.

This universe was not, of course, only expressive and symbolic. It was an instrument of social and ideological power as well as of the hierarchical segregation between colonizer and colonized and between social classes. For out of commerce, banking, landed estates, and the professions arose a bourgeoisie that moved also in the colonial world and owed its nature and place in Egyptian society to its relations with the colonial order. Its standards and styles of life derived from Europe. It adopted the new status paradigms of the colonial city, with its luxury and prestige residential quarters clearly demarcated from work and segregated by class. As land became a commodity bought and sold on the market and a prime area of investment, this class participated in turning the city and housing into a marketable object. They had a hold on space, a control of its uses and forms, which dislocated and disarticulated indigenous urban structures.

The entry of the increasing number of the urban lower classes into this universe was through the services sector — domestic servants, doorkeepers, cleaners, club attendants, vendors, waiters, nannies, shop workers, grooms, mechanics, building workers, and the army of unskilled laborers, many of whom were the product of the disruption of the rural economy. Services were so important partly because the growth in industrial employment was limited and it was not the raison d'être of the expansion of the city.

Moreover, as members of the new bourgeoisie and those members of the merchant classes who were successfully incorporated into the emerging economic and social order moved out of their old urban quarters into the new residential suburban spaces, so too social and cultural separation between classes grew greater and greater, even as their interdependency through the services sector became more intensive.

The old town became what was called the traditional city, though in fact its nature and structure and economy were related to or enormously affected by the imposition of the colonial city. It was the place of the urban masses, a model of what a modern city was not, of a displaced world of politically unstable forces and obscure native practices. It was, to the European, a *ville des indigènes* or, as one observer at the turn of the century* said of the Casbah of Algiers, "a poor little cadavre, fossilised and cancered." This profoundly ethnocentric and ideological view played its part in creating a cosmology of two separated worlds: One was the place of the irrational, secret, superstitious, dark and threatening, diseased,

* The celebrated anthropologist Arnold van Gennep.

tightly packed native quarter; the other was open, linear, public, revealing, centered, rational, and insisting on its hierarchies — the space of power and status.

This colonial city challenged and seemed to triumph over the society's sense of time and history by introducing this radical break with local forces. It threatened the society's collectively held representations of itself, its sacred configurations, as it symbolized also the transformation of the economic and social structure.

Different elements of the colonial city were reproduced even in the smaller provincial administrative centers that became local seats of government. What were the French colonial countries of North Africa, for example, are full of towns in which the square, the gardens, the military parade ground, the church, and the characteristic style of house building of nineteenth-century France were carefully constructed with the coming of colonialism. Of course, there were many variations, and a great metropolitan center such as Cairo is not typical in any simple way of these changes. But it does nonetheless show, in a very acute form, some of the processes of the formation of the modern city in the conditions of subjugation to external codes of meaning and social practice.

The other side of this unequal relationship, the supposedly traditional city in its image constructed by the outsiders, was lost to view behind the ideological screen this image created. And it is not enormously difficult to see why that image took and maintained the force it did (and still does). For indeed indigenous forms do confront the colonial and Western conception of the city with a very different logic of spatial form and practices that was either beyond the grasp of the European and was systematically misunderstood and misrepresented and/or was something to be negated.

Islam was, of course, rigorously excluded from the colonial city, which specifically rejected signs of what was the faith of the subject classes while installing all the marks of the late-nineteenth-century European cosmos of state, church, and technology. But in the precolonial town the sacred (Islamic) order played a major part in articulating spatial forms, as it still does where those areas remain significant in contemporary Middle Eastern cities.

A Sacred Geography

Studies of Middle Eastern towns reveal a broadly similar pattern here. Sacred buildings form a series of points that establish a kind of socioreligious grid that links the quarters. Small mosques, water fountains, Quranic schools, the shrines of holy men, and zawiyas (meeting places for Sufi brotherhoods) make up a sacred geography that identifies and serves as a set of reference points for the city. These buildings are likely to be on the primary routes through the quarters, the routes leading to the main mosque and market and to the "outside," the town or quarter gate and social boundary area. They are collective spaces, with their own associated rhythms of activity that are different but complementary — the mosque prayer called five times daily, the shrine visited on an individual and family basis at any moment but also perhaps the center of a major celebration of the holy man's mulid at a given time of the year, the religious school, the Sufi meeting place. To the mosque come those wishing to proselytize for a politicoreligious movement (the Muslim Brothers of Egypt, for example, frequently gain their adherents by addressing local congregations after prayers, and Sufi groups do the same), just as it serves as a point of entry and contact for strangers.

Moreover, the mosque, the shrine, and indeed the space before a given house or a whole street may be turned into religious space. Tenting or simply sacking across the narrow way between houses, lights, and chairs or mats are sufficient to create the space for prayers and Quran readings on the third, seventh, and fortieth days following a person's death, or for such celebrations as a family holding a mulid for the Prophet Muhammed as an act of piety and thanksgiving. Mats spread on the street extend the mosque or are used by men of the quarter or customers in a shop for Friday prayer (and other daily prayers where convenient) if they are not going to the larger Friday mosque.

Both time and space are punctuated, given a series of complex rhythms and movements and potentialities that are determined by custom and by the myriad local socially defined activities and social relations. There is a multiple functionality, then, characterizing the practice of space within which the sacred takes on an everyday nature as well as marking the extraordinary.

This double-sided quality means that sacred spaces and times are those in which a collective and public world is linked with the more individual and private world of social identity, family, and house, and a series of exchanges and interconnections are made between the two. It also means that the mosque is a natural rallying point within the quarter in times of crisis and a point at which those from outside can penetrate legitimately into the social world of the locality in a conventional way.

The shifting but ever-present boundaries of public and private, open and closed, that are so difficult for a stranger to apprehend become relevant here. We have already seen their operation in our picture of the Lebanese village. In the cities, too, we find that judgments about which social spaces are exterior and outside and which interior and inside, and to whom under what conditions, are crucial. Here also the houses are, as it were, turned in on themselves and present a virtually inaccessible aspect to the world. Within is the zone of closeness, the sacredness of family, honor, and the integrity of women; without is a series of degrees of greater openness, depending on relationships of kinship, marriage, neighborhood, personal status, time of day, and practical activity.

The houses constitute a set of enclosures each centered on a court or yard off which, perhaps in several storeys, are the series of rooms. As children of the family themselves marry and have children, they can take over separate rooms, all looking into the same yard and sharing the same form. Again, flexibility in the management and occupation of space is vital, particularly for the women, for whom the house is a place of relative freedom of movement and meeting. In contrast, in this sphere men obey a more rigid and public set of norms. Furthermore, in poorer areas the streets outside are themselves almost annexed to house and family space and are much less restricted in their use and definition than in the wealthier quarters. Among the poor the inside-outside opposition may be less marked and even some of the women's social encounters and activities may go on in front of their houses, a space that then becomes effectively an adjunct to the family domain. So the ways in which the sanctity of the family is guarded and practiced is also something that differs considerably between social groups in the city.

It cannot be stressed too much that boundaries are shifting and relative to many factors rather than simple blocks of given territory. It is clear from Dale Eickelman's study of Boujad (a Moroccan city), for example, that the local definition and use of the concept of a "quarter" is associated very much with fluctuating patterns of influence and political, economic, or religious clout.* For a quarter to be spoken of as a collectivity there has to be a person or several individuals and families of social standing, with "word." There must be "big men" capable of exercising some authority, of mobilizing groups and followings when necessary, of obtaining services for the area (such as water, electricity, sewage, paving, transport), of seeing that clients and dependents get what they need, and so on. "Closeness" of the people is associated with the "word" of the big men.† The meaning of the term *quarter* in social use is therefore flexible and sensitive to changes over time. Moreover, poor areas lacking in wealthy or influential families and composed of lower-class populations and unskilled laborers and rural migrants may not be regarded as being quarters at all.

The shrine of a holy man and the presence of a family or families claiming to be his descendants or in some way the legitimate guardians of his resting place, are identifying points around which a sense of being a quarter may crystallize. But a shrine in itself is not sufficient to guarantee that the quarter takes on a lasting form.

Holy men's reputations rise and fall, too, though at any given moment they may be felt to be fixed and unaltering stars in the human firmament. They have to be active. Signs of their power have to be visible, which is to say that people must have living practical reasons to sustain the belief in grace and blessing. A family that is socially on the way up or seeking to consolidate a reputation as people of influence and wealth may piously repair the tomb, claim kinship with the venerated figure, hold mulids for the holy man, distribute

* Dale F. Eickelman, *Moroccan Islam: Tradition and Society in a Pilgrimage Center* (Austin, Texas, and London: University of Texas Press, 1976), pp. 99-105.
† "Closeness" is a translation of an Arabic word, *qaraba*, which refers to a wide range of meanings around a basic notion of group feeling, mutual obligation and kinship. Eickelman, ibid., p. 96.

alms and food at his feast *if* the religious form retains a wide range of social acceptance and a sense of being imperative and proper. In such a way, if all else goes right for them, they may succeed in activating or reactivating the idea of a quarter, where people share some collective identity around the shrine and its new servants and maintainers. Other tombs may have a transcending fame far beyond the purely local shifts of social relations and may draw pilgrims, not only at specific seasons but throughout the year, becoming crucial to a whole urban economy in cases where a town is the site of such a holy place.

The Changing of a Holy Town: Boujad

Let us now be more specific and look in greater detail at the town of Boujad.* It is particularly interesting because it illustrates a whole series of social processes of change following colonialism in a North African provincial town famous as a religious center. Here, as in so many settlements of the area, shrines were the symbolic and social center around which the population was clustered. In Algeria and Tunisia in the nineteenth century the zawiya (meaning here the tomb of a marabout, or holy man) was highly significant in this way, not least because in both those societies nomadic groups predominated over sedentary populations in numbers and in economic and political terms. When tribal sections did settle, it was often at such holy places which then formed a series of interlocking points between tribal, peasant and urban societies. The pattern, then, is widespread for the region.

Boujad, too, though in the more urban and sedentary context of Morocco, was focused on the tomb of a marabout, or rather, upon the tombs of marabouts (there were twenty-six such maraboutic shrines). Again, not uncharacteristically, there was a major family of marabouts who wielded enormous influence and power in the town and its surrounding region. The family of the Sherqawa (one of the key marabout's names is Sidi Mhammed Sherqi) controlled twenty-three of the twenty-six shrines and the mosques that adjoined some of them. Sacred geography with a vengeance! The main market

* Eickelman, *Moroccan Islam*, is the source for material on Boujad.

was held in front of the shrine of Sidi Mhammed Sherqi. The maraboutic notables used to act as guarantors of the peace of the market through their baraka and would collect the arms of tribesmen coming into the market and restore them on leaving. Sanctuary also meant that alliances between tribal factions were made binding at a shrine, oaths were sworn there, communal meals eaten to seal such agreements, and offerings and sacrifices were made. Since the town was also a pilgrimage center and had a large religious hinterland, the income generated for the guardians of the holy places as well as for associated traders was considerable. The income was distributed partly within the family and partly as alms to the needy, though it is not surprising to find that in the early period of the French protectorate (which began in 1912) the Sherqawa had a council charged with the distribution of the income of its members.

The links through market and offerings, sanctuary and protection, pilgrimage and caravans, were obviously pluri-dimensional and complex. The circuits of exchange and distribution in which the sacred played a key part in the pre-colonial period are very like those in many other such settlements throughout the Middle East. The "holy family" itself was deeply embedded in local and wider political relations. The leading members had their followings and clienteles, their alliances with tribal groups, their economic interests. Certain fractions of the family were far more important than others, of course, and the less successful (again a characteristic of this kind of system) became de facto dependents or clients of the more powerful cousins whose hold on baraka was stronger. That baraka represented a power that indeed extended throughout social life, passing down from the dominant forces to the town in general and renewed through the shrines' part in the political economy. It was strongly delineated, located, and identified in the web of Sherqawa relations and interests.

What kinds of transformation did the colonial period bring to this structure, in which symbolic capital was so closely intertwined with other kinds of relations?

One important dimension seems to have been the way in which class, commercial, and political oppositions expanded and were, initially at least, contested in religious terms (that is, on the Sherqawa's own ground and in a discourse in which so much of social life might be framed "traditionally"). As the economic predominance of the Sherqawa in the region declined in the 1920s because of French restrictions upon them, some of the Sufi orders (the turuq) enjoyed a period of growth under the leadership of non-Sherqawa elements of the middle class; merchants, craftsmen, and traders. Eickelman quotes the interesting case of a leading merchant who made a fortune out of the period of French "pacification" of the region, a pacification that had robbed the Sherqawa of one of the main elements in their political relations with the tribal populations. This man joined with others to make financial donations to mosques and religious institutions the Sherqawa did not control.* They had also been hit by the diversion of trade away from the caravan routes of which Boujad had been the entrepôt. At this early stage of the protectorate, therefore, one wing of the bourgeoisie rivaled the other in the religious and well-established idiom for such competition through religious offerings and the Sufi orders.

The town slowly became of more limited importance. French colonial settlers took over significant interests in mining and agriculture. Investment was located elsewhere; industries, sugar refineries, and administrative centers were placed in other towns.† Boujad's political and administrative decline relegated it to the status of minor provincial town. The tribal groups whose connections with the Sherqawa had been so marked lost pasture lands and access to grazing because of French controls and a policy of sedentarization and the move, now familiar, to transforming land into private instead of collective property as a commodity for sale on the market. Powerful rural-based political figures emerged who had their own connections and had no need of ties with the religious notables and the shrines.

More dramatically, the period immediately following World War II accelerated these processes and even saw a qualitative, not merely quantitative, change in social organization. Both urban and tribal land became prey to those members of the new bourgeoisie that had arisen (rich merchants and notaries; the professions had by this time become

* Ibid., p. 255.
† Ibid., p. 70.

a force in their own right). Some of them had made fortunes in the famine of 1945. The land market became crucial to the power of this class, who acquired property in town and land from the tribesmen. The latter became sharecroppers, the townsmen paid rent. A different structure of exploitation crystallized in which religion was no longer the chief ideological, economic, or political instrument and identifying idiom.

There is a very interesting shift in social forms, which should be stressed here. The poor, the *lumpenproletariat*, were drawn into the older quarters of the city, often around the shrines as the Sherqawa and the new bourgeoisie of whom some of the Sherqawa were a part moved out into the quite different space of the French-constructed, villa-dominated space of a new city, a modern city, New Boujad.

> Since the Second World War, prosperous Sherqawi merchants in some of the less prestigious quarters have moved to New Boujad and have downplayed their Sherqawi identity. Rural immigrants moving into such quarters then try to claim Sherqawi descent as one means of upgrading their own prestige. The "closeness" of the remaining original inhabitants can no longer be expressed in social action. Not infrequently, entire quarters disappear over relatively brief spans of time as a consequence of this process.*

There develops a much sharper and more distinct set of class-linked separations in the structure of social relations, not least in religious terms. The bourgeoisie is increasingly marked by a stress on sober, reformist, *textual* religious ideology that does not serve as a global basis and legitimation of their economic and political dominance. They move away from the shrines in more than a literal sense. Their new collective representation is the town of the *évolués*, New Boujad, with all that it so well symbolizes of the changes in culture, class, and the wider set of relations that have formed them in the colonial and postcolonial periods.

Sherqawa descent is now in part a language of the lower classes who drift into the traditional space, while the

* Ibid., p. 99.

dominant groups move out. The meaning and ideological significance of the shrine changes as the town's economic and political position in Moroccan society as a whole is transformed. The town remains a religious center, but *not* in a simply continuous sense nor because of some supposed traditionalism of its people. An Islam in which the shrines of the marabouts are a vital center of activity, power, grace, healing, hope, and identity playing an important role more and more associated with the lower classes is placed within a quite different overall framework of power and social organization from that before the protectorate. The tribesmen are now in the city as immigrants, located in the economy as unskilled laborers and in petty services. The state's obsession with sedentarization of the tribes and the land market speculation push them relentlessly off their traditional territories. The forces that determine their position and their ideological affinity with baraka and the shrines are qualitatively distinct from those of the precolonial time.

We cannot leave Boujad without referring back more generally to the question of space, which here as everywhere contains more than its own share of paradox and irony. Images of contradiction, incoherence, and surprising transpositions and remodeling occur. In the late 1920s, for example, a French officer of Native Affairs built arcades around three sides of the main market on the inspiration of a photograph of the arcades around the sacred shrine of the Ka'aba at Mecca. As Eickelman dryly observes: "Since Boujad is also a pilgrimage center, he felt it appropriate that it replicate the Ka'aba. Strictly speaking, tribesmen and Boujadi-s distinguish between the pilgrimage (*hajj*) to Mecca, made during a specified season during each year, and 'visits' (*zyara*-s) made to the shrines of marabouts. . . . Nevertheless, construction of the arcades presumably improved the view of Boujad from the Bureau des Renseignements [Intelligence Office]."* The colonial officer as religious innovator in the name of proper respect for religion!

There are more general unexpected combinations of form and structure. The French geographer Raoul Weexsteen, who has worked on the Algerian town of Blida, notes that the old town is more European than indigenous in appearance. Much

* Ibid., p. 73.

of it had been destroyed in an earthquake and it was rebuilt in colonial style. With one difference. The basic organizing plan remains as it had been before; narrow paths, many cul-de-sacs, and, for the European, a confusing maze of houses. The colonized might use the French building forms, but in indigenous ways, refusing the basic structures and conceptions that underlie them.

Most important of all, Eickelman points to a crucial element in the colonial enterprise: "French policy for Moroccan towns in general divided the city for planning into three zones, for 'traditional' Moroccans, 'evolved' Moroccans, and Europeans. *Each zone was presumed to conform to the 'mentality' of certain elements of the population.*"* This notion of corresponding to a "mentality" perfectly reflects a colonial image of its own order in its relation to the colonized and the "nature" of the colonized, which is held to be expressed in the traditional medina.

The Ideology of the City

In time we have seen that the medina becomes, behind the apparent continuity of its organization, based on different social classes. To the bourgeoisie it is a symbol of archaism, of rejected, backward traditionalism, not part of an embodiment of history and memory that are actively present in the life of society. If anything, it is to be feared as the home of the "mob," politically troublesome and difficult to control. The old center is considered peripheral and full of a marginal, if numerically large, population.

The Moroccan writer Tahar ben Jelloun has spoken of this movement with reference to Fez, the ancient celebrated center of learning and urban culture of Morocco: "Fez, the old town. . . . Will it become a place of pilgrimage and nostalgia? Place of roots, of origins, of knowledge, it is becoming broken by time, lassitude and negligence."† A further possible development is the reappropriation of the old town by the culturally and socially dominant classes as a kind of museum organized according to their (and

* Ibid., p. 74. My emphasis.
† *Le Monde*, January 9-10, 1977, p. 8.

international) conceptions of the "traditional" and of the "Islamic thought" that are taken to have informed it. The elite will recapture the traditional city, with a kind of unquestioning innocence almost, displacing the inhabitants whose practices of the city and of Islam are not suitable for consideration as a fit representation of religion and culture. And so we find a brief announcement in a newspaper as witness to a new version of tradition:

> UNESCO is about to launch next year an international appeal for the restoration of the old imperial city of Fès, in Morocco. A blueprint, elaborated by international experts . . . provides that the historic buildings should be restored and their inhabitants rehoused elsewhere, in order to create centres dedicated to Islamic arts and thought.*

This brief note hides much in its evocative appeal to the idea of restoration. The restoration is not a social one, but rather relates to a surface and functional change. The dwellings now classified as "historic" houses will no longer in fact be houses. They will actually be converted to a totally new and characteristically modern use — as museums, constructions of a distinctly contemporary and class conception of the appropriate material setting for "Islamic thought." The removal of the inhabitants, taken as unproblematically a sine qua non of restoration, shows how easily in the name of a dominant model of religion and culture one can displace a social group as not part of the proper practice of religion and culture.

This displacement is part of the overall process whereby certain classes and groups that are politically and economically dominant in society legitimize a form of religion that increasingly relates to a specifically class view of how Islam is to be defined, practiced, studied, taught, and authorized. This will be the "real" and legitimate Islam, which will be sanctified by its concentration in shrines of modern study and display.

The purposed depossession of the inhabitants of the old city of Fez reaches very deeply, therefore, into transformations of the social practice of Islam in the modern period. It touches on an enormous number of culturally and socially

* Ibid., August 8, 1977, p. 4.

significant elements in Moroccan society and is not untypical of developments elsewhere in the Middle East. The irony is that the very bourgeoisie that moved out of the medina as it emerged under colonialism now, as a crystallized and formed class in the postcolonial period, reappropriates the medina in the name of a supposedly historically conscious desire to preserve an unchanging set of sacred Islamic values. In doing so, of course, it changes once again the social pattern of the city and of religion. Furthermore, its conception of history is limited to a static and elitist view.

This small episode is only one illustration of a much wider trend that has its roots throughout the Middle East in the colonial period: the segregative conception of the urban center. In this case it is instanced by the idea of the setting apart of a cultural center of a particular kind in which "Islam" can be appropriately reproduced and admired. More generally it refers to a linked but must broader set of changes that hinge on this notion of segregation — segregation by class, wealth, function, and political power.

Not only has this occurred, but the ideological and symbolic conception of the city has changed, particularly in its relation to the countryside. The objective basis of this change I have already indicated. In Algeria, Morocco, and Tunisia, for example, in the colonial period peasant and pastoral society became subordinated to urban-based powers and economic relations as capitalism took a greater and greater hold. In economic, political, and social terms, therefore, city and country were more closely bound together within the total framework of colonialism and capitalism. Towns came to dominate society and culture. Urban space was privileged as one of the major defining characteristics of civilization in the new modern order. As states were brought into being, centralized administrations established, bureaucratic apparatuses expanded, the nature of the market shifted, property forms in rural and urban areas modeled on European (in this case French) law instituted, the cities took on a new significance.

Now centuries before this the great North African thinker Ibn Khaldun had seen towns as the real aim of civilization. He had seen, too, a cycle of growth and decay in which they inevitably became centers of inflation, prestige expenditure, and decadence that reflected a loss of social and political solidarity and will on the part of ruling dynasties. These latter are replaced and the town renewed by the desert tribes who take over by conquest and the force of their tribal solidarity. So the desert, in so many ways for Ibn Khaldun the antithesis of urban civilization, serves in these circumstances to recharge the energy and purpose of the city.

An ideology of the town as fundamental to civilization and to Islam has a new significance. In the colonial and post-colonial period the historical setting is quite different from that of any previous period. The town is a conquered place that becomes the center of a new system and new set of economic structures. It becomes the privileged place of the new bourgeoisie, particularly as land and other forms of property become increasingly subject to the market. It is this bourgeoisie that elaborates ideologies of the great importance of urban life for a "true" Islam, in opposition to what it sees as the superstitions and barbarisms of the countryside and nomadic life (both of which are being brought within their control, as we have seen in the case of Boujad). Kenneth Brown's illuminating work on the Moroccan port and market town of Salé in the nineteenth and twentieth centuries shows very well how this ideology of the urban elite intensified specifically in a period when there were enormous upheavals in social status and conceptions of hierarchy, class relations, wealth, and trade.*

The fact that the meaning and practice of contemporary urban life contains these complicated historical transformations has to be grasped if we are to understand forms of Islam in the modern world. Cities involve perceptions and ways of seeing and experiencing that we are still a long way from really being able to describe, let alone in any sense explain. Religion is only one dimension of life that is entailed in this experience, and it is deeply intertwined with many others.

The changing field of the sacred is linked both with changes in rural-urban relationships and with the way in which different classes and groups think and represent those relations. We have seen that modern structures of power and domination have made of the city a particular instrument and

* Kenneth L. Brown, *People of Salé* (Cambridge, Mass.: Harvard University Press, 1976).

expression in ways that are separated from previous indigenous forms of life. The creation of this city is born out of what for many of the population is an alien force, experienced as overthrowing and contradicting not only explicit propositions about the world but also the implicit, commonsense dispositions and ways of acting with which daily life is impregnated without people even being aware of them. The modification of specific institutions under the impact of the commercialization of the city is only the most obvious sign of what is an immensely profound chain of processes. The obliteration of the memory and history of the town marks millions of people's daily existence.

We should not therefore be astonished to find that in times of crisis the modern city is itself called in question, taken to symbolize forces of oppression or a non-Islamic way of life. In this context the hotels, nightclubs, and cinemas that are attacked and burned down have a greater symbolic weight than their apparently banal function might merit them. For radical and millenial groups the city is a home of unbelief, not of sober, textual Islam. The true believer should, in an image that has great historical resonance, go out from the city, leave as the Prophet Muhammed did the hypocritical and unbelieving citizens of Mecca. Everything about the colonial and postcolonial city may be seen as a flagrant demonstration of all that the true believers should refuse and struggle actively against. It is to forms of this refusal and their Islamic dimensions that we must now turn.

CHAPTER 10

The World
Turned Inside Out

FORMS OF ISLAM IN EGYPT

The modern city as it has emerged in a country such as Egypt is a center, image, and form of a particular set of relations. Those relations have changed over time. The city is now apparently possessed by those upon whom it was once imposed. Yet for many a sense of contradiction between the forms of the city and the "real" nature of society remains. It is not too surprising that this city and what it is held to represent should be apprehended and experienced still by members of some groups and classes as symbol and material home of what is opposed to the authentic, indigenous bases of society in faith, law, morality, and social life.

It is out of the arena of these rapidly changing and expanding cities that religious movements of different kinds have arisen to present a whole series of possibilities of association and action. In many cases they had and have at their center the conception of a transformation of the whole nature of society. In fact this sense of totality in the aims and tasks of the movements has been a characteristic organizing notion.

In the 1920s, 1930s, and 1940s such movements were directed both against the foreign holders of power and against those forces that were held to be responsible for the subordination of the nation and the entire Islamic community (the umma). In the 1980s, however, though much of the language and ideology seems almost identical to that of the previous periods, there is a major and quite vital difference. No longer are external powers (colonial, Zionist, or communist) the only cause of our ills or the principal targets of assault. Rather it is the *internally* generated sources of corruption, unbelief, hypocrisy, weakness, and betrayal that are increasingly identified as objects of rigorous criticism or even violent struggle. The entire social order should be overthrown by the righteous, and an Islamic state should be established. Though there is much that remains virtually unaltered in the message of such movements, the social implications have obviously changed in a radical way.

The word *radical* is certainly appropriate for the most important of the plethora of groups that arose in Egypt in the interwar period, the Ikhwan, or the Muslim Brothers. Much of their vital impulse has been to re-create an indissoluble identity of "being a Muslim" from the roots of history and faith upward. I mean by this that they both look to the origins of the Islamic community in seventh-century Arabia as a model and assert a unity of faith and social and political action for the modern world. Being a Muslim, in this view, integrally entails the identification of an Islamic community, a political project that is in turn founded on the Quran and the Sunna and the Holy Law and the imperative to struggle for the realization of an Islamic society. This sense of an indissoluble link of faith, group, and action, the conviction that by being Muslim one is also inexorably bound within a global universe of belief and practice, social, political, and economic, is at the center of the movement's appeal.

The significance of such a refusal to acknowledge a split between religious identity and all other collective and individual dimensions of life can be better appreciated if we look at the origins and evolution of the Muslim Brothers within Egyptian society before considering why it is that they should still be important today.*

The founder, Sheikh Hassan al-Banna, was a young teacher who established the movement in 1929 in the relatively new

---

* The indispensable source for any discussion of the Muslim Brothers is Richard P. Mitchell, *The Society of the Muslim Brothers* (Oxford University Press, 1969).

Suez Canal port city of Ismailia. He came from a religious family (his father was a sheikh and the Imam of a mosque), and he was much influenced by Sufism and Sufi practices. But if he had something of a traditional cultural background, in many other ways he was part of a very new set of social circumstances. The authority of that entire cultural tradition had been challenged by the triumph of colonial, non-Muslim forces both over the Ottoman Empire, which had lost its Middle Eastern provinces to the British and the French following World War I, and more especially over Egypt since the British invasion of 1882. At the very period that the young Hassan al-Banna was founding the Muslim Brothers, there was an efflorescence of groups that were established as nationalist and/or religious movements in an effort to respond to this challenge. Others, less overtly political, came into being as cultural, recreational, and religious clubs, associations, and circles.

More specifically, in the economic and social realms he was part of a new class from which many members of these other groups were also drawn. It was a new class that may broadly be called the petite bourgeoisie that emerged in the context of the colonial economy and the domination of commerce, services, industry, and land by either foreign interests or what had become the Egyptian bourgeoisie of landowners, bankers, merchants, industrialists (and members of the liberal professions). Many of this class of the bourgeoisie, blocked from full development by British control of an economy in which the production of cotton for export had been made the predominant factor, were nationalists. But they were seldom concerned with making some kind of conjunction between nationalism and Islam and indeed were often hostile to the very idea of making such a conjunction. Rather they sought an independent Egypt on models of party political activity and democratic forms that owed a great deal to Europe and the influence of European nineteenth-century thought and practice. It was not clear that there would be any radical transformation of Egyptian society or Egypt's place in the world economy should political independence be achieved under their aegis.

Under pressure from these forces the petite bourgeoisie — artisans, the lower levels of the professions, clerical workers,

small business and enterprise owners — were nonetheless outside the numerically large ranks of the urban working classes
and the mass of those who serviced the cities. These latter
sold their labor when, where, and however they could on a
day-to-day basis in a world without predictable expectations
of work or livelihood. Yet the petite bourgeoisie often had
many ties with these strata: ties of kinship, neighborhood,
social origin, perhaps religious brotherhood or other associational links. And their own economic position was often
insecure enough to threaten a slipping away into the proletariat or the mass of the disinherited.

The economic crisis that, with fluctuations, lasted in Egypt
through the 1930s and 1940s was a constant source of
precariousness to this class and brought them up hard against
the realities of economic life in a dependent society. For
them the political and economic paths also seemed to be
blocked, and they were culturally outside the field dominated
by English and French language and culture that was so
important to the social world and thought of the bourgeoisie.
Their culture was betwixt and between, invaded by the power
of another society whose whole structure was radically other
and which imposed its own order on Egyptian life in many
dimensions. They were dependent on the capitalist market
and involved therefore in a whole series of forces and relations that it seemed could not be analyzed or given any
conceptual, symbolic, or practical order save in Western
terms. And these were terms from which they felt excluded,
which were part of the apparatus dominating Egypt and
which many refused. Thus in some ways they had close
cultural affinities with the traditional sectors, rural and urban,
even if the collective life of those same sectors had also been
systematically ruptured by economic and political change
since the nineteenth century.

A whole series of blockages operated upon them, as upon
all classes in Egypt. In the new towns of the Canal Zone, and
later in a rapidly expanding Cairo, Hassan al-Banna found
large numbers of adherents in this dislocated and fragmented
class. He moved naturally and with a trained conviction in
the Islamic discourse that precisely seemed to transcend all
these blockages, exploding them as it were through the power
of the Word and the vision of a society whose integrity was

that of the true sources of the community back at the time of the Prophet Muhammed's mission. The Holy Law would be the social foundation. Islam was both religion *and* framework of the state *and* a community that went beyond national boundaries. A return to first principles and the practice of the authentic community would transcend with its own imperative coherence the incoherence of Egyptian society.

Since both the Sufi orders and the Azharite sheikhs had failed to confront the problems of the community, a new kind of organization and activity was necessary. The ideology of the Muslim Brothers was not unlike that of many other groups and had a host of antecedents, as did their methods of propagandizing. Members would be recruited through traditional means: by making local mosques and religious institutions the target for proselytizing, spreading the call of the group to different congregations in the cities and later the countryside. Sermons and addresses on the iniquities of the situation in which Muslims found themselves, adherence to nationalist goals of freedom and independence but within an Islamic order that would somehow both retain the original purity of the first community and at the same time confront the contemporary world order in a planned and active way, all won over new members.

There were, as I have said, many groups at this period with approximately the same message, and they pursued other political and associational options. But few had the clarity of organizational conception that was part of the Muslim Brothers from the beginning. Banna was an organizer of extraordinary and very modern gifts. He envisaged three phases for the movement:
1. Winning adherents through "propaganda, communication and information"
2. "Formation, selection and preparation," in which cadres would be chosen, members ranked according to their status and kind of activity in the movement, and an enormous emphasis would be placed on publications, journalism, and meetings
3. "Execution," in which all kinds of changes in society would be struggled for
As time went on, the movement became both complex and

highly efficient. There were "rover" groups that went into the villages and urban quarters on literacy and hygiene campaigns and spread propaganda. A "battalion" system was started. The movement grew and the task of directing it and maintaining control and unity became more difficult for the leadership. It was grouped in "families" and operated a system of cells run, as Richard Mitchell says, primarily as indoctrination units. There were district branches, different sections charged with the supervision of specific activities (for example, physical training, liason with the rest of the Islamic world, dealing with the professions, and so on). Sections were established for doctors, engineers, teachers, lawyers, and other professionals as the movement broadened its social range.

At the head was Banna himself as Supreme Guide and presiding over a Guidance Council to which six main committees reported. A "special section" was founded in 1942, and its operations, mostly secret, became part of a quasi-autonomous and paramilitary organization within the Brotherhood.

The insistence on political and economic activity combined with the capacity to organize and mobilize as the crises of Egyptian society became more and more acute made the Muslim Brothers a most formidable entity and arguably the single most important mass movement in modern Egyptian history. It is very important to note that their apogee was reached in the critical decade of the 1940s. World War II brought with it the black market, profiteering, inflation, and economic crisis. It sharpened the sense of internal class antagonisms and of the military and political implications of British domination of Egypt and the way that domination might be fought.

The movement had an added impetus. By the start of the war the Muslim Brothers were thought to have as many as five hundred branches and a membership of over a million. Throughout the next few years this number increased as a wide range of people found in the Brothers an organizational and ideological response to, and a proffered resolution of, their own and the collective crisis. The bankruptcy and class nature of the political parties hardened a conviction of the need for a total transformation. Some sought it on the left, in the Communist Party, in workers syndicates, or in groups combining different fractions of the left. These were ferociously opposed by the Brothers, who were resolutely antileft and certainly saw no salvation in a revolution in Egypt's social structure.

The young were an enormous reservoir of political support, not only in the universities and schools but more generally among the mass of the population. In the villages, for example, increasingly dislocated by inflation and drawn ever further into the modern market system, established notables and leaders and solidarities had no interest in challenging a social system from which they themselves derived economic and political power. The Muslim Brothers, on the other hand, appeared both as a new, vigorous, and energetic presence, which at the same time was within the framework of a traditional call of Islam. The Brothers satisfied the need to confront in some way the forces they identified as disrupting society (the unbelievers and those who were "against religion") and ministered to what Berque calls "the nostalgia for a cloudy and unlocatable past which was easily subordinated to ideas of Islamic restoration."* Village communities, already acutely vulnerable to the pressures of the market and dependent on a new range of processed goods, had suffered enormously from pauperization and migration. In the 1940s peasants with small and medium-size holdings were under constant economic threat from rising rent costs and inflation. Below them the landless laborers and sharecroppers worked in conditions of poverty and precariousness. They, of all the social classes of Egypt, were outside the political process and severely exploited. Among the peasantry, as in the rest of society, the divisions between the classes were becoming stronger and stronger. Yet they also shared elements of a religious and cultural tradition from which they were by no means totally uprooted: a sense of the powers of Divinity and the Word, and a set of rituals and festivals that punctuated the year and the stages of the individual biography with its own time, rhythms, and kinds of sociability. This tradition was a world apart, or it might be seen to be: a refuge, a source of authority, a denial of those forces oppressing the community.

Banna was always sensitive to the importance of this tradition as to the significance of local spiritual hierarchies and

* Jacques Berque, "Dans le Delta du Nil," *Studia Islamica* 4 (1955): 107.

the prestige of men who held religious positions. The Muslim Brothers' insistence on the fulfillment of religious obligations anchored them in this sea of belief and practice. They added a further dimension of collective organization beyond the boundaries of the local community that accounted for the crises of the changing present in terms deriving from an unchanging and eternal scheme. Their mythologizing of the nature of the beginnings of the Islamic community as a model in some way for the present gave depth and resonance to that nostalgia to which Berque refers. But they did not invoke a passive withdrawal into tradition and religion. The organization offered what it presented as a practical means of realizing this utopian vision and an explicit as well as implicit critique of other religious groups and leaders who had failed in their opposition to non-Islamic forces.

This, in very simple terms, was the basis of the organization and appeal of the Muslim Brothers. There were internal stresses, and it would be wrong to present the movement, particularly after the assassination of Banna himself in 1948, as a totally solidified group. Some felt that a more openly violent struggle should be waged, some that the national leadership failed the movement. The problem of succession on Banna's death was acute, and in another area the relations of the "special section" to other chains of command and decision making were often a source of difficulties.

Their influence, however, was immense, not least among pious and nationalistic young army officers. The latter were often themselves drawn from the petite bourgeoisie, fiercely opposed to imperialist control of Egypt. They were determined to liberate her from that control but at the same time had no developed radical strategy for the transformation of Egyptian society. They would destroy the power of the great landowners which might threaten the revolution, but they were resolute defenders of private property and certainly no more moved than the Brotherhood by sympathies for socialism. Only a minority of the group called the Free Officers who led the coup of 1952 against the monarchy actually belonged to the Muslim Brotherhood, but they shared much of the ideological milieu of its adherents.

The revolution of 1952 left the Brotherhood as the only recognized and permitted political organization apart from the Free Officers. But the relation with the officers, under the emerging leadership of Gamal 'Abd el-Nasser, changed as the wielding of state power and policy came in question. Eventually, in 1954, the Brotherhood was suppressed and effectively driven underground. At different times during the Nasserist period suspected members and leaders were imprisoned and even executed following charges of attempting the assassination of the president and plotting against the state. The movement was apparently crushed.

Arab nationalism and a cult of the leader (the *za'im*) became the dominant ideologies of the state, particularly in the period following the Suez crisis of 1956, in which the British, French, and Israelis were forced to abandon their invasion. "The nation" and "the people," those huge cloudy symbols, were part of this ideology. There was a struggle against colonialism and reactionary regimes in the Arab world, which occurred in the context of an emerging Third World conception of neutralism and anticolonialism that became extremely important in world politics at exactly this period. The ideology was one of change and transformation, of independence and struggle against the powers that had for so long dominated Egypt, of autonomy and progress in history that would be made by the people under the za'im's leadership. No other political organizations were permitted.

Despite this repression during the Nasserist period, however, the Muslim Brotherhood survived. One of the striking things, indeed, about Egypt under Sadat has been the reappearance of their publications, some of their old leaders, and the clear impression that, if the organization is less widespread and elaborate than before, it nonetheless has many sympathizers and followers. Moreover, and this is initially somewhat surprising perhaps, the organization uses the same language and terms, almost the same call and discourse as it did in the 1930s. There is a strong sense of a repetition of unchanged formulas, or reiteration of a message that has been frozen into immobility. And that message clearly has appeal after twenty years of Nasserism and in the very changed political position of contemporary Egypt.

The Free Officers appeared to produce a sense of an Egyptian history that was made by Egypt, not by others, and that referred forward to a series of inevitable nationalist victories over colonialism and a reordering of the entire political map of the Middle East, not back to the time of an "original" Islamic state. The breakthrough in the ideological and political realms may have been less than was thought at the time, but until the humiliating defeat of 1967 it appeared to be something irreversibly achieved. In addition, there was an immensely powerful state apparatus that was developed to ensure control. Religion was certainly part of that control and was not to be left to the Sufi orders or the Azhar, let alone such movements as the Muslim Brothers. It could be molded into "Islam and nationalism" or "Islam and socialism," but it was not a primary grounds of appeal or legitimation.

This ideological control exerted during the Nasser years depended for its efficacy not only on the state but on the conviction of the mass of the people that history was being autonomously realized by Egyptians (for the first time for many centuries), that the za'im did incarnate a capacity to resist external and internal forces identified with oppression and exploitation, and that the gain embodied in Egypt's new position in the world was worth the price paid.

That price included the failure — or, as some would say, the refusal — to develop any genuine political party or movement from the base or to attempt seriously to politicize the Egyptian masses. It seems to me that in practice the state was therefore always seen as a separate entity acting on society from above, despite the identification of the person of the leader as an overarching symbol of the unity of society. Furthermore, a bureaucratic-managerial class control of major sectors of the economy and the emergence of army officers as an elite and privileged stratum were very tangible evidence of a new kind of hierarchy in Egypt. Reforms of agriculture and landholding were certainly far too limited to effect anything like a real transformation of economic and political relations in the countryside.

It is not too much to say that the crushing defeat of 1967, with the destruction and humiliation of the Egyptian army and air force by Israel, was a trauma within society. The total nature of the disaster irreparably damaged the prestige, legitimacy, and ideological dominance of the army and the state. Egypt's economic situation was already precarious, she had very large external debts, and her political standing was threatened by the rise of the conservative, Western-backed oil states to greater and greater significance in world strategic and energy considerations.

It is from this springboard that, following the death of Nasser, in 1970, the Sadatian order in Egypt took off: dominance of the state and technocratic management cadres, the re-emergence of private enterprise as a keystone of policy, the development of the service and construction sectors particularly, and the "opening" to the West in both economic and political terms.

To this must be added the attempt to use religion very much as an ideological support, particularly against the left and those who continued to see themselves as Nasserist. As Nasserism was being discredited and socialism rejected, and as nationalism itself had failed to sweep the Middle Eastern board, there was an urgent need for a legitimation that was not based on any of these elements. What is especially important here is that "Islam" is completely free of any taint of the crises that overtook the country in the late 1960s, that it is not identified in any way with what many pious Muslims believe and are encouraged to believe was an era of communism and materialism, and that it is a total language of fundamental significance and power to legitimize.

Members of the Muslim Brothers were released from jail. The movement, or rather groupings of slightly different tendencies but identified as being Muslim Brother in color, began again the publication of magazines and books. And they did so, as I have said, very much in the language of the first two decades of Hassan al-Banna. There is a feeling, to the observer, of something that is at once intensely dynamic and yet in key dimensions ossified. This time the enemy is within, the problems arise within and must be answered within, yet the solutions are the same and are cast in the same terms as they were forty years before.

This need not astonish us. It is one of the strengths of utopian belief to be free of too precise a grasp of the historical forces, concrete event, and crisis that it places within what is taken as a more real, truer, and deeper scheme of meaning and purpose underlying the unbelief of perversion or deviations of the present. It is the refounding of the original community — or whatever the utopian model is — that is the issue and not specifically an analysis of economic and political elements and relations save in the most general and moral terms. The ideology of the Muslim Brothers consisted in a remorseless reassertion of a limited repertoire of key elements that were mythologized and represented as a once-existing ideal state: the purity and examples of the first community of Islam formed around the Prophet himself, the necessity of the application of the Holy Law as the law of the state, the return to the rigorous principles of true faith.

A second theme derives from this. It is that at the very same time such a message is given as transcending the blockages of an Egyptian society in transition, it in actuality reinforces and reproduces those blockages by displacing the nature of the crisis onto the level of utopia. It helps to negate the energies it releases and to turn Egyptians away from a grasp of the factors determining the conditions of their society at all its different levels.

For the state, for whom the petite bourgeoisie is an important constituency, the Muslim Brothers seem a useful force against the left. Yet this raises considerable problems. For the Brothers' ideology, with its strongly populist overtones, which has great appeal to sections of many different strata in Egyptian society, is still opposed to the West, as a source of corruption and dependence, and equally opposed to the wealth and ostentation of the new class of wealthy *arrivistes* who make a considerable public display when the mass of Egyptians is suffering from inflation and economic difficulty. The glittering hotels that, along with the foreign banks, are a symbol of the Egypt of the 1970s, are also a sign of the hypocrisy of those who preach Islam and piety while living in luxury. Religious hypocrisy, one of the most serious charges made in the Quran against some of the secret enemies of God and the Prophet Muhammed, is charged against the dominant forces in society that seek to use religion for their own purposes. All the resentment of the petite bourgeoisie and lower classes might therefore easily take a religious form, at the very time that the state is seeking to bolster itself ideologically and politically with religion.

Since the Brothers have failed, and are bound by the character of their utopian ideology to fail, to produce an analysis of the processes and structures of Egyptian society, there are only limited possibilities for development from such a base. The language of religion becomes used in a more and more repetitive and magical way, as though it could act on circumstance merely through the power of the Word and its reiteration. It is treated as a power in itself. This in turn increases the separation between Word and social reality (which increases the insistence on magical repetition . . .).

As one extension of this process and as a break out of this spiral, utopia can be transformed into millennial expectancy and a drive to explode the blockages through an apocalyptic and radical pattern of action that will realize or bring about the power of the Word in fact and deed. Believers will return to the mountains or barren places in the desert, as the Prophet Muhammed did when receiving the Revelation, thus re-creating and reliving the originary paradigm experience of the first true model leader and community. They will, when the time is ripe, sweep down on the forces of unbelief that surround them. All those outside the group are unbelievers. All those who leave the group are apostates. All those who oppose the group oppose God.

Such is one ideological extension of the message and ethic of the Muslim Brothers. As an ultimate end point it comes from the most radical tendency of the movement, which emerged largely in the shadow of the persecution of the Nasser years and from the experience of jail and prison camps. Whereas some of the Brotherhood drew from that experience a sense that in some respects elements on the left were struggling for the true independence of Egypt and social justice, even if cast in a different mold, others shifted to a more total and pure sectarianism that excluded modification and compromise. As the former began very tentatively to reflect that perhaps the state sector and the army might have a positive role to play in the community (the alternative of retreating from the fuller implications of the call for a return to the original community to a more limited call for gradual changes and reappraisals), the latter developed as an uncompromisingly hostile enemy of the whole social order.

They, too, were initially seen as a force against the left, but the dynamic of political sectarianism could not be contained within such tidy boundaries. The group (the *takfir wa higra* movement, which developed in the middle of the 1970s) had a leader who came from the rural petite bourgeoisie and had been a follower of the most radical of the imprisoned intellectuals of the Brotherhood. They claimed to be the only true community of believers. They had access to funds that permitted them to establish the members in Cairo. They were mostly in their twenties and early thirties and therefore reared during the Nasserist period. They seem to have encouraged early marriage between members (women being admitted to the group) and an enormously strong sense of being the elect.

The campaign against unbelief was to be waged by violence. A sheikh of the University of al-Azhar (who was also an ex-minister of religious endowments) was assassinated, and there were clear threats of a far wider campaign. The state pursued one of its alternatives in this situation and attempted to eliminate the group. The leader and several of his associates were hanged and others imprisoned. Repression became essential to the government, which could not control the religious impulses it had helped to encourage but which had come to contradict its very existence.*

The simple and misleading label of religious revival thus covers a very wide spectrum of ideology and practice that does not follow neat lines of class, age, occupation, income, or whatever, even if certain tendencies can be observed. And it is always dangerous to take any one element and assume that we are dealing with some kind of unitary social and ideological formation.

The call for a return to the full application of the Holy Law, for example, is a far more complex one than it appears on the surface. The Muslim Brothers make it central to their group. Certain judges and lawyers are interested in such a course in an attempt to develop an Islamic law that will avoid what they see as the limitations and alien nature of laws derived either from capitalist or socialist models. They are concerned, therefore, to develop the concept of Islamic law in personal, civil, and criminal cases in a "modern" way. Many other lawyers, no less serious Muslims, are quite indifferent or opposed to such trends. One finds, too, some

---

* The assassination of President Sadat four years later has been the most dramatic outcome of these processes.

intellectuals teaching in the universities whose interest in the Holy Law is almost purely in its repressive and punitive aspect. For them a return to this law means the reinstatement of the harshest penalties for breach of public order and infringements against property. This is a call for the protection of the new elite and the bourgeoisie in traditional terms. As the gap between these levels and the rest of the population becomes greater (fueling the appeal of such groups as the Muslim Brothers), we should not be astonished to find the most unlikely converts to what are usually taken to be fundamentalist causes.

Some of the sheikhs who argue for such a return to the full application of Holy Law evoke the weight of tradition and the path of the Companions of the Prophet and the consensus of the community. In the contemporary situation these are the traditionalists. Some of those who call for a return rather to the Book, to the Quran, are in fact the sheikhs who are more flexible in questions of interpretation, are opposed to fundamentalist literalism and to being bound by a conservatively defined "practice of the community." But it does not necessarily follow that those who cite them or state the same view do so with the same meaning and implications.

There are other forms of religious association in Egypt, however, which have been part of religious practice for many years and which might have been expected to participate in a religious resurgence. I refer to groups that have for long been attacked by reformers and traditionalists and radicals alike: the Sufi orders.

Trajectories of Contemporary Sufism

In the middle 1960s I studied a Sufi brotherhood (*tariqa*, plural *turuq*) in Egypt. At the time any talk of Sufism, and certainly of the turuq, seemed positively anachronistic. The then dean of the College of the Foundations of Religion, Sheikh 'Abd el-Halim Mahmud (later to become an extremely stern rector of the University of al-Azhar) told me that I was not studying Islam at all if I wasted my time on the brotherhoods. Nor did he mean that there were, relatively speaking, so few members left that it was hardly worth my while, though many people were of that opinion. His view was rather the same as that of many others of the 'ulema as well as people from many different levels of Egyptian society and particularly the middle classes: that popular Sufism and the brotherhoods were not truly Islamic. Their practices and beliefs were delusions and distractions from the truth at best, and at worst (and it was implied that the distance between best and worst was not great!) downright superstitious and heretical. This opinion came from someone regarded not only as a stern legist but as one who was well known as a student of mysticism and its paths and who was often identified to me as "a Sufi."

Sheikh 'Abd el-Halim went on to explain to me that asceticism, about which I had questioned him, was an interior condition of the heart and most secret recesses of the self and not a matter of external show or form of poverty and self-denial. What passed for asceticism to my friends in the tariqa was, in his view, a false, deluding shape of asceticism without its inward reality. A man could be rich, indeed have millions, and still be an ascetic. The sheikh said that the association sometimes made by brotherhood members between wealth and being a bad Muslim was nonsense. They mistook the form of asceticism for its substance. They were ignorant and my work, as long as it focused on them and took them as in any sense valid representatives of an aspect of Islam, was totally wasted. I should rather go back to the texts, to the lives of the great Sufis and thinkers, and leave "the religion of the streets," as he called it.

One of the ironies of our encounter was that the Sufi brotherhood that I was particularly studying, the Hamidiya Shaziliya, was exercising enormous care to avoid anything remotely dubious in religious practice and teaching. To this end it had taken on what might be seen as very much the image of its own time. That is to say, it had evolved an immensely elaborate bureaucratic scheme for the administration of the brotherhood, for a series of offices pyramidally arranged one above the other from the broad base of the humble ordinary member at the bottom to the sheikh of the brotherhood himself at the top, passing through half a dozen different positions on the way.

There were rules for disputes, rules for everyday behavior,

rules for ritual comportment and sequence, for the correct way of filling in report forms for the central office of the group, for establishing precedents, for hymn singing, for looking after the shoes at prayer, for eating, dress, and an entire practical and moral order.

Part of the function of the 329 laws (*qānūn*), and the officials charged with ensuring their application, was to guarantee the brotherhood against just such attacks as those made by Sheikh 'Abd el-Halim. They were also, in a much less direct way, intended to defend the brotherhood against specifically political suspicions. In the eyes of many of the Free Army officers who made the revolution of 1952 in Egypt the Sufi orders had been identified with too many of the forces in Egyptian society that the revolution sought to destroy or neutralize.

The brotherhoods were taken to be too close to powerful, "feudal" rural class interests, too open to manipulation of the ignorant masses by the British, or the palace (the regime of King Farouk), or the upper bourgeoisie.* They were too liable to mystify the people and divert them. Popular Sufism was accused of substituting non-Islamic ecstatic rituals for the political mobilization and consciousness that the revolution sought to achieve in the name of the independent nation. And there was a great deal of justice in this view.

This was not all. To many members of the petite bourgeoisie the Sufi brotherhoods epitomized the ignorance, backwardness, and non-Islamic practices from which many members of this very heterogeneous class particularly sought to separate themselves. The brotherhoods were ferociously opposed by most sections of the Muslim Brothers, for example, a movement whose membership was drawn predominantly from that class. In the rapidly changing urban world, in the new cities that grew from small beginnings or were founded in the late nineteenth and early twentieth

---

* See Jacques Berque, *Histoire Sociale d'un village Egyptien au XXème Siècle* (Paris: The Hague, Mouton, 1957), p. 66. In this study of the history of an Egyptian village, Berque notes that national politics in the shape of the liberal bourgeois nationalist party, the Wafd, came to the community through a committee organized by a local head of the Khalwatiya order. He organized a campaign of sabotage and boycotts. As Berque says, political agitation and tariqa propaganda went hand in hand at this period (the 1920s). In this instance at least the accusations were only partially true.

centuries, the Sufi brotherhoods had few social roots and found it difficult to establish any. I suspect that for many of the clerks, office workers, petty bureaucrats, small shop-keepers and traders, students, young officers and NCOs, and school teachers who were part of this stratum the turuq represented forces from which they wished to free them-selves. Popular Sufism was associated with what was coming to be seen as a stigma of traditionalism, from which this stratum had either liberated itself or which it hoped to leave behind, along with poverty, clientelism, the power of rural notables, illiteracy, passivity, and all that was held to be responsible for Western domination. A certain powerful element of class antagonism was present here.

Where could the Sufi brotherhoods contribute to Egypt's struggle against imperialism and for the achievement of her national independence? Where did they offer a rethinking or reworking of precept and practice that might bring out the full force of Islam in its "pure" form against the non-Islamic forms? How, if they were deeply linked with old alliances and social structures in the countryside and the city, could they ever be part of a religious and social renaissance?

In the rural areas, once the sheikhs of the turuq had lost much of their control over land in the nineteenth century, political and social forces crystallized in the latter half of that period around a new landed bourgeoisie, whose class relations frequently owed little or nothing to such traditional ties and saw them as either manipulable, obstructive, or merely as a useful opiate for the masses. In at least some of the villages also, as Jacques Berque notes, the men of religious, political, and economic prestige, often associated with leadership of Sufi turuq, were increasingly subject to competition from the new educated and professionals whose socioeconomic bases became more and more detached from land and local patterns of production and cultural life. The laborers and lower peasantry remained profoundly attached to ecstatic zikr rituals and the powers of shrines and talismans, and this too fueled the opposition, often uncertain and very ambivalent, of the new groups to what they identified as a degraded "popular religion."

Given this complex of antagonisms and oppositions, it was difficult to preserve let alone create a religious and social space for a brotherhood by the 1930s. Yet it was precisely at this period of economic and political turmoil that the founder of the Hamidiya Shaziliya, Sheikh Salama ar-Radi, attempted to build up a tariqa.

A minor bureaucrat in a government office himself, he followed a double path. On the one hand, he began by pursuing a completely traditional and stereotypically rigid form of holy personal activity and behaviour: extreme ascetic practices, endless prayers, seclusion, fasting, self-mortification. He blended into the general image or icon of how a man *becomes* a sheikh, making himself into another order of being, stripping himself of individuality in totally life-transforming practices that absorb him into a picture of holiness. He lived the social imperatives of sacredness and took on all the signs that might legitimate the founding of his own tariqa.

On the other hand, once he had founded the brotherhood, after a decade of moving around the poorer quarters of Cairo and the towns and villages of the Nile Delta, he both abandoned extreme forms of asceticism and formulated and produced an innovative kind of rule within popular Sufism. This was what can only be called the bureaucratic rule. He insisted on a totally orthodox, law-bound, theologically correct way, indistinguishable from that of any of the great reformist trends of the nineteenth and twentieth centuries: "Our way in Holy Law is built on the Quran and the Sunna and it is free from blameable heresy" (law 2). He also constructed an elaborate armor of prescriptions and organizing principles that owe perhaps more to his own office and work experience than to tradition. It is not an exaggeration in fact to say that the bulk of *The Laws* are bureaucratic and administrative in nature.

The initial emphasis is the appeal to the poor, precisely the increasingly large numbers existing on the social margin of the new colonial urban and economic order:

Law 4. One of the principles of our way is humility, for it is the wealth of the poor.

Law 11. Sitting with the rich hardens the heart.

Law 16. Helping the poor and being sympathetic to them materially and spiritually as far as possible [is one of the principles of the Brotherhood].

The call is also traditional in its nature. Humility is the capital or resource of the poor. It is a state of being to be poor, and it is spiritually blessed. There is no questioning of the social origins and nature of the poor, no suggestion that poverty can be transcended in this world, no indication that humility and the pursuit of the Way might relate to a critique of society or to the kinds of action against the colonial forces that so many groups were undertaking at the time *The Laws* were written in the 1930s.

I shall return to this question of religious ethic and politics shortly. For the moment let me stress that the main emphasis in *The Laws*, as indeed it was in practice during my study from 1964 to 1966, was on order, organization, efficiency, and a theological and ritual coherence and control that would both give identity to the members (who, unlike the members of all the other Sufi brotherhoods of Egypt, were expressly forbidden to belong to any other kind of religious organization) and serve as a defense against authority, political or religious, should it attack popular Sufism.

Perhaps curiously I found myself more personally moved by this attempt to buttress the religion of the street with the instruments of what had become its opponents (the centralizing state, bureaucratic control, theological and textual rigor) than by any other element in the Hamidiya Shaziliya. Yet it created an enormous tension. At best it might be a positive and creative tension and combination of elements at the heart of the brotherhood, between *The Laws* and the other side of popular Sufism — egalitarian fraternity, ritual performances of huge emotional, psychological, and physiological power, intense personal relations and the immediacy of face-to-face contact, brother to brother.

On the other hand, it contained the possibility of a clash and contradiction between the bureaucratic principles and the most painful desire to see and experience the hand of God working in the grace acts (karamat) of the now dead holy man, Sheikh Salama. Each seemed to threaten the other. The rules might be produced by the sheikh and maintained by the officials, but the practical meaning of the brotherhood centers on the grace and power of the sheikh and on the experience of his holiness in everyday life that baraka and karamat and the ecstasies and intensity of experience offered by the zikr rituals provide.

During my stay (1964-66), when the brotherhood was headed by Sheikh Ibrahim Salama (one of the founder's sons), it was commonplace to see the officials severely reprimanding those of the members who were seized with ecstasy in the ritual and began to cry out and move violently out of rhythm with the others, shattering the carefully constructed harmony of breath, sound, and movement. And the officials also played the classical role of disciples, which I might call "stopping the little children from coming unto the Lord." That is, they turned away the devout from the sheikh's presence if he was tired or occupied. They were the ones who prevented the brothers from seizing the sheikh's hand as he passed, his eyes cast down, his right hand over his heart in silent acknowledgment of their cries and supplications. They pulled back those who wanted to touch the hem of his robe.

The officials created the distance between the faithful and the source of grace without it ever being felt that the source itself, in the person of Sheikh Ibrahim, was denying them. Whereas the founding holy man had been accessible to his followers, his son, at one remove from the power of his father and with a tariqa grown to a far larger size, withdrew into a holy distance that made those rare moments when he did wave the officials aside and require them to admit a child, an old man, a small visiting delegation from a village in the delta all the more rhapsodic and exalted. Their role was thus both creative and restrictive.

There was, moreover, another associated issue around which certain ambiguities clustered. This related to the notion of hierarchy in a Sufi brotherhood. In theory hierarchy is a matter of degree of illumination, of having passed through certain stages on the way of mystical knowledge. But it was stressed that the officials were not necessarily in their posts as a spiritual hierarchy in the Hamidiya Shaziliya, but rather for the imperatives of administration. Their bureaucratic status sometimes seemed to combine uneasily with their role as ritual organizers and de facto guardians of the sheikh. The aspect of control occasionally appeared to dominate over direct contact with what is taken to be the real form of life, the pattern of power and blessing lying behind the world's facade.

It should be added that in the many local centers or lodges of the brotherhood the khalifas (deputies) who run the centers (zawiyas) *are* supposed to be men capable of taking the place of the sheikh in more than an organizational sense. They have to teach, advise, watch over, serve, and co-ordinate mutual assistance and the practical dimension of fraternity as well as deal with disputes, guard money, write elaborate reports to the head office, recruit, and defend the group against local opposition where it occurs.

Many of the officers were legitimated, not only by the fact that they had been chosen by the sheikh but also by the fact that many of them were still first-generation followers and had taken the oath of allegiance to Sheikh Salama himself. They were often poor men themselves, usually workers of different levels but sometimes teachers in primary schools, clerks (by now often retired) in government offices, shop workers or storekeepers on a very small scale. Such men had the authority of "first followers," not officials. They were part of, and a link for those younger to, the original mission of Salama ar-Radi himself.

There was, however, another group that had no formal rank but that formed a circle around the sheikh of a rather elite kind. These were mostly businessmen, small company owners, a senior airline pilot, a high-ranking officer and engineer, and one or two government officials. They dominated the sheikh's meetings and the religious discussions. Their own image and understanding of religion was very close to that of reformist and strictly orthodox groups. Their conceptions of the miracles wrought by Sheikh Salama have nothing to do with those of the ordinary members, which are full of astonishing escapes, sudden discoveries of money, dream visions, or the voice of the dead but still powerful holy man whispering in the ear. On the contrary, they refer to his intellectual gifts, his mastery of Holy Law, and his ability to confound the 'ulema, who came to challenge him on their own ground, even though he himself had no formal training in law. Their class situation, position in the brotherhood, and religious perspective were and are, therefore, significantly different from that of the mass of the members.

There existed powerful tensions in the brotherhood, tensions that arose partly out of the very success of the group and the quality of its internal relations. There were certain critical elements or focal points at which such tensions and distinctions of belief and practice were at least potentially crystallized. What would happen if there were a crisis? Would the organization be able to ensure a smooth succession? If it came to it, could bureaucracy in fact guarantee and legitimate the supposedly central and determining forces of power and grace?

I was aware, of course, that the Sufi brotherhoods frequently split into different branches and groupings. Any number of factors may be operating when this occurs, and the multiplication of branches of turuq tracing their line of spiritual descent from the same founder but following a specific holy individual who institutes his own branch is totally characteristic. It has been part of the flexibility and responsiveness of Sufism in history.

But in a new group in the context of contemporary Eygpt and given the massive elaboration of the organizational arm, everything seemed propitious and a serious split hardly imaginable. Yet there had been one on the death of Sheikh Salama, when a large faction refused to follow the choice by some of the followers of one of the sheikh's sons (the Sheikh Ibrahim referred to) as his successor and united around the man who had been the dead founder's deputy and one of his first disciples. This crisis had gradually been overcome. Sheikh Ibrahim had become undisputed leader, and the central *maglis* (office) of the brotherhood was notably strengthened in his time to guard against the possibilities of disruption. Such was the situation when I left Cairo in 1966.

When I returned to the city over a decade later, in 1977, I was confronted by several surprises. After many enquiries at the mosques where large congregations of several hundreds of the brothers used to perform the zikr regularly had revealed no apparent activity, I was eventually astonished to be directed to a new mosque built in one of the most fashionable and modern luxury areas of Cairo. My surprise was all the greater when I found the half-built shell of a massive construction still covered with scaffolding on what was in effect a huge traffic island behind a chic sporting club and surrounded by a dual-lane carriageway.

The doorkeeper brought me in to see the interior of the yet uncompleted prayer hall in beautiful and costly marble brought from Europe. Most significantly, he took me "to see the sheikh." And I found myself before an ornate tomb that was surrounded by a brass rail and rested on the unfinished concrete. Sheikh Ibrahim had died two years before, and his shrine lies in the symbolic center of the new mosque. I was left alone with him, to be "in his presence," amid the wooden poles and supports holding up what will one day be a dome above the shrine. A large empty space beside Sheikh Ibrahim's shrine is reserved for his father, the founding holy man. But, for the moment at least, Sheikh Salama's body remained in the tiny mosque in the old former port quarter of Bulaq, an area that is very much one of the great popular and mass quarters of the city. It was the social center of the founder's mission in Cairo in the 1930s and of the mulid celebrations held every year since his death to commemorate and celebrate his life. His shrine is the core and source of baraka and pilgrimage, not only for the brothers but for those many persons who seek blessing at the tombs of holy figures.

Now, the move to the new mosque was astonishing enough. Nothing could be socially more distant from Bulaq than the ostentatious upper-middle-class wealth of Zamalek, where the new building is located. This curious transplantation to a high-prestige site, the marble carved prayer niche, the plans for a clinic, the teaching center, a library — all were a very different image of the tariqa that had dominated ten years before.

The significance of this shift quickly became apparent. At the sudden death of Sheikh Ibrahim, the brotherhood had split. Part had followed the sheikh's younger brother, who is a graduate of the Faculty of Commerce and played in the 1960s only a very limited role in the group. The other section was under the joint leadership of a committee composed almost entirely of the inner circle of businessmen and professionals to which I have referred. The precise sequence of events was difficult to establish. What is important is the extent of the change in the tariqa that has occurred.

To understand this we have to realize that there is a conjunction btween the crisis of succession and a process of change in Egyptian society as a whole. The division of the brotherhood is not only an internal question. It relates in part to transformations in the role and attitude of the state and the global political and social context within which popular Sufism now exists.

Since the economic and military catastrophes of the period from 1965 onward, the policies of Arab socialism and the whole heterogenous political order and ideology of Nasserism have been under attack. The traumatic defeat of Egypt by Israel in 1967 and the death of Nasser in 1970 were part of a transitional period toward a far more explicitly Western model of economic policy. Private enterprise was to be encouraged, economic liberalism and an "open door" policy to Western goods and interests became part of a reorientation of Egypt's position and relationships in the world at large. State controls were relaxed, the apparatus of intelligence (particularly its military organization) and the dominance of the army were diminished. The financial, commercial, and industrial wings of the bourgeoisie would be given the opportunity to come to the forefront of the economic and social order.

In the ideological field, with nationalism itself in its Nasserist forms seriously compromised, socialism also identified as having been tried and found wanting, and the regime of President Sadat seeking to distance itself from its own army and Nasserist legacy, there was a new space for religion and religious movements in state ideology. Groups such as the Muslim Brothers, which had long been proscribed, were tacitly allowed back into public life. Muslim groups were encouraged in the universities, particularly against any forces identified as being Nasserist or of the left. Other states, such as Libya and Saudi Arabia, were allegedly funding in Egypt Islamic movements cast in their image and for political purposes.

In this context there re-emerged an ideological and tacitly political arena for popular Sufism. The Hamidiya Shaziliya, already much the best organized of the brotherhoods, flowered more freely. The prestigious new mosque was planned, and Sheikh Ibrahim and trusted colleagues made trips to Europe to arrange the importation of building materials. A site of great social standing was made available and funds acquired. The tariqa enjoyed an emergence into official approval as an example of what a true and proper collective form of Sufism might be.

Sheikh Ibrahim's death, however, abruptly posed the problem of succession. The division that followed between the essentially middle-class elite of the brotherhood and those who followed the Sheikh's younger brother occurred with (to me) surprising swiftness. It is significant that the larger fraction of the members, drawn from the social world of Bulaq, outside the benefits of the shift of state policy, most exposed to the economic problems that that policy has entailed for the poor and working classes, should have remained with the sheikh's brother. A friend who is of a very high position in the brotherhood, and to whose kindness I owe much, regretfully admitted to me that in the new mosque he administers I would no longer find the great crowds I had known in the difficult years for popular Sufism of the Nasserist regime. Only a minority have made the move to Zamalek. The building has yet to take on any content and practical significance. There is a kind of social and religious emptiness, despite the tomb of Sheikh Ibrahim and the splendor of the marbled prayer hall.

The ironies are illuminating. The move to Zamalek and into such a mosque was to be a mark of flowering, of new prestige, of social re-emergence into a form of religious practice that would establish Sufism in its tariqa forms as once again acceptable and respectable. In fact it helped to divide the brotherhood and to sharpen cleavages (what were partly divisions of class) that had until the sheikh's death been contained. The members were ready to follow the sheikh. They were not ready to follow a middle-class elite nor to break with their social and symbolic anchor in Bulaq. The economic divisions in Egyptian society that have both grown and been increasingly revealed in social behavior in the decade of the 1970s have no doubt exacerbated the real significance of the move to Zamalek and the sense of very contrasting interests within the brotherhood. The elite of the tariqa, but its assertion of dominance, undermined that very dominance.

Furthermore, the whole organized structure — so elaborated, so precisely detailed, so hierarchical, so ambiguous in effect — proved quite unable to hold the tariqa together, since it generated as many tensions as it resolved.

The division also intriguingly demonstrates that state support for what might crudely be called a cleaned-up version of the "religion of the streets" can be *more* productive of contradiction than state disapproval or even quasi-repression. The tacit attempt at an *embourgeoisement* of sectors of street Sufism in alliance, or what is seen to be an alliance, with the state largely disqualified itself. It failed, and it seems to me that the members were implicitly refusing that kind of incorporation into an ideology and form of Sufism that was alien to them and the position in the social order that the vast majority of them occupy.

Is it reasonable to suggest that what we see here is a renewal in a particular form of the theme of (tacit and muted) opposition between the religion of the streets in its popular Sufism manifestation and the state and central authority? Is it an opposition now felt more from the side of popular Sufism than by the state, in contrast to the whole of the Nasserite period?

I have already remarked as a very general principle, on the subversive and covert elements present in baraka and miracles, which potentially always threaten to elude religious, not to say political, authority, however much effort may be made to strengthen the controls (in the past the banning of saint's day celebrations, with their potent and dangerous concentration of large masses of people; the intimidation of the leaders of the turuq or their followers; the removal of shrines or severe government discouragement of "saint worship"). Yet in the nineteenth century in Egypt many of the leaders of the brotherhoods were instruments for the channeling and restriction of popular religion by the dominant social strata in the towns and countryside. They were often from those strata and integral to local power structures. In that sense the turuq were incorporated by the ruling forces of society and formed an ideological and social bridge to the peasantry and the urban masses.

It was indeed this identification with rural landlords

and notables, government manipulation and established political structures, that in the twentieth century caused them to be stigmatized by fundamentalist and reformist groups, who were hostile both to what they criticized as magical and un-Islamic practices and to the power with which Sufism was associated. The complex of social forces that went into the revolution of 1952 attacked the brotherhoods as reactionary and "feudal." Sufism became more and more peripheral and confined to marginal groupings, excluded from ideological and political space by the development of the independence movement, fundamentalism, nationalism in its different forms, and the association of the colonial and postcolonial state with textual orthodoxy and legalism.

In Egypt, therefore, the brotherhoods were displaced and lost support in part because of their subservience to the precolonial and colonial state. They had not been, as in other social settings in North Africa we have seen they sometimes were, hostile to the emerging forms of the state in the nineteenth century. Even where given local sheikhs or religious notables might, as in the case mentioned by Berque, support the Wafd party in its nationalist program, this was still a relationship with local rural power structures. So popular Sufism came to be seen as traditionalist and repressive by many elements of the petty bourgeoisie and indeed the middle classes in general, who excluded it from their own organized political and cultural alternatives. At the same time, reformist and fundamentalist groups, drawn from those same classes, denied the brotherhoods' authenticity as practical and theological forms of Islam. Saints' shrines and pilgrimages remained as foci of any number of different kinds of imagined power, hope, promise, blessing, but the turuq were not structurally necessary, even to the saints.

The late 1970s saw the emergence of a different kind of ideology; the West and the economic "opening" replaced Nasserism. The state and those interests it now represented began to engage in a recuperation of religion as a major ideological support and legitimation. As a small part of that attempted recuperation (of which more in a moment) popular Sufism was to be permitted and even discreetly encouraged. But it proved not always easy to manipulate. Its social base had changed, and it had also diminished. Though its ethic of humility, reliance on the baraka of the holy man, acceptance of poverty, and proper and scrupulous attention to personal manners and conduct posed no threat, neither did they lead to an identification of the state with religious legitimacy and beneficence. The gulf had widened between social classes whose life chances (in Max Weber's phrase) are becoming more obviously separated and unequal. Since the economic policies of the state did not benefit those classes from which were drawn the members of the turuq, it was all the more unlikely that the former would be successful in its attempts to use and revitalize this religious form for its own purposes. The Hamidiya Shaziliya divided. The new mosque, splendid on its traffic island amid the luxury apartment blocks, remains empty.

A Sufism of the Elite

This is not, however, the only form that Sufism takes in Egyptian society. I have already mentioned that Sheikh 'Abd el-Halim Mahmud, who was to become rector of the University of al-Azhar (until his death in 1978) and who was often cited as increasingly fundamentalist in his calls for the strictest interpretation of Islamic law and his attacks on anything he took to be an expression of unbelief, was a "Sufi." That is to say, he was a student of the great Sufi mystics and thinkers of the classical period and certainly saw no contradiction between their teaching and Holy Law in a rigorous form. Contempt for the religion of the streets went hand in hand with a Sufism of and for a spiritual and religious elite. In the changed circumstances that followed the defeat of 1967 such a position might go along with virulent public attacks on any signs of "socialism" and "communism" — defined in terms of great elasticity and often meaning a conflation of what was taken to be a Russian model of government and economy, and all the disparate currents that fed into Nasserism. In this aspect it could be a force against the left, against proponents of a state-controlled economy, against much that the revolution of 1952 had come to stand for. At the same time, such a view might be extremely critical of the state for failing to realize the truly Islamic nature of society and for refusing to take all necessary steps to bring about a fully Islamic social order.

So such a figure as 'Abd el-Halim Mahmud was viewed with profound ambivalence by the regime of President Sadat. He was both a welcome support and a source of most unwelcome criticism, even challenge, on grounds that many supporters of the government would certainly not accept. Insofar as he mobilized religious forces against the left, he was an ally. Insofar as he stirred up those same forces for extreme fundamentalist programs (which the total application of Islamic law would certainly be considered to be by the state), he might be dangerous. He might help to release and legitimate religious energies and groupings of which the ruling strata were extremely nervous and which might well be exceedingly difficult to control. His Sufism went together with not only a high official position but also what became an activist and unyielding attitude to the proper nature of the relationship between religion and society.

His was by no means the only kind of elite Sufism or blend of beliefs and practices in which a version of Sufism was one important component. There were others that were already discreetly present in the 1960s and which in the following decade began in limited ways to expand. Circles of adepts formed around Sufi teachers, often but by no means always drawn from the universities and intellectual circles. The figure of the *murshid* (the guide, a traditional term for a Sufi teacher or sheikh and one used, for example, by Sheikh Salama ar-Radi) has become a renewed part of the experience of religion for some members of the middle classes, and by no means only the intellectuals.

Some middle-class adherents have grown up in a milieu in which Islam and its classical traditions played only a relatively limited role. Frequently, they are well educated and comfortably placed in social terms but feel themselves to be without an overall framework for life or any certainty as to their true roots and place in society. Such persons find the small group around a teacher an ideal channel for the discovery of and immersion in their own religion with all its wider resonances for personal life and conceptions of the world. Their interest is less in the Holy Law, though they may support the cause of bringing it much more prominently into Egyptian legal codes, than in the philosophy, meta-physics, poetics, and spiritual pathways of Sufism. All the more is this the case if they are hostile to the social and religious fundamentalism such movements as the Muslim Brothers advocate, movements that make a great deal of a rigid interpretation of the Holy Law as the basis of a revolution in the foundations of society.

Such small circles may include academics, journalists, businessmen, bankers, insurance brokers, engineers, and a whole wider range of professionals. For them the "true" Sufism is not the religion of the streets (from which they are totally cut off). It is rather a journey on a path to illumination that requires that one see behind the mere appearances and forms of religion — where they consider the turuq to be hopelessly trapped — and into the concealed reality, the batin. This may also mean that a member of such a group experiences no sense of contradiction between his Sufism and business affairs, the acquisition of wealth in a highly competitive situation, or a privileged place in society, or all the appurtenances of Western values and life-styles. These are surface matters and the reality exists beneath. In that dimension of reality he, too, is an ascetic. Political questions or reflection upon the nature and structure of society are irrelevant. Society is not a problem. One looks into the heart of things, not at the outward forms. Nasserism, to which they are usually hostile, was falsely and materialistically concerned with social forms. Now there is the chance to escape from such a restricted vision.

The nature of this conception of Sufism does not exclude affinities with all sections of the bourgeoisie. It appeals also to those who have a very well founded and "traditional" pious upbringing. It must be stressed again that there are no simple patterns, no neat correlations of economic and political interests and religious ethic; often quite different kinds of propositions, conceptions, practices, and representations at different levels are held by the same person or by people who broadly share the same range of life chances. So while it is possible to say that this kind of Sufism is probably only of very limited appeal to those who are deriving the greatest profit from the "opening to the West" or to the upper reaches of those of wealth and social status, the possibility exists, of course, that such individuals may embrace membership in this kind of Sufi circle.

There is no sense here of a real withdrawal from social life, but rather what might be called an ascetic and intellectual indifference to the outward appearance of things. That said, we should note that this indifference does not in fact preclude strong political attitudes to the Nasserist period as one of communism and atheism. There is a *combination* of ideological currents, of which Sufism is only one, that flow in these social channels.

In many respects members of such groups, feeling themselves to have been politically, culturally, and socially blocked in the period of later Nasserism especially, show hostility to any suggestion of a critique of post-Nasserist developments. For them, as for many drawn from these classes, a new freedom has come. Egyptian society is not to be understood in materialist and power terms (shorthand for the period 1952-1970) but in terms of an inward quality, which makes any critique of material conditions irrelevant if not downright un-Islamic. In this sense such groups are allied with the dominant forces in Egyptian society in the late 1970s, forces they represent and idealize in images of piety and asceticism.

This particular form of Sufi asceticism is worlds away from those radical groups I have mentioned who believe in the necessity of the kind of "going out," or withdrawal from the current social order as part of a fundamental antagonism to that order; which, on religious and therefore also social grounds, deny the very legitimacy of the state and the structures of domination and regulation; and which conceive of society as corrupt and ruled by hypocrites and unbelievers who must be turned against when the time is ripe. Instead, these small intellectual Sufi groups find an unproblematic place in society. But it is a very different place from that occupied by those turuq who are part of the religion of the streets, streets from which such an elite fastidiously separates itself, of which it has perhaps increasingly less comprehension, and with which it has very little direct social relation.

The current forms and practices of Sufism in Egypt seem to illustrate two main points: The first is that among the masses the turuq offer no real practical and ideological way of confronting the economic, political, and cultural problems increasingly posed by contemporary history. In periods of crisis and transition in a society such as that of contemporary Egypt it is difficult to see in what social space they can operate. The state attempts to create such a space for them for its own purposes, but we have seen the limited results of such efforts. Furthermore, the state's position is somewhat contradictory, for it would certainly try to block or rigidly control any serious renaissance of the brotherhoods (assuming that to be possible) among the most exploited and deprived strata for fear of the potentially dangerous and unpredictable results. A heavily centralized bureaucratic modern state, the bases of which are not necessarily secure, is going to be extremely wary of baraka and loyalties to holy men. Even the bureaucratic apparatus of the Hamidiya Shaziliya, with all the official approval that it enjoyed, proved too weak to contain the stresses posed by succession and class differentiation.

The social and political membership of the brotherhoods is limited largely to individuals drawn from the lower reaches of the petite bourgeoisie — small shopkeepers, traders, and clerks, for example — and from the working class and the whole host of marginal levels. A brotherhood such as the Hamidiya Shaziliya can serve important functions of mutual help for its members, but even there its resources are limited. The sheikhs lack the power or economic base to be mediators for the members with the institutions and forces that dominate their lives, though in purely internal matters, of course, they have clear authority. The specific economic and social pressures on these levels of the population cannot be resisted and transformed through the turuq, while religious training, education, cultural legitimacy, and organized calls for wider, structured social action on the basis of a given vision of Islam have passed outside the arena of the brotherhoods.

Sufism as a part of the religion of certain members of the middle classes is another matter altogether. The cultural and symbolic space is there. The roles of sheikh and adept require no political or economic power or influence. Any sense of crisis or contradiction in Egyptian society is held to be insignificant in the inner and spiritual perspective of mysticism and the path to illumination.

Theirs is a reflective, pious vision offering a deepening of knowledge of the classical writings of mysticism. It is a reflective vision that also goes together in this instance with strong hostilities to certain kinds of social order stigmatized as communist and anti-Islamic. The members are not therefore simply Sufis in an ideological and cultural vacuum. They have affinities with wider attitudes and conceptions of the social world that do not only relate to or derive from religion, however centrally defined religious practice is to them. These attitudes are certainly not all uniform, any more than is the life experience of the members, their social positions, or their personal histories. They meet in the framework of weekly or monthly discussions, not as followers of a group that constantly brings the collectivity together in a whole series of ritual and social occasions (as the Hamidiya Shaziliya does). Political views are not formally relevant to membership and their form of Sufism. But such views exist and contribute to an underlying and generalized set of perceptions of Egyptian society.

Such groups return to a specifically religious conception of mediation centered on the teaching of the sheikh-as-guide (murshid) on the path (tariqa). Such a view poses neither doctrinal nor political problems, and it occupies a long-existing cultural space sanctified by tradition. For the sheikhs of the popular turuq, however, mediation was a rather more multistranded conception and activity. It could be said of them that in Egypt in the nineteenth century, for instance, they mediated between social groups in many different ways. The tariqa, or more specifically its sheikh, might make possible communication between groups where none had existed before, or where none *could* exist because of coded oppositions of descent, blood feud, social distance, contradictory interests, and so forth. The sheikhs might construct a mutually acceptable language that was recognized to transcend the limits of a given situation or to be a translation into higher terms of messages that were otherwise socially mutually exclusive. They might thus unblock social avenues that were impassable by other means.

Precisely this capacity, founded on the ideology and symbolism of baraka, holy texts, and the powers deriving from these two sources, made them both valuable, and under certain circumstances a threat, to the ruling groups. It also meant that to a centralized, relatively well organized auto-cratic state (such as emerged in Egypt in the first half of the nineteenth century under Muhammed 'Ali) or to a bureaucratic-military state in its modern forms (up to and after the revolution of 1952) such mediation would be a political and social infringement in realms where the state increasingly exercised, or sought to exercise, a monopoly. The economic and political bases of the brotherhoods were controlled or removed, and the capacity of the sheikhs to mediate in the social and ideological realms became more and more objectively limited. Without powerful tribal or regional bases, or semiautonomous powers derived from control over important cultural or economic resources, the sheikhs of the brotherhoods, and therefore the whole hierarchy and organ-ization the turuq supplied, slowly foundered. Regulation of conflict by the legal authority of the state, control and elaboration of the entire educational and religious apparatus also by the state, the development of the modern machinery of political activity and administration — all were factors tending to the elimination of this type of sheikhly practice.

Such factors do not, however, eliminate the significance of the shrines of dead holy men. Mediation outside the channels of government apparatuses and with "higher" powers is closely linked to these shrines and to what the dominant groups classify as magic and superstition. Theft, adultery, infertility, ill fortune, envy, loss, peril and threat, vengeance, health — the list is endless of individual problems that may be brought to the shrines or directed through locally res-pected figures who are held to have special effectiveness in the writing of talismans and the operation of powerful signs to reveal, cure, protect, strike. The acts of the jinn that harm, of the good spirits that bless, the meaning of the dreams and visions that may portend who knows what, require in turn the proper responses, interpretations, acts. Theirs is a logic of power and the unseen that demands very specific modes of behavior and mediation.

A field so wide of religious and social practice often eludes and is meant to elude the knowledge, let alone the control of the state. And where it is known, it is ignored as the superstitious ideas of the peasantry or the urban illiterates. The domed shrines of the holy men are only the visible tip of an iceberg of practice, knowledge, and relations that have their deeper and vaster mass below the surface of an outsider's regard.

CHAPTER 11

Islamic Signs and Interrogations

My experience of Islam had begun with an encounter in a street in South Arabia. Green-banded turbans stood for holy sherifian descent, learning, true Islam, and membership in a religious and social elite, but their wearers, those bored young men, longed for Indonesia and felt themselves trapped in a provincial backwater, surrounded by ignorant peasants. To the boy who kissed their hands in apparent respect, those same marks of sanctity were read as signs of a control of land, alliance with the British colonial power, and a parasitical existence. Moreover, this rural worker's son had come to Nasserism through a colonial school that all unawares had served as a breeding ground for nationalist sentiment. The student who, again in apparent respect, called a young and ingenuous English teacher sir in a class devoted to subordinate clauses, saw that teacher, in his colonial uniform of white shirt, white shorts, long white socks, and heavy black walking shoes, as representing the other partner in the alliance with the green turbans.

I think that he was right on both counts. But I must qualify the term *apparent*. It is too glib to say that either the hand kiss or the address as sir was mere convention and mere show. Islam needed no mediators, but the Prophet's family and the ideal of religious learning were certainly respected, whatever their local representatives happened to be. Similarly, the young English teacher was, after all, a teacher, an *ustaz*, and as such might serve as an introduction to learning for which a genuine reverence was felt. And I noticed that the boy himself was an ustaz and a sheikh to his laborer father by virtue of his period in school. As a learned man in his turn, he had become of a higher authority than his father in his own family, a reversal of hierarchy that in other circumstances would be unimaginable.

This anecdotal moment can be used as a lens through which to view a wider scene, or as a tangible sign that points to far greater meanings than it can itself contain. A colonial era was ending. Aden and the Protectorates, as they then were, stood as one of the last domains of the British. They lay both geographically and politically on the periphery of a shrinking empire and of the Arab world itself. Without material resources of their own, their chief importance to the imperial power was strategic, guarding the routes of the Red Sea and serving as a natural harbor and fueling station for shipping between the Indian Ocean and the Mediterranean.

Yet peripheral though Aden was in many ways, there were vaster forces to which it was intimately linked. The port was still seen as crucial to Western power in the region. The British Petroleum Company ran the gigantic refinery. There was a large Royal Air Force base and an army barracks. Within three years of my encounter there would be a full-scale urban colonial war fought in the narrow streets of Crater, the "Arab town." The sherifs would lose their position in the Hadhramaut, and the Arab world's only Marxist state would be born. No hands would be kissed.

The young descendants of the Prophet found the Hadhramaut both central and peripheral. Their families originated there. Their claims to holy lineage were rooted in a series of great holy sanctuary cities strung along the broad valley of the Hadhramaut like so many glowing pearls. There was a powerful tradition of 'ilm, of learning, and of mediation between the Beduin tribes. City and desert interlocked in a very direct way. The sherifs dominated the local trade and the ownership of land. On the other hand, Hadhramaut had nonetheless also been a backwater for many years. Their

252

most important economic and religious links and investments were with the East African coast, the Gulf, India, and Java. Some had made fortunes in those areas. They were part of a wide network spanning the entire Indian Ocean, a network of learning, trade, Sufism, and power.

There were other emigrants from South Arabia who did not wear the green-banded turban. People from the peasant farmer and tribal strata also went to India and the Far East, and it was in Indonesia as early as 1914 that these migrants formed the Irshadi, or Reformers Association, to combat the power of the elite in the Hadhramaut and the whole system of sanctified inequality.*

One of the main signs of such opposition was to refuse all the marks of respect given to the sherifs, of which the most prominent was the hand kiss.

The signs of hierarchy were therefore already an area of struggle long before the student explained his own seeming deference as hiding opposition. But by his time it was no longer a question of confronting an inegalitarian ideology of Islam with a reformist one. It was rather a matter of attaining total independence from a local economic and political system and from a world system of domination that helped to determine it, and to give a new shape and practical form to Islam in that region.

For his generation, therefore, religion and the symbols were no longer the overall framework within which the world order could be interrogated and denied. That could only be done through a triumphing Nasserism, a form of nationalism that appeared to incarnate an irreversible move forward. The age of colonialism was passing; the age of the newly independent nations was beginning. Though the practice of Islam and what Islam really ought to be were themselves at issue locally and internationally, by the late 1950s the instruments of the struggle were seen to be anticolonial movements in which Islam was only one dimension.

Insofar as the Islam that was identified with state systems was concerned, as in South Arabia, it was viewed by the students as a reactionary force propped up by Britain and

* A.S. Bujra, *The Politics of Stratification: A Study of Political Change in a South Arabian Town* (Oxford: The Clarendon Press, 1971). (See especially chapters 3 and 6.)

America, who had sought "Islamic pacts" as a resistance to radical nationalism. The kind of Islam represented in the conservative dynasty of Saudi Arabia, where the luxury of the few and the repressive interpretation of the Holy Law for the many seemed inextricably linked, was to be fought tooth and nail.

An armed and shining nationalism was to be at the bright center of the time. It seemed to crystallize and define the fundamental contradictions within society that the colonial system had helped to produce. What was experienced in daily life often in indirect, mediated, and blurred ways became direct and immediate in anti-imperialist ideology and politics. The student, the sherifs, and the English teacher meeting in the outpost of a declining empire at a key moment of historical transition each in his small way stood for different elements in these contradictions.

Tradition and the Vision of History

Twenty or so years later the contradictions are undiminished. The inadequacies of nationalist movements in the post-independence period and the powers of neocolonialism are revealed more clearly. An ideology of Islam as a total scheme within which society can be reordered on the basis of what is conceived of as the primordial model of the Quran, the Tradition, and the Law is resurgent among certain strata and political groupings of very different composition.

As the previous chapter showed, such groupings make constructions of what the religious tradition was, is, and should be. They do so precisely because what were before felt as self-evident and natural forms of everyday life have been ruptured by historical changes. Forced to reflect on what had been previously practiced rather than thought, they have often produced an unreflective version of what they define as traditional.

Out of the contemporary realities have been conjured visions of a religious transcendent power both outside and within time, untainted by history yet lying behind and able to determine it, transforming and yet for ever the same.

These visions have taken on a renewed magical vitality

among those social strata that were particularly supporters of the nationalism of the 1950s and 1960s, those whom I shall call the urban masses, for want of a better term, and the petty bourgeoisie. Both had found in nationalist movements a mobilizing force, powerful because it promised not only a restoration of an old cultural and political identity, which actually the members of these strata have not experienced, but also a break with the colonialism out of which they had essentially been brought into being. Nasserism would destroy the structures of exploitation and somehow — but how? — forge an autonomous state. "The people" following "the leader" would enter a phase of history in which national identity and the homeland would break free into an utterly changed and egalitarian world.

If a mystified notion of the nation was created as well as at least a partial political and military independence, the reality of the state apparatuses became predominant in practice. The army, the police, the bureaucracy, and the technocratic elites that developed, often drawing their members from the petite bourgeoisie, did not structurally change the social order. As the forces of liberation became the forces of power, they frequently degenerated into forms of government with an arbitrary character. This arbitrariness, first, derived from the contingent and personal nature of the omnipresent patronage networks both inside and outside the institutions of the state. Second, it derived from the labyrinthine operations of self-reproducing bureaucracies of military and civilian kinds whose intrusions into people's lives are both systematic and unpredictable. And third, that arbitrariness derived from the discrepancies between the ideologies of nationalism, independence, and state legitimacy and the realities of social inequalities, dependence, and rulers who often owe more to the army and the secret service than to popular support.

The sign systems of power and the practices of power are disjoined. When Islam is invoked by states, it is treated as false coin, debased in the way that socialism or nationalism have been through people's historical experience. Societies continue to be marked by skewed and dislocated social and economic relations, in which a sense of being blocked becomes predominant.

No strata feel such distortions so acutely as do the urban

masses and the petite bourgeoisie.* Both have come into being, by definition, in the cities. And this tautology points toward one of the absolutely fundamental characteristics of modern times in the Middle East: the enormous expansion of towns and cities and the relegation of rural society to the status of an undeveloped, or even dedeveloped, periphery.

Consider the urban masses first. Many are villagers, laborers, sharecroppers, small farmers, or artisans who have migrated to the towns. Often they are part of the sea of those casually employed in all that range of activity making up what is often called the informal, or black, economy. They are part of the ever vaster world of bidonvilles, slums and densely packed "old cities" that so mark the region as a whole.

The many who live in this degraded state become an image of the "other" of the city, its dark side to those who see themselves as its light and civilized face. It is all too easy to cast them in the mold of Marx's brilliant and vicious diatribe against the *lumpenproletariat* of mid-nineteenth-century Paris:

> Alongside decayed *roués* with dubious means of subsistence and of dubious origin, alongside ruined and adventurous offshoots of the bourgeoisie, were vagabonds, discharged soldiers, discharged jailbirds, escaped galley slaves, swindlers, mountebanks, *lazzaroni*, pickpockets, tricksters, gamblers, maquereaus, brothel keepers, porters, *literati*, organ-grinders, rag-pickers, knife grinders, tinkers, beggars — in short the whole indefinite disintegrated mass, thrown hither and thither, which the French term *la bohème*.†

It is all too simple for us to take up this tone toward what Marx called "this scum, offal, refuse of all classes" and to generalize from his rhetorical characterization about

---

* *Urban masses* is a vast and vague term, and I am aware of having used *the poor* and *the urban poor* and *the lumpenproletariat* in a very slipshod way in this book. But I do not know a terminology that comes anywhere near naming these levels of society, and such words as *subproletariat* are no less crudely manufactured pigeonholes. This is a totally unsatisfactory position to be in, but I am unable to resolve the problem.

† Karl Marx, "The Eighteenth Brumaire of Louis Bonaparte," *Selected Works* (Moscow: Progress Publishers, vol. 1, n.d.), p. 442. *Lazzaroni* is glossed as an Italian term for declassed, *lumpenproletariat* elements.

something called the *lumpenproletariat* everywhere and any-where. This picture of the *bohème* of Paris in the late 1840s becomes a model, and we forget that it is a characterization founded on a very particular historical moment and place and phase of capitalism.

By one of the many curious paradoxes in the mind of the intellectual of the left, it is the most exploited of society who become the most contemptible because they are least able to participate in a transformation of their own social conditions. They can be written off, as they are here by an Iranian leftist Bizhan Jazani. In distinguishing a subproletariat — whose "lives are characterised by employment in temporary jobs requiring hard work with low pay, peddling, scavenging, living off food thrown away by people in the prosperous residential areas and army barracks" — from a *lumpenpro-letariat* of contemporary Tehran, the author has this to say about the latter:

> As for the lumpenproletariat, they come from that section of society which, despite economic deprivation, lacks any productive role and because of the ignorance and corrup-tion prevailing in society have lost their class charac-teristics. . . . Slovenliness, ignorance, superstition, para-sitism, vulgarity and violence, sexual perversion and sloth are the main features of their culture. These economic and cultural conditions prepare this class for use by internal reactionary forces for their counter-revolutionary aims.*

Marx's key point, that *lumpen* elements are the instru-ments of, in the French case, that "Prince of Clowns," Louis Napoleon — which is to say, of reactionary forces in society — is also Jazani's analysis of the Tehran gangs of young men who charge around the city doing the will of the most conservative and repressive clergy. These *hizbollahis*, the party of God, seem to confirm the view that religion and politics at this level can only be a kind of brutal masquerade in which the most oppressed become the doltish and blind

---

* Bizhan Jazani, *Capitalism and Revolution in Iran: Selected Writings of Bizhan Jazani*, trans. the Iran Committee (London: Zed Press, 1980), pp. 141-42. Jazani was one of the founders of the *Fedaii e Khalq*, the Organisation of Iranian People's Fedaii Guerillas, a secularist and socialist organization that opposed the regime of the shah and now opposes that of Ayatollah Khomeini.

instruments of their oppressors, to be used against those groups seeking a real transformation of society to democratic socialism.

Their religion can only be a compound of hired-gang, bully-boy macho sanctified as the purification of society by the elimination of "demonic" elements. New migrants, hurled into life in the shah's Tehran, where "modernization" had created a paradise for some out of a hell for many, what can they be save prey to every charismatic image and promise of sacred violence? They certainly have at least this in common with Marx's *bohème*: They come into being as the result of massive structural changes in society that occur over relatively short and intensely concentrated periods of time. Such elements are thus peculiarly representative of all the most disorganizing features of transitions to particular forms of dependent capitalist society at particular phases of the latter's development.

A totally contrary view is to see the rural migrants on the fringes of town life, along with other "marginals," as still bound up in a continuous universe of religiously grounded meaning essentially shared with the rest of urban society. This perspective informs Clifford Geertz's discussion of the Moroccan town of Sefrou. He speaks of

> the formation by the immigrant Arabs and, to a lesser extent, the Berbers of a kind of bazaar rabble of market-place peons — the flunkies, menials, and the hangers-on of commercial life. . . . The line between being a casual laborer in the bazaar and a lowly assistant or apprentice (or, indeed, between being a casual laborer and outright unemployed) is far from sharp, and most of the rural Arabs and Berbers in these categories are in fact at the bottom edge of them.*

Even though he qualifies such people as being in the "ancillary, marginal, and, as population grows, outright redundant jobs" around the social and economic center of the bazaar,†

---

* "Suq: The Bazaar Economy in Sefrou" in C. Geertz, H. Geertz, and L. Rosen, *Meaning and Order in Moroccan Society* (Cambridge University Press, 1977), p. 143.
† Ibid., p. 145.

he does not, manifestly, regard them as anything like a Moroccan equivalent of the Tehrani *lumpens*. For Geertz they are not a class, nor even the declassed fragments of a peasantry without a culture; they are part of a "mosaic" in which the bits are constituted by social provenance and label and occupation. Exchange and revelation dominate their world as much as the world of the bazaar center.*

Aside from the theoretical differences that separate him from Jazani, there are surely actual historical distinctions that make Geertz's interpretation possible. In this small, declining market town change has been relatively slow and undramatic in pace and scale. Though I consider that he gives far too much stress to a continuing unity of a cultural world, I think that Geertz's material serves as a caution of the greatest importance. It warns us against making the assumption that the rural migrants in this situation are always and everywhere in the same sociological and cultural position. His account pushes us to acknowledge the specific elements in a given historical setting.

This is particularly important, because this stratum is numerically of ever-increasing significance in Middle Eastern societies. There are many points at which they have crossed these pages: in Vincent Crapanzano's account of the Hamadsha tariqa (chapter 4), Pierre Bourdieu's interpretation of the meaning of baraka for the Algerian victims of a French policy of systematic displacement of population and of a savage colonial war (chapter 7), and in my own discussion of the dramatic and personal nature of miracles for many of the lower ranks of the Hamidiya Shaziliya in Cairo (chapter 4).

In each case there are very specific circumstances that set off one urban world from another. Bourdieu's picture in his book *Algeria 1960* is very much a portrait of Algeria in 1960 and not, for example, of Cairo in 1965.† At one level this is quite obvious. But it is easy for a sociologist, eager to make generalizations and to abstract from the order of the event, to forget the obvious. I may slip unseeing into an elision of the two settings into one "class type" constructed on similarities in the treatment of baraka but missing the very

---

* Ibid., p. 197.

† (Cambridge: Cambridge University Press, 1979). This book is an important source for our discussion.

different historical developments that have brought about the Algerian or the Egyptian *lumpen* strata. I may implicitly equate them with the "scum, offal, refuse of all classes" of Marx's Paris of 1848.

Yet clearly for a sociologist it is most important to pay scrupulous and respectful attention to the complexity of culture at these populous margins, not merely to portray them as dislocated and potentially always reactionary. We are only at the beginning of this task. Since the processes that lead to the formation of such strata show little sign of diminishing, the task becomes all the more pressing. For religious responses at these levels may determine the character of what Islam actually means for growing numbers of Muslims.

What does the religious tradition signify here? Eickelman's work on the Moroccan town of Boujad (chapter 9) shows how the poor and the migrants move into what becomes the "old city" and make it their own. The people of the margins take over, or are forced into, the one-time but now displaced social center. They surround the shrine of the saint, spurned by its former keepers, and refound a sacred geography with quite other social reference points. The saint, for so long an inestimably vital part of prestige and legitimation, relatively swiftly becomes something that both old and new bourgeoisie regard as part of popular religion. He becomes, indeed, a key marker of separation between social strata rather than of association. Theological glosses are put onto this contempt to mask the fact that it derives from new class relations and recent historical developments. The worship of saints is presented as being part of the nature of the dwellers in the old city, and this element is abstracted from its real anchoring in social relations. Popular religion is then treated as a static, quasi-sociological type that essentially just "is so."

Versions of this process whereby tradition and an essentially new stratum of urban dwellers become linked have occurred all over the Middle East since the middle of the nineteenth century. In chapter 2, though there with reference to the 'ulema and not to the saints, I referred to migrants coming into Istanbul in the later period of the Ottoman Empire. It was suggested that the religious schools gave "a subsistence living to many of the impoverished peasant youths who were entering the cities in large numbers" (to use Richard Chambers's words again).

Religion became closely entwined with the lives of displaced rural migrants at the period when the state was explicitly separating it from political and economic power. Later, in the 1920s, when the policy of subordination of religion to the state was at full flood under Kemal Ataturk, was not Islam called by that same ruler "the symbol of obscurantism," "a putrified corpse which poisons our lives," and the enemy "of civilisation and of science"? It was. Were not the Sufi orders likewise suppressed by this powerful regime? They were. The 1980s begin, however, with a manifest flourishing of both Islam and the orders in Turkey. The fact that the state itself has identified hostility to its ideology with religion is part of the reason for the identification of religious movements with conservative opposition to the political center.

What we might call a kind of populist opposition to a ruling "them," to big business, to foreign capital, and to the power of the banks easily takes on a religious form. The seeds of this identification were sown by that very set of reforms, one of whose major purposes was to pre-empt such a possibility. Tradition, then, appears in many forms on the banner of resistance of the most exploited of the ruled against the ruling elites, and this makes the political manipulation of Islamic feeling a key feature of contemporary Turkish politics, and not only of Turkish politics.

It is not only at these levels that the idea of tradition re-emerges with enormous force. In the previous chapter I mentioned that the original source of the Ikhwan, or Muslim Brothers, in Egypt in the late 1920s was the petite bourgeoisie. The movement has grown since the late 1960s in Egypt, in Syria and Iraq, and even in North Africa, where it had previously had only the most limited appeal. Nearly always it is in the towns among the students, minor officials and clerks, school teachers, small-businessmen, shopkeepers, small property owners, and civil servants that it flourishes. This is, of course, a very varied set of social strata. They can be lumped together as the petite bourgeoisie:

The petty bourgeoisie included all those who possessed a small amount of capital, a small plot of land, specialized training, or a level of culture which enabled them to live from their work by utilizing their own financial, technical, or intellectual instruments of labor without having to sell their labor power and without buying the labor power of others, except marginally.*

This certainly fills up the category of the petite bourgeoisie, but at the same time I have to acknowledge that it encompasses so much and such a range of possible relations and politics and attitudes and ideologies that it barely retains sociological value. Nonetheless, it is from these strata, however crudely indicated, that supporters of Arab nationalist movements in the struggle for independence came, as I noted a few pages ago. In one sense they benefited from nationalism, but in another they remain in an ambiguous and contradictory position. Abdallah Laroui has highlighted this double character. He refers to the petite bourgeoisie as politically dominating the national state because public administration, the technical services of public and private organizations, and teaching and culture are in their hands. But at the same time they often possess neither power nor economic preponderance nor military backing.†

As the sheer scale and complexity of state forms and of the cities has expanded over the 1960s and 1970s, the petite bourgeoisie has become numerically and socially even more important. Yet members of these strata are no more in control of their life chances than they were before what seemed to be the triumph of nationalism. They are perhaps even more fragmented than they were, and this time without the focus of the external oppression of the colonial power as a directly experienced agency of exploitation.

In addition to economic crises in dependent economies, the degradation of political and cultural opportunities threatens many with the loss of the possession of the means of economic and cultural production and thus with decline

---

* Mahmoud Hussein, *Class Conflict in Egypt: 1945-1971*, trans. Alfred Ehrenfeld and Michel Chirman (New York and London: Monthly Review Press, 1973), p. 28.

† *The Crisis of the Arab Intellectual* (Berkeley/Los Angeles: University of California Press, 1976), pp. 160-61.

into the mass of those compelled to sell their labor. Party apparatuses, bureaucracy, and patron-client relations reinforce the arbitrary and uneven determinations of existence.

If even Algeria, where hitherto the fundamentalist movements have been virtually unknown, now sees the appearance of the Muslim Brothers, then it must surely be traced to a global expansion in the role and contradictions of the petite bourgeoisie. The ideology of the Salafiya reformers, clerics, and urban elite can be stigmatized by workers and members of the petite bourgeoisie alike as part of a mere class manipulation by the culturally privileged.

Crucially it is the students of the provincial towns and the capitals, of the secondary schools and the universities, who are the spearhead of the new tendencies that are loosely categorized as Muslim Brothers. They, after all, are drawn from the age group that represents the great majority of the population of Arab states, that of the fifteen- to the twenty-five-year-olds. They have been brought up in a different atmosphere from that of the 1930s and 1940s. A French or British presence is no longer part of power structures seen in a thousand local and suffocating ways. International, particularly American, banks and intercontinental hotels now stand on the former sites of occupying-army barracks. Villas and expensive boutiques furnishing luxury consumer goods witness to the life-style of a national, not an external, privileged class. A rhetoric of liberty and independence breaks on the barren shore of food scarcity, or low-paid and dead-end government jobs, or a "guest worker" hostel in Europe, or the crowded and expensive flats of a city that consume far too much income to allow for the costs of a marriage for an individual from these strata until perhaps the middle or late twenties.

Out of this instability, unease, and immobility comes the call to a transformation of society through the application of the Quran and the Holy Law to the whole of social life. It is, on the one hand, practical and organized around specific projects, and on the other hand, utopian and repressive, excluding those who do not follow the regulations and traditions as defined by the group.

There are many possible variations, just as there are in the forms of Sufism that make their reappearance among these strata. But all of them represent an interrogation and a judgment on contemporary society in the name of an Eternal Truth, the ambiguities of which are invisible to the believer. A true Islamic society must be reinvented. But what would it look like? Certainly not like any state that calls itself by that name, except, for some, Iran. Is it compatible with socialism, as so many have asserted? Or is that merely a demogogic promise by military-backed elites? Is that student who kissed a sherif's hand to feign respect in a dusty street in South Arabia twenty years ago now a contented citizen of a Marxist state, a Muslim Brother, an exile?

A reinvention, to be authentic and creative, must make possible an expansion of the social and cultural universe. It must never be completed nor return endlessly to earlier material in a closed, ritualistic incantation.* Does the example of the ruling mullahs of Iran or of the Muslim Brothers of Egypt or Syria show this sense of creative uncompletion? I think not. But there are many other forces coming into being in these societies that resist such closure either within or outside a specifically religious tradition. Other readings of Revelation remain possible, other alliances, other revolts. Iran has shown that apparently impregnable power can be overthrown by mobilization in the name of Islam. The triumph of the mullahs neither was nor is inevitable, and everything is still at stake. Increasingly everything is in question, including Islam itself. Purely rhetorical and ritualistic answers will yield nothing but a destruction of what is to be resurrected by the very people who imagine themselves to be the instruments of rebirth. Is that to be the final irony?

Image and Intimacy

These are very public ideologies of Islam. They are versions of "unchanging tradition" reinvented either by elites as a language to fit society for a transforming world and for "reason and progress," or by such movements as the Muslim Brothers in contempt of the modernists and the classes from which they sprang. Only at the level of the masses do the

* I adapt here some comments of the French composer Pierre Boulez on the work of a modern German predecessor, Alban Berg.

apparently clear lineaments of ideologies become blurred, unsystematized, nonprogrammatic, even less self-deceptive?

This is one of the great contrasts and it points to a suggestion I made at the beginning of this book: Different and sometimes mutually exclusive apprehensions and practices of Islam are emerging that separate societies and classes as much as they unite them. Rhetorical unity may be easily achieved, but in the subterranean world there are social forces that push and thrust at the shell of dessicated formulas. Class divisions are becoming stronger, and this is the key process in the culture of contemporary Islam.

I may say, to take another image, that the currents below the river's surface are quicker than its seemingly lazy movement, they swirl this way and that, and run at different speeds. But how do I come to a sense of that level of reality? These more concealed motions, marked only by tiny, almost invisible signs, are at the heart of the matter, but how to sense and show this?

I have tried only a few of the many paths available to reach towards these hidden layers. The discussion of sexuality, pollution, and the position of the Lebanese sheikh, who must be regarded as seeing the secret if he is to be accepted as an icon of holiness, aims at one of the crucial life centers. The transformations of the dialectical, transforming, maglis into the motionless, one-dimensional salon, points at another, where crucial spaces that articulate the outer and inner worlds are themselves changed. The power of the straight line and the right angle over Gérard de Nerval's decaying old city of Cairo in the 1840s is a third attempt.

I turn back again to my own experience. If I am asked, out of the blue, what moments crystallize my experience of Islam in its more specifically religious dimension, I know my immediate responses. They are two.

When I first went to Cairo and began, week in, week out, to go to mosques and to sit in self-conscious jacket-and-tie piety while members of the Hamidi... ...ment that fundamentally disturbed all my efforts at perception and a feeling for the real meaning of the event. It was not my inability to follow the hymns, or the enormous gaps in my knowledge of the language, or my incapacity to follow the chanting of the

Quran. It was something far more subtle and far more disorienting, yet I could not locate it.

One day I realized what the discordant phrase in the music was: Neon light. All around the interior of the mosque there were verses from the Quran in *neon* light. In green neon light, as it happens, but what matter the color? Neon. Advertisements, shop fronts, Piccadilly Circus, plastic, flashing, hard, cheap. . . . A host of submerged echos flooded the mind and blocked out everything else. It drove the Quran out of my ears, threw out whatever internal calm and equilibrium I had or sought, and sounded like a constantly hit flat note disrupting the whole tonal world of a symphony.

For months neon light subverted my every solemn ritual attendance. Each time I glanced up at the Quranic verses, reading the Arabic, "knowing the meaning" in a dictionary sort of way, the neon would interpose itself, the medium would dominate. Then, one day, perhaps eight or nine months after my first hesitant observations of the zikr, I turned unthinkingly away from the swaying bodies and the rhythms of the remembrance of God and saw, not neon, but simply greenness. Greenness, and letters that did not "stand for" anything but simply were powerful icons in and of themselves. No gaps existed between color, shape, light, and form. From that unreflecting and unexpected moment I ceased to see neon at all.

This cannot be prepared for intellectually, though trained intuition plays its part. My own straining for "meaning" had done quite as much as the neon itself to ensure that I never found it. Even the word *meaning* itself is neither apt nor useful. Neither is *history*. It adds nothing much to know a history of "green" as the color of the Prophet, of the angel Khudr, of life, and to follow it through the ages. It is the direct, self-creating, and re-creating experience of greenness that "just is" for Muslims in a particularly ordinary way, both intimately the same as and distinct from our own, that is so vital.

There is nothing mystical here, nor even mysterious. There is rather the problem of finding a discursive way of expressing a timeless and endlessly repeated instant that has its own autonomy. Perhaps in phenomenology such an essence can be written out, perhaps not. No local explanation, which in any case would never be offered and could never be formulated, could serve to make me apprehend it. And, having once passed that first instant of recognition of green and form, I am quite unable to say what effect it had on my experience of the brotherhoods or of Lebanon. It is simply there.

The other moment that has stamped my consciousness of Islam also occurred in Egypt. We were sitting in a room in a poor quarter of Alexandria, listening to a local leader of the Sufi order reading a letter from the sheikh of the order in Cairo. We had made the zikr in a small mosque. My attention had been mostly taken up by the attentiveness to me of a captain in the military intelligence who was far more intrigued by my presence than by any presence of the saint himself in the ritual. It was hot, and my show of pious absorption had long since become nothing more than a show.

The khalifa, or deputy, droned on. This and that regulation, these and those pieces of sententious advice, the interspersed laments at the corruption of cards and coffee houses. Irritation and boredom and knees that seemed locked in an unbreakable stiffness after hours of sitting cross-legged on the floor created a longing for escape.

Then, still reading the sheikh's letter aloud, the deputy said something like the following: I have heard that you do not use the Name of God, *Huwa* ("He," chanted as *Hū* in the zikr), in your ritual, and this is a great error and nullifies the whole ceremony. This is the most concentrated of all the Names used in the zikr. Why is that? Because if we take the Name of God, *Allah* and take away the first letter, we still have a divine word (that is, *Allah* becomes in Arabic *lillah* when you drop the initial alef, or *a*), which means "for God." But this can be reduced yet further. If we take away the second letter we are left with *lahu* (which in Arabic is two letters only), "for God." Finally we can take away the third and penultimate letter, and then we reach the ultimate, irreducible form — *Hū*, "He" (one letter in Arabic, a softly breathed *h* made by the lips forming a circle, so there is a kind of homology of written and spoken, an identity of breath and sound). This is why no zikr is truly completed unless the essential *Hū* is chanted.'

Breath, barely a sound, a circle, all in one word that is

scarcely anymore a word.

This kind of occasion and this kind of teaching were absolutely routine and elementary and carried a long tradition behind them. Most of my friends, many of whom were semiliterate, could discourse about such guidance for hours with the appropriate quotations. Yet it indelibly marked my imagination. It imaged Islam, like a poetic image or a musical phrase that, for reasons you neither know nor need to know, will mark your barely conscious being and can never be erased, even if it may seem forgotten and is never made an object of reflection.

The dialectics of these levels of Islam with class and political experience — just as profound and elusive, too — I have barely begun to treat in this book. That all remains to do, and, to return to the composer's words, it must never and can never be completed.

A Way of Walking

This book has been a kind of excavation and a wandering. It is hard to use either of those words without seeming pretentious, but they express my experience and will have to stand for it.

The sense of moving through a city, through spaces that others define in ways the wanderer only dimly intuits and which seem sometimes frightening, sometimes empty, sometimes so full as to be overwhelming, is very strong to me. *How* should we walk, never mind where are we going? Friends in Lebanon were always amused at my striding off determinedly with long paces, eyes forward, heels clipping hard onto the path, self-conscious purpose in every move, *going somewhere* even if only — ultimate laughter — "for a walk." They knew that the appearance of purpose covered a confusion of aims, an uncertainty about what I would find or whether I would find it or whether I should even find it down that path, on that way. The only real dupe of this oh-so-determined stride was the walker himself — looking direct when he should be glancing sideways, cutting a straight line when everything — tact, manners, self-interest, knowledge — demands that he move in the slow, wide meandering stroll of his friends with frequent stops at almond trees, shoulders loose, hands arcing expansively through the air, knees almost disjointed with relaxation, having some interchange with everyone they saw, apparently going nowhere, sitting, and then, only then, approaching on an apparently momentary wish, the house of such a one. How disoriented these drifting, stone-scuffing amblings were to me. Yet they were a central thread in the labyrinth of the village as it drew me in, though it is only now that that clearly strikes me and can emerge as words on a page, that I have the uneasy smile of one who says: "So that's how it was!"

Didn't those strolls — whose whole form denied time, effort, goal, direction, end — didn't they always follow such defined ways? They never crossed those fields, now that I come to think of it, never randomly halted at that house or in that quarter, always skirted that olive grove, never included picking grapes from that apparently wild vine or eating apricots from that tree. There were endless absences and unseens which everyone saw, just knew, except me. Innumerable possible ways we might have gone, too, though I chafed endlessly for the one I had defined as leading to that piece of information, that insight, that slice of family history, or property relationship, or death. Wasn't the way of walking my education so much more than all the moments of knowledge consciously acquired, which in any case turned out frequently to be a snare set deliberately to catch anyone whose eyes did not dart and glance as warily as a bird's? Those sentences so laboriously written down in the red-backed reporter's notebooks at one or two in the morning gave me such a sense of having achieved something concrete, having at last *found out* something. But weren't they mostly remarkable for the days it took to realize their slippery and obscure nature? They were out and out false, nuanced this way and that, incomprehensible, if seen from such an angle there were facets to what appeared plain glass: X had lied, Y was bored, Z thought he would use this curious personage with this extraordinary innocence of relations and hidden purposes to cast a misty screen across his own intentions concerning another.

It is the way of walking that now quite unexpectedly comes out to teach me about that culture and its unspoken premises, its acting on time, its assumptions about intention, and the constraints that rules, unconscious predispositions, codes, and forms place on deliberateness. To absorb that walk in one's own body was far closer to "speaking the language" than any half control over words and stumbled formulas. Behind its apparent formlessness and disinterest there was a readiness, a sense of options, even a practical and quite specific awareness of risk.

It is only now that I realize how much language I picked up in that way. Certainly only now that I understand what the German writer Walter Benjamin was doing when he spoke of "the art of wandering":

> Not to find one's way in a city may well be uninteresting and banal. It requires ignorance — nothing more. But to lose oneself in a city — as one loses oneself in a forest — that calls for quite a different schooling. Then, signboards and street names, passers-by, roofs, kiosks, or bars must speak to the wanderer like a crackling twig under his feet in the forest, like the startling call of a bittern in the distance, like the sudden stillness of a clearing with a lily standing erect at its centre.*

All this talk of forests and bitterns filled me with the same impatience as strolling used to do in that Lebanese village. It looked a bit precious and self-conscious, or, at best, too close for my comfort to the *flâneurs*† of nineteenth century Paris about whom Benjamin loved to write. Anthropology ought to be straight lines to a place, like my English walk. But that isn't very practical, as my friends knew. It closes off too much, misses too much, violates too many other ways of reaching the point one hopes to reach but of whose exact nature and significance one is not exactly aware. If there is a sociological imagination, it must move like Benjamin's *flâneurs*, or rather, as he himself learned to move over years and years of losing himself in order to be schooled and schooling himself to be able to be lost, as distinct from merely confused or not knowing where he was.

* Walter Benjamin, "A Berlin Chronicle" in *Reflections*, edited and with an introduction by Peter Demetz (New York: Harcourt, Brace, Jovanovich, 1978), pp. 8-9.

† A master of the art of straying, a stroller, a virtuoso of wandering in the streets "botanizing on the asphalt," to use Benjamin's evocative phrase.

Accepting that, I begin to accept his sterner and more intimidating insight with a little less fear: "It is likely that no one ever masters anything in which he has not known impotence; and if you agree, you will also see that this impotence comes not at the beginning or before the struggle with the subject, but in the heart of it."*

I can pretend to myself this is not true, or use it as an excuse, or run away from it with a determined walk of purpose even if my mouth is dry and I am only able to head in this direction because I am so ignorant of the fact that, to those who do know it, it is a minefield through which only ingenuousness and chance will bring me.

Better still, I can pretend to you that it is not true. That will leave both of us easier in our minds. The guide does not like to feel constantly that at the heart of the city is his powerlessness. The guided prefers the illusion of seeing and knowing. He has paid his money, spent that morning, that afternoon, and the tour was announced with all the usual signs of taking him around these and those monuments and places of interest. The faster and more directed the walk, the more he sees, the more he knows. Talk about impotence and beginnings looks suspiciously like a shuffling off of responsibility. "You propose to take me around. You set up all kinds of headings and names. You set this route, not I. You are providing the service and now you talk about impotence? A fine sort of guide that is."

Well, maybe at least if we both know that I see in that way or am coming to, that also will be more *practical*. You will less likely assume mastery in me or yourself, be less inclined to trust my apparently longest and most clearly determined strides and more inclined to look for what they rushed both of us past; be simply less uncomfortable with the profoundly discomforting and vital sense of hesitation and discontinuity and doubts, more aware that another guide would walk a different route and at a different pace, with different eyes, more acute and reflective attention, discovering whole quarters of the city of whose existence this particular guide is only in part aware. Perhaps this will bring you to disagreement and questioning, too? Why there and not here? Why not down that road, toward that crowd,

* Ibid., p. 4.

those buildings? And my answer would have to be, "I'm not too sure. They are certainly, possibly, interesting. But for the moment this particular guide has traced out, no, found out as he went and even in the act of writing these few pages discovers, the only route he turns out to know."

To say that the word *conclusion* would be portentous and misleading is just to say that of course we don't conclude anything here. I hope we don't. Not because I wish to leave you with platitudes about the endless pathways of truth, the unending journey, or the tangled ways of knowledge.

Just because this sort of ending is the only practical one. For the time being.

A NOTE ON TRANSLITERATION

I have used an extremely simplified system of transliteration from the Arabic and have often given something closer to a modern spoken than to the classical form of a word (as in *zikr* for *dhikr*). Specialists will recognize Arabic words without the apparatus of dots and dashes used in standard works, although I have used them at each word's first mention.

English plurals have usually been followed, though words frequently found in their plural form in Western writings have been retained (for example, *'ulema* and *turuq*). As a general principle I have glossed Arabic words where they first appear and not thereafter, and I also italicize the first use of the word and afterward treat it as though it were in ordinary English usage.

Algar, Hamid. "The Oppositional Role of the Ulama in Twentieth-Century Iran" in *Scholars, Saints, and Sufis: Muslim Religious Institutions since 1500*, edited by Nikki R. Keddie. Berkeley/Los Angeles: University of California Press, 1972.

Antoun, R., and Harik, I., eds. *Rural Politics and Social Change in the Middle East*. Bloomington, Ind./London: University of Indiana Press, 1972.

Benjamin, Walter. "A Berlin Chronicle" in *Reflections*, edited and with an introduction by Peter Demetz. New York: Harcourt, Brace, Jovanovich, 1978.

Bourdieu, P. *Outline of a Theory of Practice*. Cambridge: Cambridge University Press, 1977.

——. *Algeria 1960*. Cambridge: Cambridge University Press, 1979.

Bourdieu, P., and Sayad, A. *Le Déracinement*. Paris: Les éditions de minuit, 1964.

Brown, K.L. *The People of Salé: Tradition and Change in a Moroccan City, 1830-1930*. Cambridge, Mass.: Harvard University Press, 1976.

Bujra, A.S. *The Politics of Stratification: A Study of Political Change in a South Arabian Town*. Oxford: The Clarendon

Press, 1971.

Burke, Edmund, III. "The Moroccan Ulama, 1860-1912: An Introduction" in *Scholars, Saints, and Sufis: Muslim Religious Institutions since 1500*, edited by Nikki R. Keddie. Berkeley/Los Angeles: University of California Press, 1972.

Chambers, Richard L. "The Ottoman Ulema and the Tanzimat" in *Scholars, Saints, and Sufis: Muslim Religious Institutions since 1500*, edited by Nikki R. Keddie. Berkeley/Los Angeles: University of California Press, 1972.

Colonna, F. "Cultural Resistance and Religious Legitimacy in Colonial Algeria." *Economy and Society* 3 (1976): 233-52.

Crapanzano, V. *The Hamadsha: A Study in Moroccan Ethnopsychiatry.* Berkeley: University of California Press, 1973.

Cruise O'Brien, D. *The Mourides of Senegal: The Political and Economic Organization of an Islamic Brotherhood.* Oxford: The Clarendon Press, 1971.

———. *Saints and Politicians: Essays in the Organisation of a Senegalese Peasant Society.* Cambridge: Cambridge University Press, 1975.

De Nerval, Gérard. "Correspondance" in *Oeuvres*, edited by Albert Béguin and Jean Richter. Paris: Gallimard, 1952.

Eickelman, D. *Moroccan Islam: Tradition and Society in a Pilgrimage Center.* Austin, Texas, and London: University of Texas Press, 1976.

Evans-Pritchard, E.E. *The Sanusi of Cyrenaica.* Oxford: The Clarendon Press, 1949.

Fischer, Michael J. *Iran: From Religious Dispute to Revolution.* Cambridge, Mass.: Harvard University Press, 1980.

Geertz, Clifford. "Suq: The Bazaar Economy in Sefrou" in *Meaning and Order in Moroccan Society*, edited by C. Geertz, H. Geertz, and L. Rosen. Cambridge: Cambridge University Press, 1979.

Gerholm, T. *Market, Mosque and Mafraj.* Stockholm: Stockholm University Press, 1977.

Gilsenan, Michael. *Saint and Sufi in Modern Egypt: An Essay in the Sociology of Religion.* Oxford: The Clarendon Press, 1973.

Hussein, Mahmoud. *Class Conflict in Egypt: 1945-1971*. New York and London: Monthly Review Press, 1973.

Hourani, A.H. *Arabic Thought in the Liberal Age, 1798-1939*. Oxford: The Clarendon Press, 1962.

Jazani, Bizhan. *Capitalism and Revolution in Iran: Selected Writings of Bizhan Jazani*. London: Zed Press, 1980.

Keddie, Nikki R., ed. *Scholars, Saints, and Sufis: Muslim Religious Institutions since 1500*. Berkeley/Los Angeles: University of California Press, 1972.

Laroui, Abdullah. *The Crisis of the Arab Intellectual*. Berkeley/Los Angeles: University of California Press, 1976 (paper).

Lévi-Strauss, Claude. *The Savage Mind*. London: Weidenfeld and Nicholson, 1966.

Marx, Karl. "The Eighteenth Brumaire of Louis Bonaparte" in *Selected Works*, vol. 1. Moscow: Progress Publishers, n.d.

Mitchell, Richard P. *The Society of the Muslim Brothers*. London: Oxford University Press, 1969.

Peters, E.L. "Aspects of Rank and Status among Muslims in a Lebanese Village" in *Mediterranean Countrymen*, edited by J. Pitt-Rivers. Paris/La Haye: Mouton and Co., 1963.

——. "Shifts in Power in a Lebanese Village" in *Rural Politics*, edited by R. Antoun and I. Harik. Bloomington, Ind./London: University of Indiana Press, 1972.

Raban, Jonathan. *Arabia through the Looking Glass*. London: Collins, 1979.

Said, Edward. *Orientalism*. New York: Pantheon Books; London: Routledge and Kegan Paul, 1978.

Von Sivers, Peter. "The Realm of Justice: Apocalyptic Revolts in Algeria (1849-1879)." *Humaniora Islamica* 1 (1973): 47-60.

I have organized this short bibliography of suggested further reading around the themes in this book, though, of course, many of the works cited here are relevant to a range of topics in the study of Islam. Where books are already fully listed in the references, I give only an abbreviated title or just the author's name.

It is still very difficult to direct an interested reader to general books on Islam, especially if we are looking for a sociological or anthropological element. General criticism of much previous work is to be found in Edward Said's *Orientalism* (references), polemical, stimulating and much criticized. Bryan Turner has written two critical studies on the way Islam has been discussed in Western scholarship: *Weber and Islam* (London: Routledge and Kegan Paul, 1974) and *Marx and the End of Orientalism* (London: George Allen and Unwin, 1978). Neither Said nor Turner give any real picture of how they see Muslim societies. One view from inside is Abdallah Laroui's *Crisis* (references), which contains a chapter of critique on the work of the celebrated historian Gustave von Grunebaum.

Maxime Rodinson's *Muhammed* (London: Allen Lane, 1971) is informed by an enormous range of scholarship and is the best study available on the founder of Islam. I was brought up as an undergraduate on H.A.R. Gibb's *Mohammedanism* (numerous editions), though it is now rather dated in some respects. The translation of the Quran that I have always most enjoyed reading is the old eighteenth-century version by the remarkable George Sale: *The Koran* (London: Frederick Warne and Co., n.d.). For students, that of Richard Bell (2 vols., Edinburgh: T. and T. Clark, 1937) is more recommended. Another extraordinary document that says at least as much about a certain class of Englishman in the nineteenth century as it does about the Pilgrimage is Sir Richard Burton's marvelous and presumptuous *Personal Narrative of a Pilgrimage to El Medinah and Meccah*. Malcolm X's autobiography also contains some moving pages on the Hajj, though he clearly did not grasp much about the nature of Saudi society.

Clifford Geertz's *Islam Observed* (New Haven: Yale University Press, 1968), is a study comparing saints as sacred metaphors in two very different societies, Morocco and Indonesia, but for a reader unfamiliar with Islam it is a little diffuse. In the tradition of anthropological monographs Abdallah Bujra's *Politics of Stratification* (references) is a fascinating study of forms of Islam in a milieu of theocracy and colonialism.

Nikki Keddie's edited collection *Scholars, Saints, and Sufis* (references) contains interesting though not particularly sociological articles. Her *Religion and Rebellion in Iran: The Tobacco Protest of 1891-1892* (London: Frank Cass, 1966) and her essays *Iran: Religion, Politics and Society* (Cass, 1980) give most useful background material and interpretation. Michael Fischer's book *Iran* (references) is unfortunately rather uneven, and the author seems to have been rushed into making it relevant to the Iranian revolution in not very illuminating ways. It is excellent as an insight into the world of the medreses and religious education in a contemporary Muslim society.

The world of modern holy men and Sufi sheikhs has been rather better studied by anthropologists than have the 'ulema. There are many important listings in the references (Evans-Pritchard, Cruise O'Brien, Crapanzano, Gilsenan), and these are studies in very contrasting settings ranging from bidonvilles to the Libyan desert. An Arab friend once remarked that there are very few sociological writings on Islamic rituals, which is both true and curious, given the almost obsessive treatment ritual is given in so much other work. For the reader interested in this dimension I will immodestly recommend the chapter on the Sufi zikr in my own book on Sufis in Egypt. It does not explore nearly deeply enough, but it may give a hint of some of the complexity of this kernel of Sufism in practical, ritual experience. J. Spencer Trimingham's *The Sufi Orders in Islam* (Oxford: The Clarendon Press, 1971) is a valuable guide but analytically not very interesting.

Mention should be made of that classic statement of what is known as the segmentary view of tribal society and the place of holy lineages, Ernest Gellner's *Saints of the Atlas* (Chicago: University of Chicago Press, 1969). The religious and symbolic elements are subordinated to structural arguments about tribal society in a particular ecological setting. Clifford Geertz's work on Sefrou and the writings of Hildred Geertz and Larry Rosen (references) take a diametrically opposed view and create a Moroccan society that is formed on a different planet from that of Gellner. Both books often leave me in violent disagreement and puzzlement and have therefore been excellent for teaching! John Waterbury's *Commander of the Faithful* (New York: Columbia University Press, 1970) is in the structuralist tradition and is illuminating on the position of the sultan of Morocco, who is both political and religious leader.

In addition to his *Crisis of the Arab Intellectual* already referred to, readers will find Abdallah Laroui's *The History of the Maghrib: An Interpretive Essay* (Princeton: Princeton University Press, 1977), valuable for North African history as the perspective of a leading Moroccan intellectual. Pierre Bourdieu's work is often dense and exasperating to read in English, but his *Algeria 1960* and *Outline* (see references for both) and *The Algerians* (Boston: The Beacon Press, 1962) contain many insights into culture and practice, even if the theoretical apparatus does not always clarify as much as it is meant to.

Anthropological writing on cities is also centered on North Africa (see Brown, Eickelman, Crapanzano, Geertz, and Rosen in the references). Janet Abu Lughod has just finished a study of Rabat: *Rabat: Urban Apartheid in Morocco* (Princeton: Princeton University Press, 1980), which came too late for my own work on this book. It follows her *Cairo: 1,000 years of the City Victorious* (Princeton University Press, 1971). Material on Islam is not really central to her research, but she is good on the historical sequence in the transformation of cities, which is very relevant to my chapters in this book. Since I know of no writer who had a greater sense of how to get a sense of cities than the German critic Walter Benjamin, I must place him here in rather unaccustomed company. His *Reflections* (references) and *Charles Baudelaire: A Lyric Poet in the Age of High Capitalism* (London: New Left Books, 1973) offer still unrivaled readings of a city's texts and subtexts. He helps to restore the senses of smell, sight, and hearing, not to mention the faculty of imagination, that a writer in the social sciences can so easily and unawares lose.

INDEX